Food Lovers' London

Jenny Linford

Photography by Chris Windsor

Food Lovers' London

Written by Jenny Linford
Photography by Chris Windsor
Edited by Abigail Willis
Design by Metro

First published in Great Britain 1991 by Macmillan, updated editions published in 1995 and 1999 by Metro Publications.

Published 2003 by
Metro Publications
PO Box 6336
London
N1 6PY

Printed and bound in Spain by Imago

British Library Cataloguing in Publication Data.
A catalogue record for this book is available from the British Library.

ISBN 1-902910-12-5

*for Mummy, Daddy, Chris and Ben
and in memory of Harry Greenwald
who believed in me.*

ACKNOWLEDGMENTS

First of all, my thanks to Andrew and Susi at Metro for their enthusiasm, interest and support for the book, Rosie Kindersley for suggesting Metro, and Chris for putting so much time and energy into taking some great photographs. Many people spared time to talk to me and my grateful thanks go to the following: everyone I talked to at the BBC World Service; and especially Nina Dekhan, Jon Cannon, Antonio Carluccio, Anna del Conte, Alan Dein, Sarah Edington, Clare Ferguson, Anna Giacon, Wendy Godfrey, Pat Howard, Shehzad Husain, the Jewish Chronicle, Sav Kyriacou, Sri Own, Laki Pattelis, Mary Pininska, Claudia Roden, Evelyn Rose, Polly Russell, Margaret Shaida, Imogen Smith, Siyu magazine, Yan-Kit So, Marlena Spieler, Jan and Dinah Wieliczko of the Centaur Gallery, Kate Whiteman, John Whiting and, finally, the shopkeepers themselves who patiently answered my many questions and from whom I learned so much.

CONTENTS

ABOUT THE AUTHOR

Jenny Linford lived in Ghana, Trinidad, Singapore and Italy before settling in London, where she now works as a freelance food writer and restaurant reviewer. Her work has included journalism for magazines and newspapers including The Guardian, The Evening Standard, The Illustrated London News, Taste, Time Out and The Times. Her books include Writing About Food, Tastes of the Orient (Tesco) and A Taste of London. An inveterate food shopper, Jenny also founded the highly successful 'Gastro-Soho Tours', which have been running since 1994 (see page 267 for further details).

INTRODUCTION

When I was a child my family moved to Florence and English food took on an especial importance. Visitors were entreated to bring packets of 'ordinary' tea, cheese and onion crisps and Walls' sausages. One small shop near the Duomo, Ye Olde English Store, sold a quaint mixture of English food: tinned asparagus, lemon puffs and Gentleman's Relish. Small jars of Marmite cost a few thousand lire more than they should have but were savoured nevertheless. Now that I am back in London I buy fresh pasta, basil and parmesan and try to recreate the sunny tastes of Tuscany.

This book started out of personal nostalgia but turned into an enjoyable and fascinating journey of discovery. London, where I have lived for so many years, suddenly revealed glimpses into new and varied worlds: the aesthetic delight of a Japanese fish counter, a delicious honey doughnut in a Turkish patisserie, the hustle and bustle of Brixton Market, bagels in a busy Golders Green bakery, being offered a free soft drink in Southall to commemorate a Sikh martyr who had preached tolerance to all. Encounters have been, on the whole, enjoyable (although one Iranian shopowner accused me, only half-jokingly, of being a tax inspector!). Waiting in a Polish bakery while three old ladies bought their rye bread and sausages chatting away in Polish, I gathered, from their sideways glances at me standing notebook in hand, that they were wondering what I was doing there. As one opened her purse to pay the baker, she suddenly broke into English: "Daylight robbery!" she exclaimed, and shot a wicked, amused glance in my direction.

We are so much creatures of habit that new things are avoided almost automatically and this is certainly true with food. One of the great pleasures for me in writing this book has been the discovery of new ingredients and dishes. I had, for example, walked down Drummond Street many times to buy some barfi from the Ambala Sweet Centre but had never stopped to look at the unusual vegetables and fruits on sale. Now I know a little more about them and have tried and enjoyed many. The Japanese say that for every new food tried and truly enjoyed one lives for seventy more days.

In Britain attitudes towards food have changed enormously and more and more specialist ingredients are appearing on supermarket shelves. Supermarkets, however, cannot offer everything or keep it in the best conditions, especially 'exotic' fruit and vegetables. Tired-looking rambutans or rock-hard mangoes in a supermarket compare badly with the excellent quality fruit on offer in Gerrard Street, Asian greengrocer's or West Indian markets. Food is an important part of culture and a primary means of identification. It is a pleasure to shop at places where staff really know what they are selling, from an Italian deli assistant carefully slicing Parma ham to a fishmonger explaining how to cook an unusual fish.

The tragic thing I have witnessed while writing and updating this book is that so many of the smaller shops are being forced to close, with those in central London especially hard hit by steeply rising rents. Small shops are having to open longer to compete with the round-the-clock opening hours offered by supermarkets. As shops like these, run by people who love and take pride in what they do disappear, we all become impoverished.

Poilane

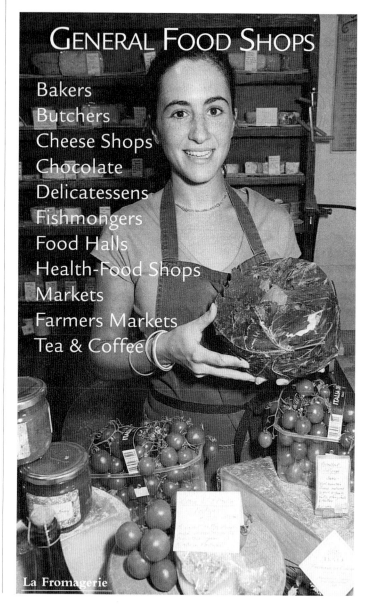

GENERAL FOOD SHOPS

Bakers
Butchers
Cheese Shops
Chocolate
Delicatessens
Fishmongers
Food Halls
Health-Food Shops
Markets
Farmers Markets
Tea & Coffee

La Fromagerie

BAKERS

ioneered by chef Sally Clarke, London's bread scene is undergoing something of a Renaissance with a number of fine quality bakeries opening in the capital while wholesaler bakers such as Flour Power find a receptive audience at farmers' markets and Borough Market. While there are now bakeries offering decent ciabattas, sourdoughs, baguettes and focaccia, the traditional English high-street bakery, selling something as simple as a decent-quality fresh tin loaf, is frustratingly elusive.

CENTRAL

De Gustibus
▢ *6 Southwark Street, SE1*
☏ *020 7407 3625*
▦ *London Bridge LU/Rail*
☺ *Mon-Sat 7am-5pm*
In a prime position backing onto Borough Market, this award winning corner shop is a London outlet for Oxfordshire-based baker Dan Schickentanz, offering the full range of his breads such as Six Day Sour (made with a sourdough starter) and Milwaukee Rye. The lunchtime trade is catered for with superior sandwiches.
Other branches: 53 Blandford Street, W1, Tel: 020 7486 6608
53-55 Carter Lane, EC4, Tel: 020 7236 0056

Exeter Street Bakery
▢ *15 Exeter Street, WC2*
☏ *020 7379 1881*
▦ *Charing Cross LU/Rail*
☺ *Mon-Fri 10am-7pm*
Tucked away in a side-street just off the Strand, this smart shop, with its chic chrome shelving, offers an excellent range of authentically flavourful Italian breads, including its bestselling dark-crusted Pugliese, slices of excellent pizza and proper crostata (Italian jam tart). (See also Italian London, p.146).

Konditor & Cook

⌖ *27 Cornwall Road, SE1*
☎ *020 7261 0456*
🚇 *Waterloo LU/Rail*
🕐 *Mon-Fri 7.30am-6.30pm, Sat 8.30am-2pm*

Gerhard Jenne's bakery is noted for its creative cakes and pastries, from wildly colourful iced gingerbread skeletons at Halloween to imaginatively personalised birthday cakes (much in demand with celebrity clients). One reason for Gerhard's success is that he firmly believes everything should taste as good as it looks.

Other branches: 10 Stoney Street, SE1, Tel: 020 7407 5100
46 Gray's Inn Road, WC1, Tel: 020 7404 6300

Paul

⌖ *29 Bedford Street, WC2*
☎ *020 7836 3304*
🚇 *Covent Garden LU*
🕐 *Mon-Fri 7.30am-9pm, Sat & Sun 9am-9pm*

This first London branch of a well-established French chain is an impressive operation. While its pastries and cakes are distinctly alluring, its extensive repertoire of French-style breads, all baked on the premises, have proved a particular forte. When the shop first opened English customers asked for "normal bread"; now this thoroughly Gallic enterprise attracts patient queues both for the bakery and the back-room salon du thé (see also French London, pages 120 & 124).

Other branch: 115 Marylebone High Street, W1, Tel: 020 7836 3304

Poilane

⌖ *46 Elizabeth Street, SW1*
☎ *020 7808 4910*
🚇 *Sloane Square LU or Victoria Station LU/Rail*
🕐 *Mon-Fri 7am-7.30pm, Sat 7.30am-6pm*

This dainty shop is a lovingly recreated replica of a famous Paris-based bakery, complete with a wood-fired oven in the basement. Regulars return for Poilane's huge, round sourdough loaves, with their distinctive, addictive tang, which are sold whole, halved, quartered or simply by the slice (see also French London, p.120).

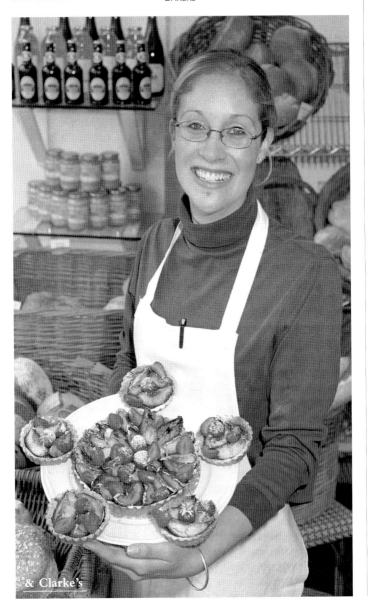

& Clarke's

St John

🖷 *26 St John Street, EC1*
☏ *020 7251 0848*
🚇 *Farringdon LU*
🕓 *Bread sold from 7am Mon-Sat*

This much-applauded Clerkenwell restaurant, noted for chef Fergus Henderson's appreciative approach towards offal, also does a side-line trade in bread baked on the premises, with the St John sourdough being particularly popular.

EAST

De Gustibus

🖷 *53-55 Carter Lane, EC4*
☏ *020 7236 0056*
🚇 *St Paul's LU*
🕓 *Mon-Fri 7.30am-6pm*

A City-based café outlet for De Gustibus breads, with diners being able to mix and match breads and fillings. The outlet also serves hot food and a good selection of wines and beers.

North-West

Baker & Spice

⌨ *75 Salusbury Road, NW6*
☎ *020 7604 3636*
🚇 *Queen's Park LU*
🕐 *Mon-Fri 7am-8pm, Sat 7am-7pm, Sun 8.30am-2pm*

On offer here is a tempting range of breads, including sourdough and focaccia and sweet treats such as muffins, cookies and pastries.

West

& Clarke's

⌨ *122 Kensington Church Street, W8*
☎ *020 7229 2190*
🚇 *High Street Kensington LU or Notting Hill LU*
🕐 *Mon-Fri 8am-8pm, Sat 9am-4pm*

An elegantly rustic shop next door to Sally Clarke's restaurant, that sells her famous breads, such as rosemary, raisin and sea-salt plus own baked treats ranging from savoury pizzas to sweet tarts, including fresh fruit and chocolate. The discerningly selected stock also features own-made chocolate truffles and chutneys plus delicacies such as fine cheeses. There is a small café section at the back of the shop where one can sit and savour the freshly baked goodies with a cappuccino.

Exeter Street Bakery

⌨ *1B Argyll Road, W8*
☎ *020 7937 8484*
🚇 *High Street Kensington LU*
🕐 *Mon-Sat 8am-7pm, Sun 9am-6pm*

Specialists in traditionally-made Italian bread, such as ciabatta or pane Pugliese (see also Italian London, p.146).

Ottolenghi

⌨ *63 Ledbury Road, W11*
☎ *020-7727 1121*
🚇 *Notting Hill*

Sophisticated bakery-cum-traiteur-cum-cafe, offering freshly-baked pastries, cakes and breads made on the premises including stirato, foccacia and cornbread.

BUTCHERS

Even the most basic High-Street butcher's is a fast-vanishing breed, while a really decent one is extremely hard to find. One encouraging thing to emerge from the aftermath of the BSE crisis is that those butchers who put the emphasis on providing quality, plant-fed, free-range or organic meat have seen sales improve, as customers have realised the value of buying meat from a trustworthy, traceable source.

Ginger Pig

CENTRAL LONDON

Allen & Co
- *117 Mount Street, W1*
- *020 7499 5831*
- *Bond Street LU*
- *Mon-Fri 3.30am-4pm, Sat 3.30am-12noon*

With its beautiful tiles and huge wooden chopping blocks, this venerable butcher's is a Mayfair institution with customers ranging from film stars to famous restaurants. Allen & Co. is noted for the quality and range of its game and also for its Scotch beef.

Biggles
- *66 Marylebone Lane, W1*
- *020 7224 5937*
- *Bond Street LU*
- *Mon & Sat 10am-4.30pm, Tue-Fri 10am-6pm*

Tucked away down a charming side-street, Biggles is a sausage specialist selling made-on-the-premises, high-meat sausages in a huge range of varieties, from Toulouse to Greek.

The Ginger Pig
- *Borough Market*
- *020 7403 4721*
- *London Bridge LU/Rail*
- *Open weekly, Fri and Sat 8am-5pm*

Anne and Tim Wilson's Yorkshire-based meat business, specialising in meat from their own-reared pork, lamb and beef has found a receptive audience at Borough Market, where regulars queue patiently for cuts of beef, lamb or pork, freshly and expertly cut on request, and the excellent dry-cured bacon. Also on offer is chef Paul Hughes' home-cooked charcuterie, including black puddings, faggots and brawn.
For mail-order contact the farm 01751-460 242.

Portwine

⌨ *6 Earlham Street, WC2*

☎ *020 7836 2353*

🚇 *Leicester Square LU*

🕐 *Mon & Sat 7.30am-2pm, Tue-Thurs 7.30am-5pm, Fri 7.30am-5.30pm*

Run with enthusiasm by Graham Portwine, who can proudly say that there's been a Portwine butcher's shop in the Seven Dials area since 1790, this small shop specialises in traditional, quality meat. Stock includes meat from rare breeds, MacSween haggis, game, geese and superb dry-cured bacon.

Simply Sausages

⌨ *Harts Corner, 341 Central Markets,*
   Farringdon Street, EC1

☎ *020 7329 3227*

🚇 *Farringdon LU*

🕐 *Mon-Fri 8am-6pm, Sat 9.30am-2pm*

Appropriately situated next to Smithfield meat market, this corner shop sells over 40 different seasonal own-made bangers at any time of the year. In addition to truly meaty sausages – such as venison or pork – seafood and vegetarian sausages are also stocked.

EAST

Leadenhall Market

⌨ *off Leadenhall Street, EC3*

🚇 *Aldgate LU*

🕐 *Mon-Fri 8am-4pm*

Inside this picturesque Victorian arcade in the shadow of the Lloyds Building, among the boutiques and eateries remains a handful of distinguished butchers and fishmongers, whose quality stock reflects the world of huntin', fishin' and shootin'. Fishmongers H. S. Linwood, 6-7 Grand Avenue (Tel: 020 729 0554) have an eye-catching display while butchers R. S. Ashby, at 8 & 9 Leadenhall Market (Tel: 020 7626 3871), are known for Scotch beef with Butcher & Edmonds, at 1, 2 & 3 Grand Avenue (Tel: 020 7626 5816), specialising in game.

NORTH

Baldwins

- 469 Green Lanes, N4
- 020 8340 5934
- Manor House LU, then bus 29, 141, 341
- Mon-Sat 8.30am-6.30pm

Attractively spic and span, this smart corner shop stocks an excellent selection of meat including more specialist offerings such as rabbit and venison. At Christmas they do a roaring trade with their free-range bronze turkeys.

Frank Godfrey Ltd

- 7 Highbury Park, N5
- 020 7226 2425
- Arsenal LU
- Mon-Fri 8am-6pm, Sat 9am-5pm

This down-to-earth family butcher's – now run by fourth generation brothers Chris and Jeremy Godfrey – has a loyal and devoted following who know good meat when they see it. All the meat sold here is free-range and very good quality, from the English corn-fed chickens to the plant-fed pork and Orkney Island beef. The brothers work closely with their suppliers to ensure high feed and welfare standards, and the results are reflected in the meat that they sell.

Graham's

- 134 East End Road, N2
- 020 8883 6187
- East Finchley LU or Finchley Central LU
- Tue-Fri 7.30am-5.30pm, Sat 7.30am-4pm, Sun 9am-1pm

Among the specialities on offer are Aberdeen Angus beef, free-range meat and organic poultry. Food writer John Whiting recommends the free-range pork.

Highland Organics

⌨ *14 Bittacy Hill, NW7*
☎ *020 8346 1055*
🚇 *Mill Hill LU*
🕐 *Mon-Sat 8am-6pm*

As the name suggests, organic meats are the order of the day here, from Welsh black cattle beef steaks to huge plump homemade sausages. Customers can also stock up on basic organic groceries, from fresh bread to baked beans.

Midhurst

⌨ *2 Midhurst Parade, N10*
☎ *020 8883 5303*
🚇 *East Finchley LU, then the 102 bus*
🕐 *Mon-Thurs 8am-6pm, Fri 7am-6pm, Sat 7am-5pm*

Tucked away in a little parade of shops between Muswell Hill and East Finchley, this small shop offers decent meat (some organic) and a picturesque range of fresh fruit and veg outside.

Moore & Sons

⌨ *25 Greenhill Parade,*
Great North Road, New Barnet, EN5
☎ *020 8440 9649*
🚇 *High Barnet LU*
🕐 *Mon-Thurs 8am-5.30pm, Fri 7am-5.30pm, Sat 7am-4pm*

A small, traditional, well-established butcher's with friendly staff. Specialities include Scotch beef, own-made sausages and game.

SOUTH-EAST LONDON

P. & J. Baker

⌨ *147 Evelina Road, SE15*

☏ *020 7732 2820*

🚆 *Nunhead Rail*

🕐 *Tue-Sat 6am-4pm*

A cheerful family-run butcher's where popular items include excellent homemade pork bangers (made to a 100 year old recipe), well-hung beef and free-range chicken.

SOUTH-WEST

A. Dove & Son

⌨ *71 Northcote Road, SW11*

☏ *020 7223 5191*

🚆 *Clapham Junction Rail*

🕐 *Mon 8am-1pm, Tue-Sat 8am-6pm*

This characterful butcher's shop, run with passion by Bob Dove, has a loyal clientele. Particular highlights include the well-hung beef, Linda Dove's frozen meat pies and excellent bronze turkeys.

M. Moen & Sons

⌨ *24 The Pavement, SW4*

☏ *020 7622 1624*

🚆 *Clapham Common LU*

🕐 *Mon-Fri 8am-6.30pm, Sat 7.30am-5pm*

This well-established butcher's boasts a distinctly upmarket stock. The meat is good quality, from homemade sausages to a range of in-season game. Additional delights include wild mushrooms and seasonal produce like sea-kale.

Pether

⌨ *16 Station Parade, Kew Gardens, TW9*

☏ *020 8940 0163*

🚆 *Kew Gardens LU/Rail*

🕐 *Mon-Fri 7.30am-6.30pm, Sat 7.30am-5pm*

An appetising smell of spit-roasted chicken wafts out from this old-fashioned butcher's. All the meat here is free-range and the shop does a brisk business in homemade pies.

WEST

Kingsland Edwardian Butchers
⌨ *140 Portobello Road, W11*
🚇 *Notting Hill LU*
🕐 *Mon-Sat 7.30am-6pm*

A bright red frontage marks out this attractive, old-fashioned butcher's shop. There is a good range of meat, from their own dry-cured bacon to Orkney Aberdeen Angus beef. The speciality here, however, is rare breeds meat, from Gloucester Old Spot pork to extremely rare, seaweed-fed North Ronaldsay lamb from Orkney. Staff are jocular and helpful.

C. Lidgate
⌨ *110 Holland Park Avenue, W11*
☎ *020 7727 8243*
🚇 *Holland Park LU*
🕐 *Mon-Thurs 7.30am-6pm, Fri 7am-6pm, Sat 7am-5pm*

A grand old butcher's established in 1850, which specialises in high-quality, naturally reared meat and poultry. Run with great expertise and commitment by David Lidgate, the shop's stock includes organic meat from Highgrove (The Prince of Wales' estate), free-range bronze turkeys and geese. In addition, this family-run business sells award-winning homemade pies such as steak and kidney, and own-cooked hams.

Macken Bros
⌨ *44 Turnham Green Terrace, W4*
☎ *020 8994 2646*
🚇 *Turnham Green LU*
🕐 *Mon-Fri 7am-6pm, Sat 7am-5.30pm*

A seemingly perpetual queue testifies to this shop's popularity. Staff are helpful and friendly and the meat and poultry excellent.

Richardsons
⌨ *88 Northfield Avenue, W13*
☎ *020 8567 1064*
🚇 *Northfields LU*
🕐 *Mon-Thurs 8am-5.30pm, Fri 8am-6pm, Sat 8am-4.30pm*

A member of the Queen's Guild of Butchers, this down-to-earth, busy butcher's attracts a loyal clientele, drawn by the quality of the meat on offer, which includes well-hung beef and award-winning sausages.

CHEESE SHOPS

CENTRAL

La Fromagerie
2-4 Moxon Street, W1
020 7935 0341
Mon 10.30am-7.30pm, Tue-Fri 9.30am-7.30pm, Sat 9.30am-7pm,
Sun 10am-5pm
See French London p.118

Neal's Yard Dairy
17 Shorts Gardens, WC2
020 7240 5700
Covent Garden LU
Mon-Sat 9am-7pm, Sun 11am-5pm
A champion of British farmhouse cheeses, this small dairy shop has an impressive range of traditionally-made farmhouse cheeses including classics such as Appleby's Cheshire, Keen's Cheddar and Mrs Kirkham's Lancashire. Other produce includes Clarke's breads and good-quality cream, yogurt and butter. Staff are both friendly and knowledgeable and customers are encouraged to taste before buying – one of the joys of artisan-made cheese is that it varies in flavour from batch to batch. Other branch: 6 Park Street, SE1, Tel: 020 7645 3555

Paxton & Whitfield
93 Jermyn Street, SW1
020 7930 0259
Piccadilly Circus LU
Mon-Sat 9am-5.30pm
This picturesque, vintage shop (over 200 years old) is a well-known name in cheese-selling. Staff are helpful and there is a good selection of over 200 classic cheeses from Stilton to chestnut leaf-wrapped Banon goat's cheese, plus an assortment of wafers, biscuits and relishes.

Rippon Cheese Stores
26 Upper Tachbrook Street, SW1
020 7931 0628
Pimlico LU or Victoria LU/Rail
Mon-Sat 8am-5.15pm
In this cool, neat shop Karen and Philip Rippon stock an astonishing range of around 550 European cheeses. Here one can find seven different Cheddars, six different bries and a choice of differently aged Crottin.

NORTH

Cheeses

⌖ *11 Fortis Green Road, N10*
☎ *020 8444 9141*
🚌 *Bus 134*
🕐 *Tue-Fri 10am-6pm, Sat 9.30am-6pm*

Tucked away in an old-fashioned parade of shops just off Muswell Hill Broadway, this tiny shop offers an excellent array of European cheeses, served by friendly and helpful staff.

La Fromagerie

⌖ *30 Highbury Park, N5*
☎ *020 7359 7440*
✎ *www.lafromagerie.co.uk*
🚌 *Highbury & Islington LU/Rail*
🕐 *Mon 10.30am-7.30pm, Tue-Fri 9.30am-7.30pm,*
    Sat 9.30am-7pm, Sun 10am-5pm

Patricia Michelson's shop is something of a Mecca for cheese-lovers. Around 150-200 cheeses are stocked, according to season with the focus predominantly on fine French and Italian cheeses, plus some British farmhouse cheeses. See French London p.121.

SOUTH-WEST

Hamish Johnston

⌖ *48 Northcote Road, SW11*
☎ *020 7738 0741*
🚌 *Clapham Junction Rail*
🕐 *Mon-Sat 9am-6pm*

Now approaching its tenth year, this dapper shop has a loyal following, drawn by the carefully chosen selection of cheeses, numbering from 100-150 depending on the time of year. Preference is given to small-scale cheese producers, with delights on offer including Vintage Lincolnshire Poacher, Cotherstone and Llanboidy. The shop also sells a good range of biscuits to accompany cheese, plus chutneys, jams and olives. Knowledgeable, helpful staff are undoubtedly part of the shop's appeal. Other branch: Abbeville Road, SW4, Tel: 020 8673 5373

Neal's Yard Dairy

CHOCOLATE

CENTRAL

L'Artisan du Chocolat

⌨ *89 Lower Sloane Street, SW1*
☏ *020 7824 8365*
🚇 *Sloane Square LU*
🕐 *Mon-Sat 10am-7pm*

This austerely smart shop showcases the considerable talents of chocolatier Gerard Coleman and his partner Anne Weyns. Here one can buy Gerard's delectable ganache-filled chocolates, with sophisticated flavourings such as sea-salted caramel, lemon and thyme, chestnut honey or green cardamom. Easter and Christmas also see the shop filled with stylish Easter eggs and moulded figures, all lovingly made from the finest chocolate.

Charbonnel et Walker

⌨ *1 The Royal Arcade,*
28 Old Bond Street, W1
☏ *020 7491 0939*
🚇 *Piccadilly Circus LU*
🕐 *Mon-Fri 10am-6pm, Sat 10am-5pm*

An elegant chocolatiers, established in 1875, which sells high quality chocolates, including classic rose and violet creams, charming novelties and smartly-packaged chocolate gifts.

The Chocolate Society

⌨ *36 Elizabeth Street, SW1*
☏ *020 7259 9222*
🚇 *Sloane Square LU, Victoria Station LU/Rail*
🕐 *Mon-Fri 9.30am-5.30pm, Sat 9.30am-4pm*

This cosy shop-cum-café offers a wide range of fine French Valrhona chocolates. Bestsellers include the handmade fresh truffles and choco-late-coated hokey-pokey (honeycomb) while their hot chocolate, made from flaked chocolate, goes down particularly well with chocoholics.

Godiva

▢ *247 Regent Street, W1*
☏ *020 7495 2845*
🚇 *Piccadilly Circus LU*
🕐 *Mon-Sat 9.30am-7pm, Sun 12noon-6pm*

Smart shop offering classic Belgian chocolates and seasonal novelties.
Other branches: 17 Russell Street, WC2, Tel: 020 7836 5706
150 Fenchurch Street, EC3, Tel: 020 7623 2287

Rococo

▢ *321 King's Road, SW3*
☏ *020 7352 5857*
🚇 *Sloane Square LU, then the 11, 19 or 22 bus*
🕐 *Mon-Sat 10am-6.30pm*

Chocolate lover Chantal Coady (a founder of the Chocolate Society) set
up this pretty shop which offers an imaginative range of goodies
(including in-house handmade chocolate bars flavoured with spices and
flowers) and a plethora of enticing chocolate novelties.

NORTH

Ackermans

▢ *9 Goldhurst Terrace, NW6*
☏ *020 7624 2742*
🚇 *Finchley Road LU*
🕐 *Mon-Fri 9.30am-6pm, Sat 9.30am-5pm*

This discreet, well-established chocolate shop offers a classic range of
homemade chocolates, including the finest dark chocolate mint wafers,
superior truffles and attractive novelties.

DELICATESSENS

Flaneur Food Hall

CENTRAL

Chatsworth Farm Shop

54-56 Elizabeth Street, SW1

020 7730 3033

Sloane Square LU or Victoria Station LU/Rail

Mon-Fri 10am-6pm, Sat 10am-1pm

This spic and span upmarket venture, run with enthusiasm by Derbyshire man Craig Gordon, is a London showcase for Derbyshire products including those from the Chatsworth estate. An eye-catching display of fully traceable, seriously good-looking meat is a particular source of pride, and features Chatsworth cured bacon, ox-tails, own-made sausages, thick rare breed pork chops and matured beef. The shop does a roaring trade in homemade dishes cooked on the premises, including pies, salads, soups.

Flaneur Food Hall

41 Farringdon Road, EC1

020 7404 4422

Farringdon LU/Rail

Mon-Fri 8am-10pm, Sat 9am-10pm, Sun 9am-6pm

Housed in attractive high-ceilinged premises this spacious deli-cum-diner has a convivial, buzzy feel to it. Distinctive design elements include tall shelves filled with oils, vinegars, condiments and confectionery and a central counter complete with a pastry chef busy producing savoury and sweet baked goods. The stock, ranging from wine and dairy produce to confectionery, is extensive and upmarket, with French goods particularly well represented.

Villandry

170 Great Portland Street, W1

020 7631 3131

Great Portland Street LU

Mon-Sat 8.30am-10pm, Sun 11am-4pm

This pioneering deli-cum-diner is now housed in large, airy premises on Great Portland Street. Attractively presented stock ranges from breads and own-baked pâtisseries and baskets of fresh produce to an enticing selection of sophisticated chocolates. Ample space allows shoppers to wander round and browse at leisure, with particular highlights being the superior cheeses and charcuterie. Diners can sample produce in the refectory-style dining room.

EAST LONDON

A. Gold

- 42 Brushfield Street, E1
- ☎ 020 7247 2487
- Liverpool Street LU
- Mon-Fri 11am-8pm, Sat & Sun 11am-6pm

Housed in atmospheric 18th-century premises, with the shop retaining the name of its original French milliner owner, this delightful shop evokes an old-fashioned grocer's or village shop. Unusually, British produce, rather than the more usual French or Italian fare, takes pride of place here – hence, an eye-catching array of old-fashioned sweets such as Uncle Joe's Mint Balls, Cornish saffron cake, Scotch bannocks, Wormersly herb vinegars and traditional tipples, such as mead, sloe gin and silver birch wine. Basics include bread, English farmhouse cheeses, Richard Woodall's bacon and quality sausages. With space definitely at a premium, owners Safia and Ian choose their stock discriminatingly, though also with an eye for attractive vintage packaging. Bestsellers include Cartmel Village Shop sticky toffee pudding, "real" Scotch eggs and pear drops.

NORTH

Myddletons

- 25A Lloyd Baker Street, WC1
- ☎ 020 7278 9192
- Angel LU
- Mon-Fri 7am-6.30pm, Sat 7am-5pm

Tucked away on a peaceful Islington back-street Myddletons evokes the feel of a corner shop while stocking a good range of delicatessen basics.

SOUTH-WEST

Mise-en-Place

- 21 Battersea Rise, SW11
- ☎ 020 7228 4392
- Clapham Junction Rail
- Mon-Fri 9am-9pm, Sat & Sun 8.30am-7pm

A stylish delicatessen with upmarket stock, including an enticing range of olives, French farmhouse cheeses, pastas and traiteur dishes.

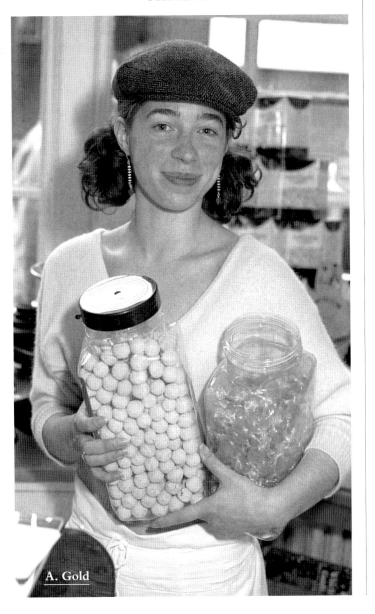

A. Gold

Troubadour Delicatessen
⌨ *267 Old Brompton Road, SW5*
☎ *020 7341 6341*
🚇 *East Putney LU*
🕐 *Mon-Sat 7am-9pm, Sun 10am-3pm*

Attractively decked out in dark green and burgundy, this smart new deli, linked to the Troubadour café next door, has been greeted with enthusiasm by locals pleased to find a proper food shop opening up in their midst. Stock includes cheese, charcuterie, wine and assorted breads – while the traiteur counter has proved a hit with weary, homeward bound commuters.

WEST

Maquis
⌨ *111 Hammersmith Grove, W6*
☎ *020 8846 3851*
🚇 *Shepherd's Bush LU*
🕐 *Mon-Fri 8am-7pm, Sat 8am-4pm*

Hidden away on a quiet leafy, residential street, next to the French restaurant Maquis, this airy food shop has an endearingly eclectic approach. Links to both Maquis and its Spanish-cum-Moorish sister-restaurant Moro in Clerkenwell are apparent in the stock with French produce including fine cheeses, wines and Normandy cider along with Middle Eastern ingredients such as dried limes, pomegranate syrup, argan oil, barberries and freekeh (roasted green wheat). In addition one finds Ginger Pig meat, an attractive display of fresh fruit and vegetables, breads and top notch charcuterie.

Mortimer & Bennett
⌨ *33 Turnham Green Terrace, W4*
☎ *020 8995 4145*
🚇 *Turnham Green LU*
🕐 *Mon-Fri 8.30am-6.30pm, Sat 8.30am-5.30pm*

This smartly tiled, well-established shop is crammed with goodies, from cheeses, salamis and pâtés, to a range of some 30 different olive oils. Sweet treats are a particular forte, including upmarket French chocolates, tempting biscuits and beautifully packaged confectionery.

FISHMONGERS

CENTRAL

Blagden

⊡ *65 Paddington Street, W1*

☎ *020 7935 8321*

🚇 *Baker Street LU*

🕓 *Mon 7.30am-4.30pm, Tue-Fri 7.30am-5pm, Sat 7.30am-1pm*

An eye-catching display of fish and seafood arranged on a marble slab marks this attractive purpose-built fishmongers, dating back to 1890. On offer is an upmarket selection of quality seafood: scallops in their shells, fresh Salcombe farm salmon, turbot and halibut. Game (in season) and poultry are also on offer, from English grey-leg partridge to Kelly free-range bronze turkeys.

The Fish Shop

⊡ *201 Kensington Church Street, W8*

☎ *020 7243 6626*

🚇 *Notting Hill LU*

🕓 *Tue-Fri 9am-7pm, Sat 9am-5pm*

This sleek annexe to the Kensington Place restaurant sells a select range of predominantly English fish, plus tuna and swordfish. The majority of the fish sold here comes from Cornwall from where it is delivered fresh and whole, daily, before being filleted on the premises.

La Maree

⊡ *76 Sloane Avenue, SW3*

☎ *020 7589 8067*

🚇 *South Kensington LU*

🕓 *Mon-Sat 8am-6pm*

This tiny annexe of the Poissonnerie restaurant offers a small but select range of seafood, including scallops in their shells and wild salmon. Prices are high but so is the quality and the staff are knowledgeable and helpful.

A. Scott & Son

NORTH

B & M Seafoods

⌖ *258 Kentish Town Road, NW5*
☏ *020 7485 0346*
🚇 *Kentish Town LU*
🕐 *Tue-Sat 9am-6pm*

A down-to-earth fishmongers which also, unusually, offers free-range and organic meat.

France Fresh Fish

⌖ *99 Stroud Green Road, N4*
☏ *020 7263 9767*
🚇 *Finsbury Park LU*
🕐 *Mon-Sat 9am-7pm, Sun 11am-5pm*

The arresting window display of brightly coloured tropical fish is a notable feature of this longstanding fish-shop, owned by the same Mauritian family who run the Chez Liline restaurant next door. Staff are friendly and happy to offer advice on the exotic stock.

Hampstead Seafoods

⌖ *78 Hampstead High Street, NW3*
☏ *020 7435 3966*
🚇 *Hampstead Station LU*
🕐 *Tue-Fri 7.30am-5pm, Sat 7.30am-4.30pm*

Tucked away off the High Street, this small shop offers a good range of quality seafood.

Steve Hatt

⌖ *88-90 Essex Road, N1*
☏ *020 7226 3963*
🚇 *Angel LU*
🕐 *Tue-Sat 7am-5pm*

An Islington institution, this no-nonsense fishmongers carries a good stock of fish, everything from herring to swordfish. The own-smoked fish is very popular.

Walter Purkis & Sons
⌨ *17 The Broadway, N8*
☎ *020 8340 6281*
🚇 *Finsbury Park LU, then the W7 bus*
🕐 *Tue-Sat 8am-5pm*

Right in the middle of Crouch End's bustling Broadway, this friendly shop offers a good selection of fish, from herring to salmon.

A. Scott & Son
⌨ *94 High Road, N2*
☎ *020 8444 7606*
🚇 *East Finchley LU*
🕐 *Tue-Thurs 8.30am-5.30pm, Fri 8.30am-6pm, Sat 8.30am-5pm*

This small, friendly fishmongers has an excellent range of fresh fish and seafood, with luxury items including clams, raw tiger prawns and frozen crabmeat.

SOUTH-EAST

Soper's
⌨ *141 Evelina Road, SE15*
☎ *020 7639 9729*
🚇 *Nunhead Rail*
🕐 *Tue-Fri 9am-5.30pm, Sat 8.30am-5.30pm, Sun 9am-2pm*

The appropriately-named Whiting family run this classic 'wet fish shop', which has been in the family since 1897. Customers come from a large catchment area to purchase prime, professionally-prepared fish and seasonal extras such as samphire.

SOUTH-WEST

Copes Seafood Company
⌨ *700 Fulham Road, SW6*
☎ *020 7371 7300*
🚇 *Fulham Broadway LU*
🕐 *Mon-Fri 10am-8pm, Sat 9am-6pm*

The sheer quality of the fresh, Cornish-caught fish on offer here has gained this fishmonger a strong reputation and loyal local following.

EAST

H.S. Linwood & Son
⌧ *6-7 Grand Avenue, Leadenhall Market, EC3*
☎ *020 7929 0554*
🚇 *Monument LU*
🕐 *Mon-Fri 6am-3pm*

As you enter the market, a splendid, show stopping display of fish and seafood marks out this long established fishmonger, proud holders of a Royal Warrant.

WEST

Covent Garden Fishmongers
⌧ *37 Turnham Green Terrace, W4*
☎ *020 8995 9273*
🚇 *Turnham Green LU*
🕐 *Tue, Wed & Fri 8am-5.30pm, Thurs & Sat 8am-5pm*

Despite small premises, veteran fishmonger Phil Diamond's shop stocks an impressive range of seafood: from fresh wild Scotch salmon to Pallourde clams and langoustine.

Goldborne Fisheries
⌧ *75 Goldborne Road, W10*
☎ *020 8960 3100*
🚇 *Ladbroke Grove LU*
🕐 *Mon 9.30am-4pm, Tue-Sat 8am-6pm*

George's bustling fish shop is a local institution, always busy with customers. The range of stock is enormous: from live eels and octopuses to tropical fish such as barracuda and parrot fish, and an excellent choice of shellfish.

FOOD HALLS

CENTRAL

Bluebird

🖃 *350 King's Road, SW3*

☎ *020 7559 1000*

🚇 *Sloane Square LU*

🕐 *Mon-Wed 9am-8pm, Thurs-Sat 9am-9pm, Sun 12noon-6pm*

Conceived on a characteristically grand scale, Terence Conran's gastro-drome is housed in the lovingly-refurbished 1923 Bluebird Garage, and offers everything from charcuterie and cheeses to fine wines and fresh seafood. As one would expect, presentation is stylish, from the Philip Starck organic groceries to an elegant array of olive oils. Highlights include the bakery section which offers 40-50 bread varieties a day (all made on the premises in wood-fired ovens), and the excellent butcher's counter.

Fortnum and Mason

🖃 *181 Piccadilly, W1*

☎ *020 7734 8040*

🚇 *Piccadilly Circus LU*

🕐 *Mon-Sat 10am-6.30pm, Sun 11am-5pm (Food Hall only)*

With its red carpeted floors, pastel-coloured walls and chandeliers, this famous high-class grocer's (established in 1707) is justly renowned for providing the finest quality products from across the world. Traditional and regional British foodstuffs are very much to the fore with luxuries such as smoked wild salmon, vintage whiskies and champagnes, pheasant's, pullet's eggs and Japanese Gyokura tea (£50 for 125g).

Harrods

⊞ *87 Brompton Road, SW1*
☎ *020 7730 1234*
🚇 *Knightsbridge LU*
🕐 *Mon, Tue & Sat 10am-6pm, Wed-Fri 10am-7pm*

These sumptuous food halls – some complete with vintage tiling – are a reminder of Harrods' roots as a tea merchant's business. With 18 departments, the range of foodstuffs is enormous: from the magnificent fresh fish display to exotic fruits and vegetables. Highlights include the wide-ranging charcuterie and cheese counters.

Harvey Nichols Food Hall

⊞ *Knightsbridge, SW1*
☎ *020 7235 5000*
🚇 *Knightsbridge LU*
🕐 *Mon-Fri 10am-8pm, Sat 10am-6pm*

This stylish food hall, with its high tec marketplace feel, adjoining restaurant and smartly-dressed customers, offers an upmarket range of products focusing on British foodstuffs. The bakery section and butcher's and fishmongers counters are all impressive. In-house goods come tastefully packaged in silver and grey.

Selfridges

⊞ *400 Oxford Street, W1*
☎ *0870 8377 377*
🚇 *Bond Street LU or Marble Arch LU*
🕐 *Mon-Wed, Fri & Sat 9.30am-7pm, Thurs 9.30am-8pm*

Immaculate and gleaming, the food hall at Selfridges reflects its cosmopolitan clientele with an excitingly international range of ingredients and ready-made foods. Particularly eye-catching is the long fresh fish counter, with its attractive display of fresh fish and shellfish.

HEALTH FOOD SHOPS

Fresh & Wild

CENTRAL

Fresh & Wild

⌨ *69-75 Brewer Street, W1*
☏ *020 7434 3179*
🚇 *Piccadilly Circus LU*
🕐 *Mon-Fri 7.30am-9pm, Sat 9am-9pm, Sun 11.30am-8.30pm*

Where there was once an old-fashioned butcher's shop, there's now a thriving, funky health food shop – a telling sign of the times. Housed over two storeys, it carries an impressive range of organic foodstuffs, plus a fresh salad bar and juice bar popular with local workers.

Planet Organic

⌨ *22 Torrington Place, WC1*
☏ *020 7436 1929*
🚇 *Goodge Street LU*
🕐 *Mon-Fri 8.15am-8pm, Sat 11am-6pm, Sun 12noon-6pm*

An attractive branch of the West London store, complete with a juice-bar and café area offering organic, vegan and vegetarian food, which is busy at lunchtime.

EAST

Fresh & Wild

⌨ *194 Old Street, EC1*
☏ *020 7250 1708*
🚇 *Old Street LU*
🕐 *Mon-Fri 9.30am-7.30pm, Sat 10.30am-5.30pm*

A small, friendly branch of the well-established organic chain, stocking organic foodstuffs, take-away snacks and natural remedies.

NORTH

Bumblebee

⌨ *30, 32 & 33 Brecknock Road, N7*
☏ *020 7607 1936*
🚇 *Kentish Town LU, then 29 bus*
🕐 *Mon-Wed, Fri & Sat 9.30am-6.30pm, Thurs 9.30am-7.30pm*

This trio of busy shops offers an excellent range of health foods, from fresh organic produce to vegetarian cheeses. Staff are very helpful.

Fresh & Wild

⌨ *49 Parkway, NW1*
☎ *020 7428 7575*
🚇 *Camden Town LU*
🕐 *Mon-Fri 8am-9pm, Sat 9.30am-9pm, Sun 11am-8pm*

This large, funky shop is very much a new wave health food shop, complete with juice bar, breakfast bar and Latino music playing in the background. Highlights include the eye-catching display of fresh organic produce and a huge array of pulses, nuts and dried fruits. The extensive general stock includes a small organic meat section and freezers filled with organic Rocombe Farm and Green & Black ice creams.

Fresh & Wild

⌨ *32-40 Stoke Newington Church Street, N16*
☎ *020 7254 2332*
🚇 *Bus 73*
🕐 *Mon-Fri 9am-9pm, Sat 9am-8.30pm, Sun 10am-8pm*

Attractive airy branch of the organic food shop chain, offering their hallmark extensive stock and friendly service. The in-house organic café and juice bar is a popular meeting place for mums with toddlers.

Haelan Centre

⌨ *41 The Broadway, N8*
☎ *020 8340 4258*
🚇 *Finsbury Park LU, then W7 bus*
🕐 *Mon-Sat 9am-6pm (Friday until 6.30pm), Sun 12noon-4pm*

Just by Crouch End's Clock Tower, this shop is a local institution. The downstairs shop sells fresh organic produce and health-food groceries ranging from goat's milk to honey; upstairs there is a health clinic.

Just Natural

⌨ *304 Park Road, N8*
☎ *020 8340 1720*
🚇 *Finsbury Park LU, then W7 bus*
🕐 *Mon-Sat 9am-7pm, Sun 11am-3pm*

Housed in an old, tiled butcher's shop in a pretty parade of shops at the foot of Muswell Hill, this health-food shop's stock is both vegetarian and 100% organic, from the wheatgrass juices and babyfood to the spices and Rocombe Farm ice cream. Staff are friendly and helpful, and mums with buggies are particularly well catered for.

SOUTH

Baldwins Health Food Centre
🏠 *171-3 Walworth Road, SE17*
☎ *020 7703 5550*
🚇 *Elephant & Castle LU*
🕐 *Mon-Sat 9am-5.30pm*

A South London institution, this established business offers a truly impressive range of herbal remedies plus good general organic and health food stock.

Brixton Wholefoods Transatlantic
🏠 *59 Atlantic Road, SW9*
☎ *020 7737 2210*
🚇 *Brixton LU/Rail*
🕐 *Mon 9.30am-7pm, Tue-Thurs & Sat 9.30am-5.30pm, Fri 9.30am-6pm*

This is a friendly, laid-back wholefood shop, so-named because its former premises were on the other side of Atlantic Road. Organic fruit and veg are delivered three times a week. The range of around 300 herbs and spices and the selection of 20 breads are particularly popular.

SOUTH-WEST

Fresh & Wild
🏠 *305-311 Lavender Hill, SW11*
☎ *020 7585 1488*
🚇 *Clapham Junction Rail*
🕐 *Mon-Fri 9am-9pm, Sat 8.30am-7.30pm, Sun 12noon-6pm*

This large branch of the new wave organic food specialists offers an impressive display of fresh produce, plus a juice bar where Claphamites can enjoy a reviving glass of wheatgrass.

Kelly's Organic Foods
🏠 *46 Northcote Road, SW11*
☎ *020 7207 3967*
🚇 *Clapham Junction Rail*
🕐 *Mon-Thurs 9am-8pm, Fri & Sat 9am-6pm*

Attractively housed in a corner site, Daniel Kelly's fresh-looking shop offers a good range of organic stock, from baby foods (jars and frozen) to bacon and wheat-free bread. Particular highlights include the fresh fruit and vegetables and the deli counter. An added draw for customers is an arrangement whereby Copes (see p.28) sell their upmarket seafood in an annexe on Tuesdays, Thursdays, Fridays and Saturdays.

Oliver's Wholefood Store

⌨ *5 Station Approach, TW9*
☎ *020 8948 3990*
🚇 *Kew Gardens LU/Rail*
🕐 *Mon-Sat 9am-7pm, Sun 10am-7pm*

This pleasant airy shop has excellent overall stock: from fresh organic produce (including blood oranges, sweet potatoes and young garlic) which is delivered daily, to neatly arranged shelves of groceries – including organic polenta and rosehip jam. Staff are friendly and helpful and practitioners of complementary medicine come in every week to offer customers free advice.

WEST

Fresh & Wild

⌨ *210 Westbourne Grove, W11*
☎ *020 7229 1063*
🚇 *Bayswater LU or Notting Hill Gate LU*
🕐 *Mon-Sat 8am-9pm, Sun 10am-7pm*

This appealing health food shop provides Notting Hill residents with a huge range of organic foods and natural remedies. The organic deli and juice bar, offering a choice of truly fresh juices, are particularly popular.

Planet Organic

⌨ *42 Westbourne Grove, W2*
☎ *020 7221 7171*
🚇 *Bayswater LU or Queensway LU*
🕐 *Mon-Sat 9.30am-8pm, Sun 11am-5pm*

This cavernous, stylish superstore offers everything for the healthy lifestyle, from freshly-pressed juices at the juice bar to organic muesli. There is a large grocery section, a seafood counter, and a particularly impressive fresh produce section and butcher's counter.

MAIL-ORDER

Fresh and Wild also supply natural remedies by mail-order; freephone 0800 03 23456 for details.

39

MARKETS

The most exciting recent development on London's food shopping scene has been the growing number of new specialist food markets. The success of markets such as Borough demonstrates that there is a real appetite for fresh, good food in the capital .

Catherine at Borough Market

Borough Food Market

🚇 *London Bridge LU/Rail*
🕐 *Fri 12noon-3pm, Sat 9am-4pm*

Housed in Borough's wholesale market (atmospherically situated under the railway arches next to Southwark Cathedral) Borough food market continues to thrive, despite current redevelopment of the site by Railtrack.

Fundamental to its success is the range and quality of goods on offer: wonderfully fragrant, mono-varietal French honeys from delicate lavender to rich chestnut honey, prime pork, beef and first-rate bacon from Nottinghamshire-based Ginger Pig and smoked eel from Brown & Forest. A fine range of take-away foods is also sold here, ranging from fiery chorizo sandwiches and free-range chicken wraps to proper pork pies and Malay curry puffs.

Borough Market also acts as a showcase for retailers such as Brindisa, offering superb Spanish foodstuffs, L'Artisan du Chocolat, with their distinctive flavoured chocolates, Stefano Cavallini's I Sapori with own-made pasta and sauces, and wholesalers including Flour Power (offering great baguettes and focaccia) and Turnips, with a picturesque display of fresh fruit and vegetables.

The nearby side-streets are also home to farmhouse cheese specialist Neal's Yard Dairy, Monmouth Coffee House and bakers Konditor & Cook with bakers De Gustibus backing onto the market.

Henrietta Green's Food Lovers' Market
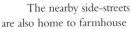 *Covent Garden Piazza, WC2*

Every second Friday of the month sees a selection of fine food stalls setting up shop in the piazza from 10am-7pm, selling comestibles such as unpasteurised cream, farmhouse cheeses and prime meat.

Organic Market
Spitalfields Market, Old Spitalfields Market, Brushfield Street, E1
Liverpool Street LU/Rail
Sun 9.30am-5pm

London's first 'organic' market draws a steady stream of devoted regulars, returning for fresh produce, organic meat, health foods and breads. A recently set up Food Market also takes place at Spitalfields Market on Wednesdays (from 10am-6pm), offering foodstuffs including cheeses, organic produce and breads.

FARMERS' MARKETS

armers' markets (an idea imported from America, where farmers and food producers sell direct to local consumers) are growing in popularity throughout Britain. London is no exception and now hosts a number of farmers' markets, each showcasing foods produced within 100 miles of the M25.

Being able to buy seasonal produce at its best is obviously one of the attractions of the farmers' markets, so in the summer months one might find zingy green watercress picked that morning, pea shoots and soft fruit such as strawberries and raspberries whereas in the autumn traditional English apple varieties and root vegetables abound.

There is more on offer at farmers' markets, however, than simply fresh fruit and vegetables: meat, fish and shellfish, breads, cakes, cheeses and fruit juices are also sold. Regular stall-holders at a number of London's farmers' markets include the Demes, selling a range of apple juices, Flour Power, with breads including notable sourdoughs, David Jennings selling shellfish and smoked fish, Quality Herbs and March House with Gloucester Old Spot pork.

Barnes

Essex House car park (opposite the pond), Station Road, Barnes, SW13
Barnes Bridge Rail
Saturdays 12noon-4pm

Blackheath

Blackheath Rail Station Car Park, 2 Blackheath Village, SE3
Sundays 10am-2pm

Camden

Camden Lock Market, Camden Lock Place, Chalk Farm, NW1
Camden Town LU
Wednesdays 10am-4pm

Chiswick

Dukes Meadows, just off A316, via the park-gates in Edensor Road or the back of Alexandra Gardens
Sundays, 10am-2pm

Dulwich

South Gravel, Dulwich College, Dulwich Common, SE21 7LD

West Dulwich Rail

Generally the last Sunday of the month, 9am-1pm

Ealing

Leeland Road, West Ealing, W13

West Ealing

Saturdays 9am-1pm

Islington

Essex Road, N1
(opposite Islington Green)

Angel LU

Sundays 10am-2pm

Notting Hill

Car park behind Waterstones, access via Kensington Place, W8

Notting Hill Gate LU

Saturdays 9am-1pm

Palmers Green

Palmers Green Rail Station Car Park, N13

Southgate & Wood Green LU, then buses 121, 299

Sundays 10am-2pm

Peckham

Peckham Square, Peckham High Street, SE15

Peckham Rye or Queens Road Rail, buses 12, 36, 171, 345

Sundays 9.30 am-1.30pm

Pimlico Road

Orange Square, SW1
(corner of Pimlico Road & Ebury St)

Sloane Square LU, or buses 211, 11 & 239

9am-1pm

Swiss Cottage

O₂ Centre Car Park, Finchley Rd, NW3 (near Homebase)

Buses 13, 82 & 113
Buses 268 & 187 go into car park

Wednesdays 10am-4pm

Twickenham

Holly Road Car Park, Holly Rd, off King St, Twickenham, TW1

Twickenham

Saturdays 9am-1pm

Uxbridge

Forecourt of Uxbridge Civic Centre High St, Uxbridge, UB8
(opposite The Chimes shopping centre, free parking in the Chimes)

Uxbridge LU

Sundays 10am-2pm

Whetstone

High St, N20 (opposite Waitrose)

Totteridge LU & Whetstone LU

Fridays 11am-5pm

Wimbledon Park

Wimbledon Park First School, Havana Road, SW19

Wimbledon Park LU

Saturdays 9am-1pm

TEA & COFFEE

William Martyn

Founder of W. Martyns
~ 1897

W.M. Martyn

44

CENTRAL

Algerian Coffee Store
⊞ *52 Old Compton Street, W1*
☏ *020 7437 2480*
▦ *Leicester Square LU*
🕐 *Mon-Sat 9am-7pm*

A vintage Soho institution, set up in 1887 by an Algerian businessman and now Italian-run. The aromatic scent of coffee and spices wafts out of the door – a clue to the extensive range of coffees and teas inside.

Angelucci
⊞ *23b Frith Street, W1*
☏ *020 7437 5889*
▦ *Leicester Square LU*
🕐 *Mon-Wed/Fri/Sat, 9am-5pm, Thurs 9am-1pm*

This tiny family-run business, housed in these premises since 1931, is best-known for its in-house Mokital blend, used a few doors down by Bar Italia (see Italian London, p.155 for more details).

H. R. Higgins
⊞ *79 Duke Street, W1*
☏ *020 7629 3913*
▦ *Bond Street LU*
🕐 *Mon-Wed 8.45am-5.30pm, Thurs & Fri 8.45am-6pm, Sat 10am-5pm*

Founded in 1942 by Harold Higgins (known as 'the coffee man'), this family-run business continues to sell quality teas and coffees. The huge copper caddies, beautiful old scales and knowledgeable, courteous service provide a glimpse into another retail era.

Monmouth Coffee Company
⊞ *27 Monmouth Street, WC2*
☏ *020 7379 3516*
▦ *Covent Garden LU*
🕐 *Mon-Sat 9am-6.30pm*

With its high-backed, wooden tasting booths and aromatic scent of coffee, this small coffee shop-cum-café is a much-loved Covent Garden institution. It offers a discerning range of carefully sourced coffee, sold whole or freshly ground, as requested.

NORTH

W. M. Martyn

⌨ *135 Muswell Hill Broadway, N10*
☎ *020 8883 5642*
🚇 *Highgate LU, then 134 bus*
🕐 *Mon-Wed & Fri 9.30am-5.30pm, Thurs 9.30am-1pm, Sat 9am-5.30pm*

The aroma of freshly-roasted coffee beans floating down the Broadway marks the presence of this small, old-fashioned grocer's, which was established over 100 years ago. While best known for its teas and coffees, the shop also stocks a range of traditional groceries, from excellent dried fruits to sugar mice and bars of German marzipan. Staff are helpful and friendly.

SOUTH

Monmouth Coffee House

⌨ *2 Park Street, SE1*
☎ *020 7645 3560*
🚇 *London Bridge LU/Rail (Borough High Street exit)*
🕐 *Mon-Sat 8am-5pm*

Right by Borough Market, in a prime corner site, this is an attractively airy, spacious café-cum-coffee shop, (sibling to the Monmouth Street establishment) offering a carefully chosen range of coffees. Coffee drinkers can sample both the coffee and a selection of Sally Clarke's viennoserie.

MAIL-ORDER

Union Coffee Roasters

⌨ *The New Roastery, Unit 2,*
7a South Crescent, London, E16 4TL
☎ *020 7474 8990*
✆ *020 7511 2786*
✍ *www.unionroasters.com*

Coffee afficionadoes Jeremy Torz and Steven Macatonia of Union Coffee Roasters specialise in hand-roasted coffee. Their carefully chosen coffees (which include organic, estate and decaffeinated) range from their popular Revolution Espresso blend to aromatic Yemen Mocha Matari. Union Coffee Roasters make a point of ethically sourcing their coffee from small family-owned farms and have cultivated close relations with growers across the world.

SPICES

Greencades

⌧ *Merton Abbey Mills, No.5 The Apprentice Shop,*
Watermill Way, South Wimledon, SW19 2RD
☎ *020 8543 0519*
🚇 *Colliers Wood LU*
☺ *Daily 9.30am-5.30pm (10am-5pm Bank Holidays)*

This long established shop is situated in the heart of Merton Abbey Mills Market, and is always very busy on Sundays when the market is in full swing. As well as gifts Greencades offers an extensive range of herbs and spices with eleven kinds of pepper and twenty six types of dried herbs. The mulling spices and spice blends are prepared on the premises and are a firm favourite with regular visitors. If you don't want to trek down to Wimbledon they offer an efficient mail order service – just phone for a price list.

The Spice Shop

⌧ *1 Blenheim Crescent, W11*
☎ *020 7221 4448*
🚇 *Ladbroke Grove LU*
☺ *Mon-Sat 9.30am-6.30pm, Sun 11am-5pm*

Birgit Erath runs this small, aromatic shop with enormous enthusiasm and energy, stocking an impressive range of spices and herbs for both culinary and medicinal purposes.

MAIL-ORDER

Seasoned Pioneers

⌧ *101, Summers Road,*
Brunswick Business Park, Liverpool, L3 4BJ
☎ *Freephone: 0800 0682348*
✍ *www.seasonedpioneers.co.uk*

An intelligently chosen selection of over a hundred spices, spice blends and herbs are on offer from this mail-order company. Spices are dry-roasted in small batches in-house and carefully blended to offer authentic flavours. In addition to more familiar spices, Seasoned Pioneers offer items such as Ras-al-Hanout, sumac, chipotle chillies and curry leaves, with the spices ingeniously packaged in funky re-sealable foil packets.

AFRICAN & CARIBBEAN LONDON

France Fresh Fish

In his monumental book, Staying Power, Peter Fryer points out that the first Black presence in Britain dates back to Roman times, when Black men were among the conscripts in the Roman army. The growth of a domestic Black community, however, was connected with Britain's slave trade, which was started in 1562-3 by the first 'triangular voyage' between Britain, Africa and the West Indies. The demand for sugar and the labour-intensive sugar cane plantation system in the Caribbean encouraged the slave trade's growth, making it enormously profitable to those running it.

Africans came to Britain as slaves until the slave trade was outlawed in 1807. Before this date some free Blacks, such as seamen, servants and street entertainers were established in Britain, with the London community living mainly along the Thames in Limehouse. But accounts, such as that of freed slave Ukawsaw Gronniosaw, give a vivid picture of ill-treatment and discrimination, which forced many into destitution. After 1807 the Black community in Britain declined, although Black loyalists returned after fighting in the American War of Independence, and some seamen settled after serving in the Napoleonic Wars (1792-1815). In the late nineteenth century a small community of Somali seamen settled in the London docks.

The coming of the First World War meant a change of attitude towards the Black community. Instead of being rejected for work on racial grounds, their help was now needed in the munitions factories. Black seamen also filled the gaps in the Merchant Navy caused by conscription. By 1919, there were 20,000 Black people in Britain. But once the war was over the picture changed again, with the seamen's unions closing the door firmly against any Black labour.

A similar pattern occurred in the late 1940s and 1950s when, as Britain struggled to rebuild its war-torn economy, a call went out to the Commonwealth for workers to come to the 'Mother Country'. The 1948 Nationality Act granted British citizenship to people living in Britain's current and former colonies. For many West Indians this was an opportunity to be seized; unemployment was high in the West Indies and in 1951 a hurricane added to Jamaica's problems. Corporations such as London Transport actively recruited labour in Barbados in 1956, and by 1966 had also turned to Trinidad and Jamaica. Between 1945 and 1958, over 125,000 West Indians emigrated to Britain.

The different stages of African immigration into London in the post-war years have been triggered by the ebb and flow of African politics. The 1950s and 1960s saw an influx of West Africans made up largely of students and lawyers. During the 1970s, African and Asian Ugandans fled Idi Amin while recent years have seen an increase in immigration from Ghana, Zaire and Ethiopia.

There is no single centre for the African community in London, with pockets of different African nationalities scattered throughout the capital. There are, however, focal points such as Brixton and Notting Hill for the West Indian community. Many of the first post-war Jamaican immigrants who sailed over on the Empire Windrush settled in Brixton, a formerly prosperous suburb which had become cheap and run-down. This community attracted further Jamaican immigrants during the 1950s and 1960s. Notting Hill, in which mainly Trinidadians settled, hosts the famous Carnival; what originated as a 1964 Bank Holiday street party for local children has since developed into Europe's largest open-air street festival. The costume parades and rhythmic steel drums all derive from Trinidad's own spectacular Carnival.

AFRICAN & CARIBBEAN CUISINE

'African food' is a blanket term covering a huge number of countries with their own characteristic cuisines. Certain staples, such as maize, cassava, plaintain and beans, are shared across different African countries and crop up in Black cuisine in many parts of the world. Dried foods, such as smoked or salted fish and meat, are another common element in the African kitchen, reflecting the need to preserve food before the days of refrigeration or canning. Many of these ingredients are still used to add a distinctive flavour to dishes.

West African slaves brought their cuisine to the West Indies and its influence remains marked in today's Caribbean cooking. Many of the staples are the same (several brought from Africa): cassava, yams, taro, plaintain, groundnuts. Dishes in common include coo-coo (cornmeal pudding) and fufu, the latter being a Fanti word used on the Cape Coast. In West Africa fufu is pounded yam, plaintain and cassava dough dipped into a soup, while in Jamaica fufu now means both the pounded yam and the soup. The slaves' restricted diet also included salted meat and fish and these are still popular, although the latter is now something of a luxury.

Caribbean cooking is very much a melting pot of a cuisine, influenced by a series of colonisers and immigrants. Chillies were brought from South America by the Spanish colonisers and 'escovished fish', fresh pickled fish, originated from the Spanish dish escabeche. The arrival in Trinidad of indentured workers from India means that dishes like roti and curry goat are popular there today; a large proportion of the island's inhabitants have Indian roots.

The fertility of the Caribbean islands allowed many plants to be introduced successfully. Staples now include breadfruit, which was introduced by Captain Bligh. Fresh seafood is characteristic of West Indian cuisine and increasingly fish such as colourful snappers are becoming available in Britain.

GLOSSARY

Ackee: a red-skinned fruit that is only safe to eat when the fruit is fully ripe. The white, fleshy base called an aril is the part that is eaten. Fresh ackee is very rarely found but it is available in tins. Saltfish with ackee is one of Jamaica's famous dishes. The Latin name of the fruit, *Blighia sapida*, is a tribute to Captain Bligh, who introduced it to Jamaica.

Agbono: sometimes spelt ogbono, this is the inner kernel of the African bush mango. The kernel is the size and shape of an almond but browner and much harder. Available both whole and ground.

Allspice: peppercorn-sized berries, with a flavour that combines cloves, cinnamon and nutmeg – hence the name.

Annatto: small, orange-red seeds, used to add colour and flavour.

Arrowroot: a starch extracted from the underground stem of a water-plant.

Avocado: this green-skinned, soft-fleshed fruit is called 'pear' in the Caribbean.

Bananas: green bananas, which are the unripe fruit of certain varieties, and ripe yellow bananas are treated as both a vegetable and a fruit in Caribbean and African cuisines.

Bitter leaf: a distinctively flavoured African leaf, related to the lettuce family. Available dried or frozen.

Breadfruit: a football-sized fruit with thick, green, pimply skin and creamy flesh, used both as a starchy vegetable and in pies and puddings.

Callaloo: green leaves of the dasheen plant, used to make a famous eponymous soup. Available tinned and fresh.

Cassava: large, brown, hand-shaped tubers of the cassava plant, also called manioc or yucca. Bitter cassava, despite the fact it contains toxic prussic acid which must be removed by either cooking or pressing, is a staple food. Yellow-fleshed sweet cassava is eaten as a vegetable. Dried, ground cassava is used in Africa to make gari. Ground cassava meal is used in the West Indies to make a type of bread and the flavoured juice of grated cassava is used to make cassareep, a key ingredient of pepperpot.

Catfish: dried: small blackened fish, with a distinctive large head, used to add flavour to soups and stews in West African cooking.

Cho-cho (christophene, chayote): a pear-sized member of the squash family, with a wrinkled skin ranging in colour from white to green, and watery white flesh.

Coconut: coconut flesh and milk are widely used in Caribbean cookery.

Cornmeal: coarsely or finely ground dried corn kernels.

Crayfish (dried): although called 'crayfish' in Africa, these are a type of shrimp. Used whole or ground as flavouring.

Custard apple: apple-sized fruit with a knobbly, green skin. The white, sweet pulp has a custard-like texture, hence the name.

Dasheen: potato-sized fibrous tubers with white starchy flesh. Some varieties of dasheen have an acrid taste.

Eddoe: a small, rounded fibrous tuber with white starchy flesh.

Egusi: pumpkin seeds, which are available shelled, either whole or ground. Egusi is used in West African cooking, providing a nutty texture in soups and stews.

Fish: *flying fish*, a distinctive 'winged' fish; *king fish*, a firm-fleshed 'meaty' fish, often sold as steaks; *parrot fish*, a brightly-coloured fish with a beaky head; *snapper*, a popular, firm-fleshed fish, available in colours from grey to pinkish-red; and *trevalli*, a large, firm-fleshed oily fish. *Jacks,* is the name given to the smaller fish of the same family.

Gari: coarsely-ground cassava, an African staple.

Guava: small, yellow-green, hard-skinned fruit with pinkish flesh filled with small seeds. It has a distinctive fragrance and is eaten raw or used to make jams and jellies.

Guinep: small, round, green fruit which grows in bunches. The pink flesh has a delicate flavour.

Irish moss: white, curly seaweed from which an eponymous drink is made. Available either in dried or drinkable form.

Jackfruit: a large, green fruit with a pimply skin, similar in appearance to breadfruit.

Kenke: West African dumpling, made from fermented maize flour wrapped in corn husks or banana leaves and cooked.

Landsnails: giant snails, sold either alive, frozen, tinned or smoked. If bought alive, keep them and feed them salad for a few days before cooking to make sure they have excreted anything toxic.

Mango: this large, kidney-shaped fruit, with its succulent orange flesh and sweet, resiny flavour, comes in numerous varieties.

Okra (ladies fingers, ochroes): finger-sized, ridged, tapering green pods, introduced into the Caribbean from West Africa.

Ortanique: a cross between an orange and a tangerine, this looks like an orange with a flattened end.

Palm hearts: tender palm tree hearts, usually found tinned.

Palm oil: a thick, orange-red oil, made from the fruit of the oil palm, which adds flavour and colour to African dishes.

Pawpaw: long, oval fruit, with soft orange flesh, varying in skin colour from green to orange.

Peppers: among the hottest and most flavourful of the peppers used in African and Caribbean cooking is the squat, rounded Scotch bonnet pepper, available in green, yellow and red varieties.

Pepper sauce: the sauce comes in a variety of textures from liquid to paste, but is always hot!

Pigeon pea (gunga): ridged pea pods, with every pea in its own section. Unusually, the peas within a single pod vary in colour from cream through green and brown. Available fresh, tinned or dried.

Plaintain: similar in appearance to green bananas, plaintain have starchy flesh and are cooked and eaten as a vegetable. They can be chipped, boiled or cooked in stews.

Pomelo: often called shaddock, after the merchant ship captain who introduced the fruit to the Caribbean, this is a large, thick-skinned citrus fruit, similar in flavour to grapefruit.

Saltfish: preserved foods such as salted fish were brought over to the Caribbean to feed the plantation workers. It is now something of a luxury item. Stockfish is a popular salted fish.

Sapodilla (naseberry): a fruit very similar in appearance to kiwi fruit, with a brown, furry skin. Inside it has pinky-brown, granular flesh with a few glossy pips and a distinctive sweet flavour.

Sorrel (rosella): the red sepals of a flowering plant, used either fresh or dried to make a dark-red, aromatic drink, traditionally at Christmas.

Soursop: a large, oval-shaped fruit with a thick, green, spiny skin. The pinkish-white flesh inside is custard-textured with a delicate, tart flavour.

Sugar cane: similar in appearance to bamboo, this plant has played a considerable part in Caribbean history as the sugar cane plantations demanded extensive labour, provided by slaves. Short lengths of the woody stalk are either chewed or sucked for their sweet refreshing juice.

Sweet potato: a sweet-fleshed tuber, available in many varieties.

Yam: a family of large, brown-skinned, starchy tubers, which come in many varieties, both yellow and white-fleshed.

FOOD SHOPS

EAST

Queens Market
▱ *Green Street, E7 (on the corner of Queen Road)*
🚉 *Upton Park LU*
🕐 *Tue & Thurs-Sat 8am-5pm*
Among the clothing and household goods are a number of stalls and shops selling Caribbean foodstuffs, such as tropical fish and halal meat.

Ridley Road Market
▱ *Ridley Road, E8*
🚉 *Dalston Junction Rail*
🕐 *Tue-Sat 9am-5pm*
A large, bustling market with a mixture of English and West Indian fruit and vegetable stalls, fishmongers and halal butchers, mixed in with fabric and hair-care stalls.

NORTH
The stretch of Stroud Green Road nearest to Finsbury Park tube station is home to a number of African and Caribbean food shops, ranging from greengrocers to halal butchers.

France Fresh Fish
▱ *99 Stroud Green Road, N4*
☎ *020 7263 9767*
🚉 *Finsbury Park LU*
🕐 *Mon-Sat 9am-7pm*
An eye-catching window display marks out this established shop, specialists in tropical fish and run by the same family who own Chez Liline, the Mauritian fish restaurant next door. Good things on offer include an array of raw prawns, samphire (when in season) and exotic fish and seafood, including barracuda, conch and parrot fish.

K. M. Butcher's Grocer's

🔲 *29 Stroud Green Road, N4*

☎ *020 7263 6625*

🚇 *Finsbury Park LU*

🕑 *Mon-Sat 8am-8.30pm, Sun 9am-7pm*

A large store, complete with a counter piled high with goat's meat and chickens, and groceries ranging from Mauby syrup drinks to bags of cornmeal.

Stroud Green Food Store

🔲 *65 Stroud Green Road, N4*

☎ *020 7272 0348*

🚇 *Finsbury Park LU*

🕑 *Mon-Sun 8am-8pm*

A neatly-arranged store with an attractive display of fresh fruit and vegetables outside, including breadfruit, mangoes, plaintain and bunches of thyme and grocery staples inside.

SOUTH

Brixton Market

🔲 *Brixton Station Road, Pope's Road,*
Atlantic Road, Electric Road and Electric Avenue

🚇 *Brixton LU/Rail*

🕑 *Mon, Tue & Thurs-Sat 8am-5.30pm, Wed 8am-1pm*

This is the best market in London for West Indian and African food-stuffs. Spread out through streets and arcades alongside a mixture of household goods, wig and fabric shops are a range of fruit and vegetable stalls, piled high with yams, red Scotch bonnet peppers, green and yellow plaintains, breadfruit, mangoes, limes and bunches of thyme. Fishmongers here sell an array of tropical fish while the butchers (some with signs advertising 'meat so tender you don't need teeth') offer goat, offal, cow's feet and pig's trotters. Saturday is the busiest market day and the noise is tremendous: music blaring from the record shops and people exchanging greetings, catching up on news and arguing over prices.

Fresh Food City
⊞ *256 Upper Tooting Road, SW17*
☎ *020 8672 0414*
🚇 *Tooting Broadway LU*
🕐 *Daily 9am-9pm*

A large well-stocked store, catering to both the local Asian and Caribbean communities, complete with fresh produce section, halal meat and fish counters and grocery.

WEST

Portobello Road Market
⊞ *Portobello Road, W12*
🚇 *Notting Hill Gate LU*
🕐 *Mon-Sat 9am-5pm*

Past the antique shops is a lively fruit and vegetable market. Several of the stalls here sell West Indian produce such as yams, Scotch bonnet peppers and okra.

Shepherd's Bush Market
⊞ *Uxbridge Road, W12*
🚇 *Goldhawk Road LU or Shepherd's Bush LU*
🕐 *Mon-Wed, Fri & Sat 9am-5pm, Thurs 9am-1pm*

A decade ago this was a larger, more food-orientated market. Among the fabric, lingerie and kitchenware stalls, however, one can still find a handful of stalls selling Caribbean produce.

MAIL ORDER

Gramma's Pepper Sauce
⊞ *PO Box 218, East Ham,*
London, E6 4BG
☎ *020 8470 8751*

Dawn Moore produces the best and hottest pepper sauce I have ever tried. She will supply jars of mild (seriously euphemistic), medium and super-hot pepper sauce.

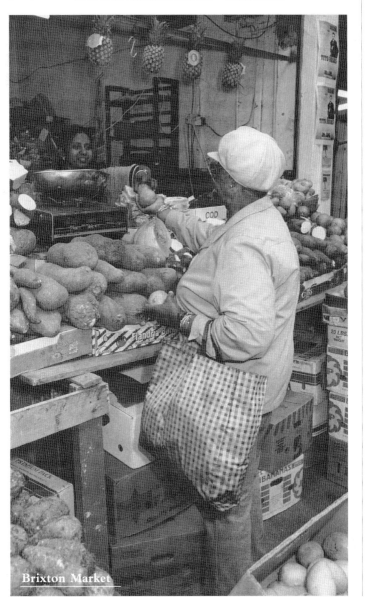

Brixton Market

EATING PLACES

CENTRAL

Calabash   £2

- 🏠 *The Africa Centre, 38 King Street, WC2*
- ☏ *020 7836 1976*
- 🚇 *Covent Garden LU*

This basement restaurant offers a range of reasonably priced dishes from across the continent of Africa.

NORTH

Cottons   £2

- 🏠 *55 Chalk Farm Road, NW1*
- ☏ *020 7485 8388*
- 🚇 *Camden Town LU or Chalk Farm LU*

Attractively decorated in bright tropical colours this funky restaurant serves up generous portions of excellent Caribbean food. Highlights include the banana leaf-wrapped ackee parcel and mixed jerk grilled fish (red snapper, squid, goat fish and mullet). Drinks include cocktails, sorrel and a serious range of rums.

Lalibela   £2

- 🏠 *137 Fortess Road, NW5*
- ☏ *020 7284 0600*
- 🚇 *Tufnell Park LU*

This small, friendly Ethiopian restaurant offers a chance to enjoy lovingly prepared classic Ethiopian dishes such as 'wot', richly-spiced stews and injeera, the flat, spongy, slightly sour bread with which one scoops up and eats the wot. Finish off with Ethiopian coffee, a pleasantly sensory, leisurely experience during which one inhales the fragrance of the freshly roasted beans, heated in a heavy metal saucepan, before being presented with a pottery flask of the freshly made coffee served with aromatic burning frankincense on the side.

WEST

BB's £££
⌨ 3 Chignell Place, Uxbridge Road, W13

☎ 020 8840 8322

🚇 Ealing Broadway LU

Hidden away down a tiny side-street this convivial restaurant, run by the genial Brian Benjamin, offers a menu of rich Grenadian food and rum cocktails. Eat here with a crowd of friends and enjoy the party atmosphere.

Mandola ££
⌨ 139 Westbourne Grove, W11

🚇 Bayswater LU or Queensway LU

This small, relaxed Sudanese restaurant, run with great charm by Yusuf and his wife, serves fresh, tasty food such as salata aswad (aubergine salad) and kustalata (lamb cutlets) at remarkably reasonable prices. Round off your meal with the delectable date mousse and traditional Sudanese coffee.

COOKBOOKS

Caribbean and African Cookery by Rosamund Grant
An informative and readable cookbook.

Caribbean Cooking by Elizabeth Lambert Ortiz
An excellent look at Caribbean cuisine.

Creole Caribbean Cookery by Kenneth Gardiner
A well-written cookbook.

Nigerian Cookbook by H.O. Anthonio and M. Isoun
A very clear and informative book.

A Taste of Africa by Dorinda Hafner
A fascinating look at African and Caribbean cookery, written with exuberance and infectious enthusiasm.

Trade Wind: Caribbean Cooking by Christine Mackie
An evocative mix of text and recipes.

ASIAN LONDON

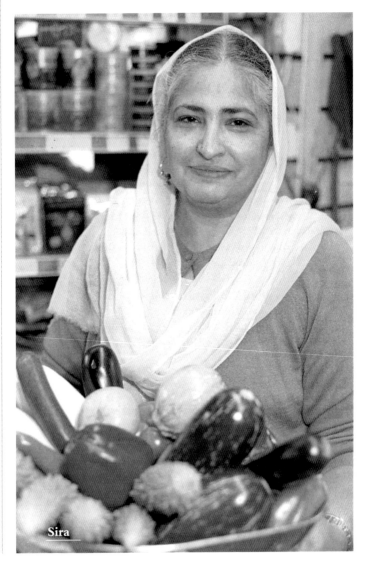

Sira

The term 'Asian' covers what was once the Indian subcontinent but is today Bangladesh, India, Pakistan and Sri Lanka. An Asian presence in Britain can be traced back to the seventeenth and eighteenth centuries. Some early settlers were performers but many were servants brought back from India by the newly prosperous nawabs. Through the East India Company others came as lascars, Indian seamen.

A fascinating book, *Across Seven Seas* (edited by Caroline Adams), describes how many of these lascars were from one small, land-locked part of Bengal called Sylhet. There was a tradition in rural India of men leaving their villages to work and support their family. Work as seamen was offered at large ports such as Calcutta. In the words of Haji Kona Miah: 'The Sylhet people were in the ship because these people follow each other, and some went there and others saw them and thought they could get jobs too'. The serangs, agents who chose workers for the ships, preferred to employ people from their own village or locality. Once Sylhetis became serangs, a pattern of using Sylheti sailors was established.

Those who settled in London lived in the East End, near the docks. For many of them earning a living was difficult; in 1858 the 'Strangers Home for Asiatics, Africans and South Sea Islanders' was opened in West India Dock Road, Limehouse. The major growth in the Bengali community came this century in 1956, when passports were finally granted and thousands of people came to London. By 1962, the number of Bengali immigrants living in the East End had swelled from approximately 300 to 5,000.

Of course, it was not only Bengali seamen who came to London: doctors, politicians and lawyers were also among the immigrants. Indeed, three men pivotal to India's independence studied law in London at the turn of the century: Mohandas Karamchand (later Mahatma) Gandhi, Mohammed Ali Jinnah and Jawaharlal Nehru. In 1892 Dabadhai Naoroji, a campaigner for Indian rights, was elected as Britain's first Asian MP by a majority of three votes.

It was in the period following the Second World War that the Asian presence in Britain expanded considerably; the 1948 Nationality Act granted the right of British citizenship to Britain's colonies and former colonies. After Indian Independence the violent partition of

India and Pakistan left thousands dispossessed. Britain officially encouraged mainly unskilled workers from India and Pakistan to come to Britain and by 1958 there were around 55,000 Asians in Britain. The next wave of immigration came in the late 1960s when Asians were expelled from Uganda, and in 1972, when Idi Amin expelled nearly 30,000 Ugandan Asians who arrived in Britain within the space of three months.

The Asian community today, like the complex Indian subcontinent, is made up of people from different countries who speak different languages and practice different faiths. Certain areas in London are linked to particular groups. Brick Lane, which over the centuries has housed different waves of immigrants, is now predominantly Bengali, the Sylhet seamen who first settled there having paved the way for others. The history of Brick Lane is encapsulated in the story of one building on Fournier Street: built as a Huguenot chapel in 1774, it later became a Methodist chapel; in 1898 it was converted into a Jewish synagogue, and nowadays it functions as the London Jamme Masjid mosque.

Wembley is a Gujarati area, while Southall is predominantly Punjabi and Sikh. There are various theories about Southall's Asian roots. One is that workers brought out to construct the new airport at Heathrow settled near their worksite. Alternatively, it is thought that work was provided for Asian labourers in local factories and the community grew up around this. Southall today is a thriving community with everything from Sikh temples to bookshops and restaurants. In South London Tooting houses a diverse Asian community, including Sri Lankans, East African Asians, Pakistanis and Gujuratis. London's Hindu community, meanwhile, is justly proud of 'Shri Swaminarayan Mandir' (Tel: 020 8965 2651), the traditional Hindu temple recently built in Neasden. The gleaming white marble temple, which rises like a mirage in an urban setting just off the North Circular, is unique in Europe as an example of traditional Indian temple construction. It is made from blocks of limestone and marble which were hand-carved in India then shipped over and assembled in London. There is an adjourning Haveli (community centre) decorated with intricate wooden carvings – visitors to the temple complex are courteously welcomed.

ASIAN CUISINE

The term 'Indian cuisine' is a catch-all phrase, covering the diverse cuisines of India, Pakistan, Bangladesh and Sri Lanka – and a huge spectrum of regional, religious and cultural differences. The hallmark of all Indian cuisine is the emphasis on spices and herbs. These numerous flavourings, from aromatic crocus stamens (saffron) to pungent resin (asafoetida), are used in intricate and varying ways: dry-roasted, fried in hot oil or mixed with other spices to form a masala (spice mix). Underlying their culinary use is an ancient belief in the health-giving properties of spices. In the Holy Hindu Scriptures, Ayurvedic scripts list the medicinal properties of herbs and spices. Turmeric and cloves both have antiseptic properties. Asafoetida, a digestive which prevents flatulence, is added to lentil dishes. Spices are divided into 'warm', generating internal heat, and 'cool', lessening it.

Underneath this culinary umbrella are diverse cuisines influenced by religion (the main Indian faiths being Hinduism, Islam, Buddhism, Jainism and Sikhism), geography and culture. Religions have laid down rules and taboos as to what can or cannot be eaten. For example, the Hindus will not eat beef as the cow (tended by Lord Krishna in myth) is a sacred animal. Some Hindus are vegetarian, while for strict vegetarians even the flavourings associated with meat (garlic and onion) are forbidden in cooking. For Muslims, pork is a forbidden meat.

When describing Indian cuisine in regional terms, it is possible to draw a crude north-south boundary, although there are exceptions. Flat wheat breads such as paratha and chapati are a staple in the north while rice is the staple in the south. Northern cuisine was influenced by Mogul rulers who came down to India through Persia and brought with them many of the dishes we now consider typical of Indian cuisine. The Persian influence is apparent in the subtle spicing, the use of nuts and in dishes such as pullao. From this luxurious court cuisine came techniques used today: korma (braising in a thick, often nut-based sauce); pot-roasting (in a traditional charcoal stove); and kebab, kofte and tandoori (dishes cooked in a tandoor oven). The Indian food that is most frequently served in restaurants is based on this Mogul cuisine. In Southern Indian cookery the coconut palm has an influential role, with sweet coconut milk used in many dishes. Rice is eaten not just as a grain but is ground, mixed with dal, and used to make light pancakes called dosai.

GLOSSARY

Angled loofah: a green gourd with distinctive raised ridges running down its length and a bitter flavour.

Asafoetida (heeng): a pungent brown resin, valued for its digestive properties, sold in either lump or powder form.

Bitter gourd (karela): a knobbly-skinned, cucumber-shaped green gourd with a distinctive bitter flavour and digestive properties.

Bottle gourd (dudi): a large, smooth, bottle-shaped, green-skinned gourd with marrow-like flesh.

Cardamom: a fragrant spice pod sold whole, hulled or ready-ground. The small green or white cardamoms are used in both sweet and savoury dishes while the larger wrinkled black cardamom is used only in savoury dishes.

Carom (ajwan): a tiny seed spice, like miniature fennel seeds, with a medicinal scent and sharp, thyme-like flavour.

Chayote (chow-chow): a pear-sized, wrinkled, green-skinned squash with a single large seed and marrow-like flesh.

Chenna: a ricotta-like curd cheese.

Chickpea flour (gram or besan): ground chickpeas are the basis for many breads and fritters. Madhur Jaffrey recommends storing it in the fridge.

Chickpeas (channa): fresh chickpeas are small, puffy green pods which need peeling to reveal the kernel.

Chikoo (sapodilla): similar in appearance to kiwi fruit with a fine brown, furry skin, pinky-brown granular flesh, a few glossy pips and a distinctive sweet flavour.

Chillies: sold both fresh and dried. Long slim green chillies and dried red chillies are used in Indian cookery to add both pungent heat and a distinctive flavour.

Chilli powder: a hot red powder made from ground, dried red chillies.

Cluster beans (guar): fine, straight green beans.

Coconut milk: a thick white liquid made from grated coconut flesh and not, as is sometimes thought, from the cloudy liquid inside the coconut which is called 'coconut water'. Homemade coconut milk can be made by blending together dessicated coconut with hot water, then sieving it. Alternatively, tinned coconut milk is a convenient, ready-to-use product; Madhur Jaffrey recommends the Chaokoh brand. Creamed coconut or coconut milk powder needs diluting before use.

Coriander: both the aromatic green leaves (similar in appearance to flat-leafed parsley) and small rounded seeds are used extensively in Indian cookery.

Spiny Bitter Gourd

Cumin: small, greenish, finely-ridged oval seeds, similar to caraway seeds, with a distinctive, slightly sharp flavour, widely used in Indian cookery. Black cumin, which is rarer, has a more pronounced herbal flavour.

Curry leaf: a spicy-smelling leaf which resembles a small bay leaf. It's usually sold dried but sometimes branches of fresh curry leaves are available.

Dal: a generic term covering the three types of pulses (lentils, beans and peas) used in Indian cookery: *chana dal*, small yellow split peas; *masoor dal*, tiny pink split lentils (sometimes called red split lentils); *moong dal*, yellow split mung beans (sold both skinned and unskinned); *rajma dal*, red kidney beans; *toovar dal*, a large split yellow pea; *urad dal*, ivory-coloured hulled black gram beans (used in Southern Indian vegetarian cookery in dishes such as pancakes and fried dumplings).

Drumsticks: long, green, ridged pods with a thick skin, fibrous pulp and a distinctive flavour. Usually available tinned but sometimes found fresh.

Fennel: aniseed-flavoured, greenish ridged seeds, valued as a digestive. Candied fennel seeds are eaten after a meal.

Fenugreek (methi): both the small, stubby, hard, yellow seeds and the spicy-smelling, bitter green leaves are used in Indian cookery. The seeds have a strong, bitter flavour and are used in pickles. The dark green trefoil leaves, which look similar to clover, are sold both fresh and dried.

Fish: *Hilsa*, a prized freshwater fish from Bangladesh; *pomfret*, a flat, round-shaped and white-fleshed fish.

Garam masala: a fragrant spice mix, available in many versions.

Ghee: clarified butter with a nutty flavour. Because of the clarification, ghee can be used for deep frying and stored at room temperature.

Ginger: this knobbly, light-brown root is a key flavouring prized for its aromatic flavour and digestive qualities.

Guava: a fruit resembling a small, knobbly pear, with a distinctive aroma, pinkish flesh and several small, hard seeds.

Hyacinth bean (seim): a broad-podded, thick-skinned, curved green bean; a member of the hyacinth bean family.

Jackfruit: a huge fruit with a thick, green studded skin. The creamy-textured flesh inside is eaten as a vegetable when unripe and as a fruit when ripe.

Jaggery: a pale brown sugar with a rich, nutty flavour, made from sugar cane juice or palm sap, and used in Indian sweets.

Kohlrabi: a pale green or purple bulbous vegetable, resembling a sprouting turnip – but with a more delicate flavour.

Kokum: an inedible variety of mangosteen, sold in dried pieces and used as a souring agent.

Lemon crystals: light-coloured crystals used as a souring agent.

Mango: a kidney-shaped fruit, with succulent orange flesh and a sweet, resiny flavour, which is enormously popular in India. Tart, green unripe mangoes are used to make pickles, chutneys and relishes while orange-red ripe mangoes are eaten on their own or used in desserts. Over a thousand varieties are grown in India, but the Alphonso mango is one of the best known in Britain.

Mango powder (amchoor): sour, beige-coloured powder made from dried, unripe mangoes, used to add a tart flavour to food.

Mustard oil: a pungent yellow oil, made from mustard seeds, used extensively in northern India and Bangladesh.

Mustard seeds: tiny, black round seeds, often used in pickles.

Okra (bhindi, ladies fingers): a tapering, ridged green pod which exudes a sticky juice when cooked.

Onion seed (kalonji or nigella): tiny tear-shaped black seeds which, despite their name, are not related to onions. Used primarily in pickles but also on tandoori naan bread.

Panch phoran: a Bengali five-spice mix, containing cumin, fennel, onion seeds, fenugreek and black mustard seeds.

Paneer: a firm white cheese, made from pressed Indian curd cheese called chenna (which is similar to ricotta).

Patra: large, green taro leaves which are spread with a gram flour paste, rolled and steamed to make a dish called 'patra'.

Phalooda (falooda): transparent, thread-like noodles made from wheatberry starch and flavoured with pine or rose essence, used in desserts, to garnish kulfi or in a drink of the same name.

Pistachio: green-fleshed, delicately-flavoured nuts, used in Indian sweetmeats and ice cream or as a nibble.

Pomegranate seeds (anardana): dried pomegranate kernels, used to add sourness.

Poppadums (papar): small round wafers made from split-peas and flavoured with garlic or spices. When fried in hot oil they puff up and become crispy.

Poppy seed (khas khas): minuscule white poppy seeds, used in ground form to thicken sauces.

Rice: the most famous and expensive of rice varieties grown in India is basmati, with its nutty aroma and flavour.

Rose essence: a delicate rose-scented essence used in desserts. Rose water is a diluted form of rose essence.

Saffron: the dried stigmas of a crocus variety, sold in both thread and powdered form.

Sevian: fine golden-brown wheat vermicelli, used in desserts.

Snake gourd: as the name suggests, a long, narrow, twisted green gourd with bland marrow-like flesh.

Spiny bitter gourd (kantola): a small, spiky, egg-shaped relation of the bitter gourd.

Sweetmeats: many Indian sweetmeats are made from milk boiled down slowly until it thickens (rabadi) or until it takes on a fudge-like consistency (khoya). Varieties include: *barfi*, a crumbly Indian fudge often flavoured with nuts; *gulub jamun*, deep-fried dumplings in syrup; *halwa*, nuts, fruits and vegetables cooked with ghee and sugar to a firm texture; *jalebi*, bright orange, crisp batter squiggles filled with syrup; *kulfi*, ice cream made from slow-cooked milk which gives a slightly grainy texture; and *rasmalai*, delicate, soft chenna dumplings served in rabadi (slow-cooked milk).

Tamarind: a brown fleshy pod with a sour-sweet flavour, used as a souring agent. Both tamarind pulp and tamarind paste are available.

Taro: the term applies to a whole range of fibrous tubers, recognisable by their brown hairy skins and white starchy flesh.

Tinda: a small, rounded member of the marrow family, with pale green skin and white flesh.

Tindola (tindori): walnut-sized 'ivy' gourds with variegated markings and a crisp, crunchy texture.

Turmeric (haldi): a small-fingered, orange-fleshed root from which comes the powdered yellow spice powder of the same name.

Vark: fine edible foil, made from ground silver or gold, used to adorn dishes on special occasions.

White radish (mooli): long, thick white radish, with a mild flavour, used to stuff parathas in Pakistani cooking.

Yard-long beans: exceedingly long, thin green beans.

Yogurt: traditionally made from buffalo milk, Julie Sahni suggests stirring a little soured cream into normal yogurt to reproduce the necessary tangy flavour.

FOOD SHOPS

The range of stock in Asian food shops is huge, from fresh fruits and vegetables to staples like dals and flours. Often the emphasis is on bulk-buying and stocking up with large sacks of basmati or huge packets of spices. Both Southall and Wembley have this kind of shop, sandwiched amongst stores selling alluring fabrics and glittering jewellery. These shops often have a paan counter (a digestive made from shredded betel nut rolled up in a paan leaf).

CENTRAL

Tucked away behind Euston Station, the quiet backwater of Drummond Street is home to a number of excellent, good value Indian restaurants, and a few food shops.

Ambala

- 112 Drummond Street, NW1
- 020 7387 7886/3521
- Euston LU/Rail
- Daily 9am-9pm

Ambala have been selling Asian sweets since 1965, when their first small shop opened on this site. Ambala is now a thriving chain and the original shop has been revamped in bright colours with marble counters. Customers return again and again for excellent fudge-like barfis, sticky jalebi and takeaway packets of rasmalai. Savoury snacks include crisp vegetable samosas and packets of Bombay mix.

Indian Spice Shop

- 115-119 Drummond Street, NW1
- 020 7916 1831
- Euston LU/Rail
- Mon-Sat 9.30am-9.30pm, Sun 10am-9pm

Catering for both the local English and Indian communities, this is divided into an off-licence-cum-corner shop on one side and an Indian grocer's on the other which offers a glorious range of spices, chutneys, papads and dals, plus huge sacks of basmati.

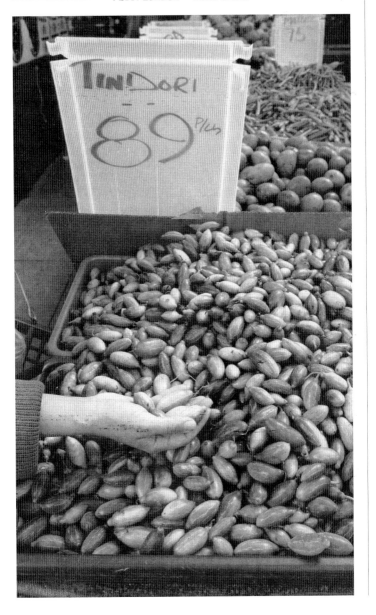

East

Focal points for Indian shopping in the East End are the area around Brick Lane (home to the Bengali community) and, further out, Green Street in Upton Park.

Ambala

⌨ *55 Brick Lane, E1*
☎ *020 7247 8569*
🚇 *Aldgate East LU*
🕐 *Mon-Sat 10am-8pm, Sun 9.30am-7.30pm*

A branch of the Asian sweet manufacturers (see under Central for more details).

Taj Stores

⌨ *112-14a Brick Lane, E1*
☎ *020 7377 0061*
🚇 *Aldgate East LU*
🕐 *Daily 9am-9pm*

A comprehensive food store, serving the local Bengali community, which combines a halal meat counter, a greengrocer's section and a mini-supermarket of grocery items such as pulses and spices.

Green Street, E7

🚇 *Upton Park LU*

This long East End road is characterised by a mixture of High Street chain stores, a jellied eel and mash shop and an assortment of Asian stores, selling everything from wedding saris and gold jewellery to bargain boxes of mangoes and sweetmeats.

Bharat

⌨ *4-6 Carlton Terrace, Green Street, E7*
☎ *020 8572 6393*
🚇 *Upton Park LU*
🕐 *Daily 9am-8pm*

This large store is aimed at those who buy in bulk, stocking things like huge 15 litre tins of ghee and 10 kilogram sacks of basmati. The freezers are jammed with Indian fast food, from halal kofta kebabs to spicy chicken nuggets. Fresh fruit and veg, such as aubergines and chillies, can be found at Bharat's small sister shop, over the road at No. 263.

Green Village

☖ 10a Carlton Terrace, Green Street, E7

☎ 020 8503 4809

🚇 Upton Park LU

🕐 Daily 8am-7pm

A large, neat greengrocer's, full of the smell of ripe mangoes at the time of my visit. Stock included more unusual items such as rolls of patra leaves, gunda (used in chutneys), sweet tamarind pods and Thai mangosteens.

Kishan The Mill Shop

☖ 20 Carlton Terrace, Green Street, E7

☎ 020 8471 0008

🚇 Upton Park LU

🕐 Mon-Sat 9am-7pm, Sun 10am-6pm

A grocer's, with a large selection of spices, cooking oils, nuts, nibbles (such as cassava chips) and pulses, and brightly-coloured garlands of flowers hanging down behind the till.

Queens Market

☖ Green Street, E7 (on the corner of Queen Road)

🚇 Upton Park LU

🕐 Tue & Thurs-Sat 8am-5pm

Stalls here sell an assortment of goods, from curtain fabric to household wares. The presence of a local Asian community is reflected in a number of halal butchers and fishmongers selling Asian fish around the edge of the market.

Sunfresh

☖ 11-12 Carlton Terrace, Green Street, E7

☎ 020 8470 3031

🚇 Upton Park LU

🕐 Daily 8am-7pm

Funky music blares in this large store which offers both an array of Indian fruit and veg and a grocery section with rice, pulses, chutneys and spices.

NORTH

Bina
⌨ *241 Golders Green Road, NW11*
☏ *020 8458 2366*
🚇 *Golders Green LU*
🕐 *Daily 8am-7pm*
This large Asian supermarket is strong on pre-packed goods, stocking an array of flours, spices, pulses, tinned fruits and vegetables, papads and chutneys.

Goodeats
⌨ *124 Ballards Lane, N3*
☏ *020 7349 2373*
🚇 *Finchley Central LU*
🕐 *Mon-Sat 9am-7pm*
This well-established, neatly arranged foodstore has an excellent range of stock. In addition to a good selection of Indian groceries, there is a fresh fruit and vegetable section, including fresh methi, mangoes and patra.

Q Stores
⌨ *19 Lodge Lane, N12*
☏ *020 8446 2495*
🚇 *Woodside Park LU*
🕐 *Mon-Sat 9.30am-5.45pm, Sun 10am-1pm*
Tucked away just off North Finchley's busy high street, this small, neat shop has a good range of fresh Indian produce, from mangoes to methi, plus store cupboard staples.

NORTH-WEST

For an excellent choice of Indian food shops, especially greengrocers, visit Wembley's Ealing Road. Be warned, however, that it becomes very busy over the weekend and parking restrictions have made it hard to leave the car nearby.

Fudco

🏠 *184 Ealing Road, HA0*
☎ *020 8902 4820*
🚇 *Alperton LU*
🕐 *Mon-Sat 9.30am-6.30pm, Sun 10.30am-6.30pm*

As importers and packagers, Fudco are a major supplier of foodstuffs ranging from spices to dried fruits. Their own grocer's shop is a show-case for their own brand goods, offering everything from chickpea flour to an assortment of dried chillies.

Obhrai

🏠 *168-170 Ealing Road, HA0*
☎ *020 8903 4450*
🚇 *Alperton LU*
🕐 *Daily 9am-7pm*

A cash and carry store with a good range of groceries including spices, pulses, flours, pickles and tinned vegetables.

Royal Sweets

🏠 *280 Ealing Road, HA0*
☎ *020 8903 9359*
🚇 *Alperton LU*
🕐 *Tue-Sun 10am-7pm*

A friendly branch of the established Asian sweetmeat shop, selling brightly coloured halvas and savoury nibbles.

Sira Fruit-Veg

🏠 *288 Ealing Road, HA0*
☎ *020 8903 5769*
🚇 *Alperton LU*
🕐 *Daily 8am-10pm*

A roomy store with a large fresh fruit and vegetable section, including okra, fresh curry leaves and bunches of methi. In addition there is a selection of basic Asian groceries.

V. B. & Sons Cash and Carry
⌨ *218 Ealing Road, HA0*
☏ *020 8902 8579*
🚇 *Alperton LU*
🕐 *Mon-Fri 9.30am-6.45pm, Sat 9am-6.45pm, Sun 11am-5pm*

A huge, neatly-arranged store, aromatic with spices and bustling with customers tracking down the numerous special offers. V.B. specialises in groceries, with a gargantuan range of spices, nuts, dried fruits, dals and flours. The freezer section contains yucca and mogo chips, samosas and samosa pastry.

Wembley Exotics
⌨ *133-135 Ealing Road, HA0*
☏ *020 8900 2607*
🚇 *Alperton LU*
🕐 *Daily 24 hours*

Mounds of chillies, root ginger and peanuts under an awning mark this cavernous self-service store, which specialises in fresh produce. Inside is a staggering array of Asian fruits and vegetables, from guvar beans and pigeon peas to guavas and mangoes.

SOUTH

The main highway through Tooting is lined with a real variety of Asian food shops (halal butchers, greengrocers, foodstores and sweetshops) and a tempting choice of eateries, ranging from veteran South Indian vegetarian to Pakistani restaurants offering halal meat dishes.

Daily Fresh Foods
⌨ *152 Upper Tooting Road, SW17*
☏ *020 8767 7861*
🚇 *Tooting Bec LU or Tooting Broadway LU*
🕐 *Daily 8am-8pm*

An eye-catching outdoors display of fresh fruit, vegetables and herbs, ranging from pumpkins and bunches of methi to passion fruit and mangoes, distinguishes this busy shop. Inside is a halal counter and a grocery section offering a limited choice of basics.

Deepak Cash and Carry

🏠 *953 Garratt Lane, SW17*

☎ *020 8767 7819*

🚇 *Tooting Broadway LU*

🕐 *Mon-Sat 9am-7.30pm, Sun 10am-4pm*

An enormous, rather ramshackle supermarket with an extensive range of Asian foodstuffs, from provisions like poppadums and chutneys to fresh fruit and vegetables.

Nature Fresh

🏠 *126-128 Upper Tooting Road, SW17*

☎ *020 8682 4988*

🚇 *Tooting Bec LU or Tooting Broadway LU*

🕐 *Daily 7am-8pm*

This large neatly arranged self-service greengrocers has an excellent selection of good quality, reasonably priced produce, including patra leaves, yellow limes and chikoo.

Patel Brothers

🏠 *187-191 Upper Tooting Road, SW17*

☎ *020 8672 2792*

🚇 *Tooting Bec LU or Tooting Broadway LU*

🕐 *Daily 9am-6.30pm*

A large store with a fresh fruit and vegetable section near the door. Stock includes shelves of pickles, curry pastes and spices, ghee and tinned foods. A side room is devoted mainly to rice, pulses and flours, including 32 kilogram sacks of chapati flour.

WEST

Southall, in London's western suburbs, is a busy Indian shopping area full of sari shops, jewellers, halal butchers, greengrocers and large-scale cash and carry stores, where the emphasis is on bulk-buying.

Ambala

🏠 *107 The Broadway, UB1*

☎ *020 8843 9049*

🚇 *Southall Rail*

🕐 *Daily 10am-8pm*

A branch of the established Asian sweet manufacturers.

Dokal & Sons

🖳 *133-135 The Broadway, UB1*
☎ *020 8574 1647*
🚇 *Southall Rail*
🕐 *Daily 9am-8pm*

What appears at first to be a small corner shop widens out into a huge store, filled with a comprehensive stock of groceries such as chutneys, flours, tinned vegetables, nuts and spices. Now in its 25th year, it is run with friendly enthusiasm by Mr Dokal and his family.

Gifto Cash and Carry

🖳 *115-119 The Broadway, UB1*
☎ *020 8574 8602*
🚇 *Southall Rail*
🕐 *Daily 9am-8pm*

Well-established and resembling a mini-supermarket, Gifto's is a classic Southall cash and carry. Stock includes basics such as rice and dal, a freezer of frozen seafood such as kingfish steaks, tubs of ghee and a selection of spices and condiments.

Sira Cash and Carry

🖳 *128 The Broadway, UB1*
☎ *020 8574 2280*
🚇 *Southall Rail*
🕐 *Daily 8am-8pm*

A roomy shop with a good range of stock including flours, pulses, spices and chutneys. In addition there is an excellent, extensive greengrocery section with an aisle of fruit including chikoo, limes, guavas and tiny green mangoes for pickling and Asian vegetables, such as karela, tindola and fresh chickpeas.
Branch at: 43 South Road, UB1, Tel: 020 8571 4529
Open: daily 8am-9pm

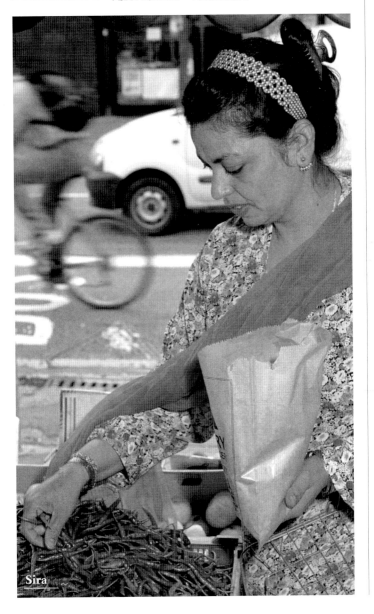

Sira

EATING PLACES

Over the last decade London's Indian restaurants have undergone a noticeable renaissance, with stylish new restaurants offering regional Indian food, often presented in a Western style but with the emphasis on authentic flavours and spicing.

CENTRAL

Café Laseez   £££

⌨ *21 Dean Street, W1*

☎ *020 7434 9393*

🚇 *Leicester Square LU*

An archetypal 'New Wave Indian', complete with modish décor and a menu offering attractively presented, carefully spiced Indian dishes such as charcoal-grilled marinated salmon and aromatic Avadhi lamb korma.

Diwana Bhel Poori House   £

⌨ *121 Drummond Street, NW1*

☎ *020 7387 5566*

🚇 *Euston LU*

Tucked away behind Euston station this well-established, unpretentious South-Indian vegetarian restaurant serves up dosai, idlee and good value thali at remarkably reasonable prices.

Great Nepalese   ££

⌨ *48 Eversholt Street, NW1*

☎ *020 7388 6737*

🚇 *Euston LU*

A Euston institution, much-frequented by hungry commuters, which in addition to standard curry house fare has a selection of Nepalese specialities.

India Club   ££

⌨ *Strand Continental Hotel, 143 Strand, WC2*

☎ *020 7836 0650*

🚇 *Temple LU*

A long-established restaurant recommended by Indian friends, this is an unpretentious, friendly restaurant which offers good North Indian food at very reasonable prices.

Indian YMCA   £

☐ *41 Fitzroy Square, W1*

☎ *020 7387 0411*

🚇 *Warren Street LU*

The appetising smell of Indian cooking wafts out from this large building, adding character to its institutional air. On offer is good home-style
food at student prices in a canteen atmosphere.

Malabar Junction   ££

☐ *107 Great Russell Street, WC1*

☎ *020 7580 5230*

🚇 *Tottenham Court Road LU*

A rather drab frontage hides a large airy restaurant complete with an
attractive glass roofed dining room. South-Indian cuisine is the speciality here, from tangy idlee (steamed rice and black gram cakes) to spicy
Keralan fish curry. Service is courteous and prices very reasonable given
the standard of the cooking.

Raavi Kebab Halal Tandoori   £

☐ *125 Drummond Street, NW1*

☎ *020 7388 1780*

🚇 *Euston Square LU*

A small, unpretentious restaurant which specialises in delicious, chilli-hot
kebabs, freshly-grilled over charcoal.

Ragam   ££

☐ *57 Cleveland Street, W1*

☎ *020 7636 9098*

🚇 *Goodge Street or Warren Street LU*

A small, modest and friendly restaurant serving excellent, good value
food including South-Indian dishes such as avial or uthappam, and delicious breads.

Rasa Samudra   ££££

☐ *5 Charlotte Street, W1*

☎ *020 7637 0222*

🚇 *Goodge Street LU*

This is the latest Rasa restaurant, specialising in Keralan seafood dishes
such as kingfish and green mango curry, and crab in coconut milk.

Rasa W1 *£££*

- *6 Dering Street, W1*
- ☎ *020 7629 1346*
- *Oxford Circus LU or Bond Street LU*

Keralan vegetarian cuisine is on offer here, giving diners the chance to try distinctive spiced dishes such as green banana and mango curry and cashew nut patties. Round off your meal with Keralan desserts such as banana dosa (pancakes) or pal payasum (cashew rice pudding).

Ravi Shankar *£*

- *133-135 Drummond Street, NW1*
- ☎ *020 7388 6458*
- *Euston LU*

A popular Indian vegetarian restaurant offering reasonably priced dishes such as masala or de luxe dosai.

Veeraswamy *£££*

- *99 Regent Street, W1*
- ☎ *020 7734 1401*
- *Piccadilly Circus LU*

London's oldest Indian restaurant has shed its Raj image. Now owned by the Chutney Mary team it has been transformed into a sleek example of new-wave Indian restaurants, complete with vividly painted walls, smartly dressed staff and a menu offering regional dishes.

EAST

Cafe Spice Namaste *££££*

- *16 Prescott Street, E1*
- ☎ *020 7488 9242*
- *Aldgate East LU or Tower Hill LU*

Chef Cyrus Todiwala is committed to bringing true Indian cookery, in all its variety and glory, to the London restaurant scene. From within a brightly-decorated old courthouse he serves up dishes from an extensive menu, including many Goan and Parsee dishes rarely-found in British restaurants.

Lahore Kebab House £
- 2 Umberstone Street, E1
- ☎ 020 7481 9737
- Whitechapel LU

One of the best known of the Whitechapel Indian restaurants, still offering bargain-price Pakistani dishes, including excellent kebabs.

NORTH

Jai Krishna £
- 161 Stroud Green Road, N4
- ☎ 020 7272 1680
- Finsbury Park LU

An unpretentious restaurant offering cheap Indian vegetarian food. Refreshingly, the menu includes unusual Indian vegetables such as tindora and dudi curries.

Majjo's £
- 1 Fortis Green Road, N2
- ☎ 020 8883 4357
- East Finchley LU

This small, smart, friendly take-away offers superior Pakistani home-cooking. The meat is halal and there is a range of more unusual vegetarian dishes such as patra. Sample tastes are offered to those trying to choose from the array of dishes on offer.

The Parsee ££££
- 34 Highgate Hill, N19
- ☎ 020 7272 9091
- Archway LU

Chef Cyrus Todiwala, himself a Parsee, offers Londoners a rare chance to sample authentic Parsee dishes such as lamb dhansak.

Rani ££
- 7 Long Lane, N3
- ☎ 020 8349 4386/2646
- Finchley Central LU

A Gujarati restaurant serving authentic vegetarian cuisine. All dishes, from the homemade chutneys to the breads, are carefully prepared, and the exciting range includes delights such as banana methi and tindora curry.

NORTH-WEST

Karahi King £

⌧ *213 East Lane, HA0*
☎ *020 8904 2760/4994*
🚇 *North Wembley LU*

Despite being distinctly off the beaten track, housed in a non-descript arcade of shops just off the North Circular, the Karahi King does brisk business – as the row of cars parked outside testifies. The décor is functional, but the service is polite and the food gutsy and tasty: from grilled kebabs to Karahi Lamb Chops – tiny, flavourful chops in a rich, thick tomato-based sauce. It's unlicensed but you can stock up with booze at the off-licence next door.

Sakonis £

⌧ *119-121 Ealing Road, HA0*
☎ *020 8903 9601*
🚇 *Alperton LU*

This bright, cheery vegetarian diner attracts queues of would-be diners (many of them in family groups), waiting patiently by the paan stall and take-away counter to sit down in the back room. The menu offers a wide range of snacks, mains, drinks and desserts: seriously chilli-hot dosai, chilli paneer, falooda, chikoo ice cream and delicious, salty-sweet freshly-squeezed lime juice.

SOUTH

Chutney Mary ££££

⌧ *535 King's Road, SW10*
☎ *020 7351 3113*
🚇 *Fulham Broadway LU*

This large, glamorous restaurant, complete with an attractive conservatory dining area, offers a chance to enjoy top-notch Indian cooking in an enjoyably buzzy atmosphere. The menu offers carefully chosen regional specialities, with the chilli-marinated lamb chops and Alphonso mango ice cream being particular highlights.

Shree Krishna £

⌖ 192-194 Tooting High Street, SW17
☎ 020 8672 4250
🚇 Tooting Broadway LU

This large restaurant is full of enthusiasts who appreciate both the good South Indian vegetarian food and the reasonable prices.

West

Madhu's Brilliant £

⌖ 39 South Road, UB1
☎ 020 8574 1897
🚇 Southall Rail

A popular Southall eaterie, attracting Asians and non-Asians alike, serving tasty Punjabi food such as Masala Fish and Karahi Chicken – good breads.

Rita's Samosa Centre £

⌖ 112 The Broadway, Southall, UB1
☎ 020 8571 2100
🚇 Southall Rail

This bright, cheery diner, complete with 'takeaway' pan and kebab kiosks on the street, offers an assortment of snacks, chaats, curries, breads and rice. Drinks include rose syrup-flavoured falooda.

Sagoo and Takhar £

⌖ 114-116 The Green, UB2
☎ 020 8574 2597
🚇 Southall Rail

A down-to-earth, self-service curry house where you can eat tasty North Indian food at very reasonable prices.

Zaika ££££

⌖ 1, Kensington High Street, W8
☎ 020 7795 6533
🚇 High Street Kensington LU

This sophisticated restaurant is a showcase for the considerable talents of chef-patron Vineet Bhatia, whose culinary skills have earned Zaika a Michelin star. Diners here are offered deftly assembled, creative Indian cooking, with signature dishes including chocolate samosas served with Indian masala tea ice cream.

COOKBOOKS

Classic Indian Cooking *by Julie Sahni*
A well-written Indian cookery book which is readable, useable and authoritative.

Classic Indian Vegetarian Cooking *by Julie Sahni*
An inspirational book filled with appetising recipes conveying the less well-known world of Indian vegetarian cuisine in all its subtlety.

Flavours of India *by Madhur Jaffrey*
An attractive regional tour of Indian cookery containing some unusual recipes.

Madhur Jaffrey's Indian Cookery *by Madhur Jaffrey*
A clearly-written, accessible introduction to the cuisine.

Fifty Great Curries of India *by Camellia Panjabi*
A beautifully-presented, in-depth illustrated guide which takes readers through the art of making curries clearly and in detail. Recipes range from classic dishes, such as Goanese pork Vindaloo, to less familiar ones such as Gujurati mango and yogurt curry.

CHINESE LONDON

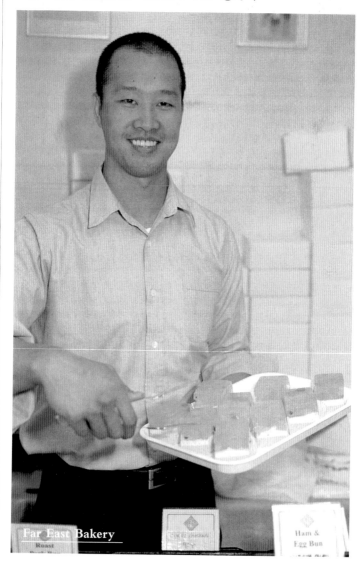

The original points of entry for the Chinese community in Britain were Liverpool and London: the ports into which Chinese seamen with the East India Company arrived and settled. The Limehouse area, near the docks in the East End, was London's first 'Chinatown', with the first immigrants arriving during the eighteenth century when Britain's tea trade with China was booming. Sailors jumped ship and set up businesses running laundries, shops or becoming ship's chandlers. In the 1950s, the development of the laundromat and the domestic washing machine adversely affected the laundry business, so catering became an alternative source of work.

Limehouse was practically destroyed in the Blitz and post-war restrictive regulations imposed on non-British workers by the Seamen's Union, hit Chinese seamen hard. So, both alternative livelihoods and accommodation had to be found. Soho, a run-down, derelict area with a bad reputation and low property prices, saw an influx of Chinese around the Gerrard Street area in the 1950s. The first Chinese restaurants in Soho were chop-suey outlets, opened in the 1940s to cater for American GIs and British servicemen who had acquired a taste for Chinese food overseas. Restaurants catering specifically for the growing Chinese community also opened in the area. The Communist revolution in China in 1949 resulted in a further wave of immigration from China into Britain in the 1950s and 1960s, mostly from the British colony of Hong Kong. As a result, the Chinese community in Soho expanded further.

The area bounded by Shaftesbury Avenue, Leicester Square, Charing Cross Road and Wardour Street is a rectangle of predominantly Chinese shops, businesses, gambling clubs and restaurants. Gerrard Street, now pedestrianized, comes complete with Chinese-style arches and 'pagoda' phone boxes.

Two annual festivals have become major events in London, attracting people from outside the Chinese community. Chinese New Year takes place either in late January or early February, and is celebrated with gifts to children and a lion dance procession. At this time special dishes appear on menus in the restaurants. Each year is attributed to one of the twelve animals in the Chinese zodiac – with the Year of the Dragon being especially auspicious – and the New Year celebrations feature the animal to which the year belongs. The autumnal Moon Festival, around September, is marked by special moon cakes and a lion dance. During both these festivals, Chinatown is filled with Chinese of all generations, colourful lanterns and decorations and street-stalls selling snacks and gifts.

CHINESE CUISINE

This ancient cuisine is both complex and various. Underlying it are the 'yin and yang' principles, translated in culinary terms into hot, cold and neutral, with ingredients allocated different properties. A huge range of ingredients is used, with nothing wasted. There is an old saying that 'A Cantonese will eat anything with four legs except for a piece of furniture and anything that flies apart from a kite'. Textures play an important role in Chinese cooking and include some that are foreign to Western sensibilities, with slippery, jelly-like textures being prized.

Each of China's regions has its own characteristic cuisine, influenced by climate and the availability of ingredients. It's customary, however, to group China culinarily into four broad geographical groups: Peking/Northern, Shanghai/Eastern, Szechuan/Western and Cantonese/Southern. The cuisine of the North is distinguished by its use of grains other than rice, such as wheat, corn and millet, in the form of breads, noodles, dumplings and pancakes. Because the ancient Imperial Court was situated in Peking, elaborate dishes such as Peking Duck are characteristic of this cuisine. The Mongols introduced lamb, which is eaten more widely here than in other parts of China.

Eastern cuisine is famous for its fresh fish and seafood. Rich, sweet seasonings are a hallmark and popular techniques include stir-frying, steaming, red-cooking (slow simmering in soy sauce) and blanching. Szechuan cooking, from the provinces of Hunan, Yunnan and Szechuan in Western China, is marked by its use of fiery chillies, garlic, ginger and Szechuan peppercorns producing a vigorous, strongly flavoured cuisine. Two regional foodstuffs are the aromatic peppercorns and chilli-pickled mustard plant.

Cantonese cuisine is the best-known Chinese cooking outside China, because of the large numbers of Chinese from southern Canton who emigrated in the nineteenth century. Strong, overwhelming flavourings are avoided and, instead, a harmonious blend of colours, textures and flavours is sought. Stir-frying epitomises Cantonese cooking, with the freshness and colours of ingredients retained and a minimum of seasonings added. Dimsum, the small steamed and fried dumplings eaten at lunchtime, are another Cantonese speciality.

GLOSSARY

Agar agar: a vegetarian setting agent obtained from seaweed which does not require refrigeration to set. Available either in powdered form or translucent strands.

Azuki beans: small red beans, used primarily in cakes and desserts and available both whole and in sweetened paste form.

Bamboo shoots: fresh bamboo shoots are occasionally available. Tinned bamboo shoots, either whole or sliced, are easily found.

Bean curd (doufu): a soy bean product which has always been a valuable source of protein in Chinese cooking. Fresh ivory-coloured bean curd has a firm custard texture and bland flavour. It is sold in the chilled section, packed in water. Deep-fried bean curd has a golden colour and spongy texture and is found in packets in the chilled section. Bean curd 'cheese', either red or white, is fermented bean curd with a strong, salty taste and is sold in jars. Dried bean-curd sheets are sold in packets.

Bean sprouts: white crispy sprouts of the mung bean; also available are the larger, nuttier soya bean sprouts, which should be cooked before eating.

Beche–de–mer: sea cucumber or sea slug, sold dried and prized as a delicacy.

Bird's nest: the key ingredient of the famous delicacy, bird's nest soup. The nests of a species of cave-dwelling swallow are coated with a gelatinous saliva and it is this which gives the soup its prized consistency. The nests are sold either whole or in fragments for high prices.

Black beans: small black soya beans, fermented with salt and spices, with a pungent flavour.

Chilli oil: a transparent oil, tinted red from chillies, sold in small bottles and with a powerful chilli kick.

Chinese broccoli (gaai laan): a thick-stalked vegetable with large rounded leaves and white flowers.

Chinese cabbage (bok choy): similar in appearance to Swiss chard, with dark green leaves and thick white stems. Green bok choy, with green leaves and stems, is also available.

Chinese chives: long, dark green, flat leaves, with a stronger and more pungent odour and flavour than English chives; also sold blanched and complete with buds.

Chinese cinnamon: cassia bark, sold in sticks similar to cinnamon but larger and rougher with a stronger flavour.

Chinese flowering cabbage (choi sum): a leafy vegetable with rounded leaves, small yellow flowers and long stems.

Chinese leaves: a large tight head of white-green crinkly leaves with a crunchy texture; widely available.

Chinese mushrooms: black, dried shitake mushrooms with a distinctive meaty flavour. Prices vary according to the size and thickness of the caps.

Chinese sausages: these resemble small, fatty salamis, but they must be cooked before eating. There are two sorts: pork and pork and liver, the latter being darker in colour. They are found in packets or hanging up in bunches with other dried meats.

Coriander: this green herb, similar in appearance to flat-leaved continental parsley but with a distinctive sharp flavour, is one of the few herbs used in Chinese cooking.

Five-spice powder: fragrant, golden-brown powder made from five or sometimes six ground spices, with the four base spices being star-anise, Chinese cinnamon, cloves and fennel seeds. Szechuan peppercorns, ginger and cardamom are the additions.

Ginger: an aromatic root available fresh.

Glutinous rice: rounded rice grains with a sticky texture when cooked, used in both sweet and savoury dishes.

Golden needles: long dried buds of the tiger-lily flower.

Longan: a small brown-skinned fruit, related to the lychee, with translucent flesh and glossy black seed (also known as 'dragon's eye' fruit). Available either tinned or fresh.

Lotus leaves: the large leaves of the water-lily plant, available dried and used to wrap food for cooking.

Lotus root: a crunchy root with a decorative tracery of holes, available fresh, in sausage-like links, or tinned.

Mooli: a large, long white radish, with crispy white flesh.

Mustard Greens (gaai choi): a green large-leafed plant. The bitter varieties are pickled rather than cooked.

Noodles: *cellophane noodles* (also known as beanthread, glass or transparent noodles), fine thread-like noodles made from mung beans and need soaking before they can be easily cut; *egg noodles*, made from wheat flour, egg and water, distinguished by their yellow colour; *rice noodles* and *vermicelli* are dried, white noodles of varying widths made from rice flour which need soaking before use; *river rice noodles (sarhor noodles),* made from ground rice and water, steamed in thin sheets and cut into strips. Fresh-river rice noodles are sold in clear packets, and usually stored near the chilled section.

Potato flour: fine white flour, made from cooked potatoes, used as a thickener.

Rice vinegar: mild vinegars, ranging from delicate white rice vinegar to sweet red rice vinegar and rich black rice vinegar.

Rice wine: made from glutinous rice, yeast and water, this is used for both drinking and cooking.

Sauces: *chilli bean sauce,* a hot, spicy, dark sauce made from soya beans and chillies; *chilli sauce,* a bright red sweet chilli sauce; *hoisin sauce,* a thick, brown fruity sauce; *oyster sauce,* a thick, brown sauce made from oysters; *soy sauce,* a dark brown salty liquid made from fermented soya beans (available as thin, salty Light Soy Sauce or as thicker, sweeter Dark Soy Sauce); and *yellow bean sauce*: a thick, brown sauce made from fermented yellow beans.

Sesame oil: a nutty, golden-coloured oil made from sesame seeds.

Shrimps dried: small, shelled, dried pink shrimps, with a strong salty flavour.

Spring roll wrappers: white paper-thin wrappers, available in different sizes. Found in either the chilled or freezer sections.

Star-anise: dark brown, star-shaped pod with a distinctive licorice flavour and scent.

Straw mushrooms: cone-shaped mushrooms, usually available canned.

Szechuan peppercorns: fragrant, reddish-brown 'peppercorns', which are the dried berries of a shrub.

Szechuan pickled vegetables: mustard green roots, pickled in salt and hot chillies, which are a speciality of Szechuan province.

Tangerine peel: in its dried form, in dark-brown pieces, this is used as a flavouring in Chinese cooking.

Thousand-year-old eggs: preserved duck eggs, with a pungent flavour, which are in fact only about a hundred days old.

Water chestnuts: the crunchy bulbs of a waterplant. Fresh, brown-skinned bulbs are sometimes found, but tinned water chestnuts are easily available.

Water spinach (ong chai): a triangular-leafed plant with a mild, spinach-like flavour.

Winter melon: a large green gourd with white flesh, available whole or in pieces, and often used to make soup.

Wonton skins: small squares of yellow egg-noodle dough, used to wrap up dumplings. Found in either chilled or freezer sections.

Wood ears: black, crinkled, dried fungus with a beige underside.

FOOD SHOPS

CENTRAL

Far East

⌨ *13 Gerrard Street, W1*

☎ *020 7437 6148*

🚇 *Leicester Square LU*

🕐 *Daily 10am-7pm*

During the day this functions as a friendly bakery cum tea-shop selling Chinese cakes and pastries freshly baked on the premises (including sticky, glazed char-siu buns, curry beef puffs and egg custard tarts); at night it metamorphosises into a restaurant.

Golden Gate Grocers

☐ *16 Newport Place, WC2*

☎ *020 7437 6266*

🚇 *Leicester Square LU*

🕐 *Daily 10am-7.45pm*

A small but well-stocked food shop with a good range of Chinese vegetables displayed outside: boxes of bok choy, gaai laan, mooli, piles of durians, boxes of Thai mangoes and mangosteens – helpfully labelled in English.

Golden Gate Hong Supermarket

☐ *14 Lisle Street, WC2*

☎ *020 7437 0014*

🚇 *Leicester Square LU*

🕐 *Daily 9am-8.30pm*

Boxes of fresh fruit and vegetables under a canopy signal this pleasant, neatly-arranged shop. The vegetables inside are labelled in English and there is good basic stock.

Good Harvest Fish and Meat Market

☐ *14 Newport Place, WC2*

☎ *020 7437 0712*

🚇 *Leicester Square LU*

🕐 *Daily 11am-7pm*

Chinatown's only fishmonger offers fresh scallops in their shells, live lobsters, raw king prawns and more unusual fish including catfish, seabass and pomfret.

Loon Fung Supermarket

☐ *42-44 Gerrard Street, W1*

☎ *020 7437 7332*

🚇 *Leicester Square LU*

🕐 *Daily 10am-8pm*

Over thirty years old, Loon Fung is the oldest and largest Chinese supermarket in Soho, occupying a key site on Gerrard Street and always bustling with customers. Boxes of fresh fruit such as lychees, longans and persimmons, are displayed outside on the pavement with a large fresh vegetable section inside. A butcher's counter sells basic cuts plus more unusual items such as duck and chicken feet and ducks' tongues. All the staples are stocked across a wide range.

New Loon Moon Supermarket

⌨ *9a Gerrard Street, W1*

☎ *020 7734 9940*

🚇 *Leicester Square LU*

🕐 *Daily 10.30am-8pm*

In the heart of Gerrard Street, this veteran foodshop draws attention with an attractive display of consistently good quality fresh fruit and vegetables, such as gai lan and longans and Emperor lychees. Inside the busy shop is crammed with Chinese foodstuffs: noodles, sauces, tinned ingredients and teas. A large backroom contains chilled and freezer sections, cookware and an impressive range of spices.

Newport Supermarket

⌨ *28-29 Newport Court, WC2*

☎ *020 7437 2386*

🚇 *Leicester Square LU*

🕐 *Daily 10.30am-8pm*

This corner supermarket has an excellent selection of Chinese vegetables and fruit on display outside. Inside, the roomy shop, complete with frozen and chilled sections, contains a good choice of ingredients.

See Woo

⌨ *19 Lisle Street, WC2*

☎ *020 7439 8325*

🚇 *Leicester Square LU*

🕐 *Daily 10am-8pm*

This sprawling shop has an excellent, comprehensive stock: chilled, frozen, dried, tinned and bottled. There is a large fresh fruit and vegetable section, which regularly stocks more unusual items. A basement room contains bowls of all sizes, woks, steamers and other Chinese cookware.

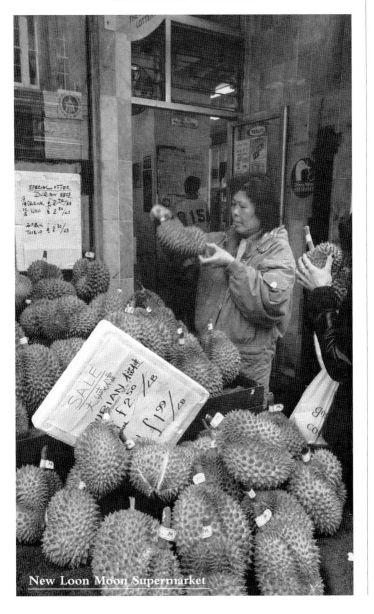

New Loon Moon Supermarket

NORTH

Maysun Markets

⌨ *869 Finchley Road, NW11*

☎ *020 8455 4773*

🚇 *Golders Green LU*

🕐 *Mon-Sat 9am-7.30pm*

A small, pleasantly ramshackle shop, run with friendly cheerfulness by its owner, selling a mixture of household goods and Chinese foodstuffs. It has a basic stock of dried, bottled and tinned ingredients and a few fresh ingredients.

Wing Yip (London) Ltd

⌨ *395 Edgware Road, NW2*

☎ *020 8450 0422*

🚇 *Colindale LU*

🕐 *Mon-Sat 9.30am-7pm, Sun 11.30am-5.30pm*

This enormous superstore at Staples Corner is the place for bulk-buying Chinese food. It has an impressive selection, ranging from freezers of dim sum to delicacies such as bird's nest and shark's fin. There is a small selection of fresh vegetables and foodstuffs such as beancurd and noodles.

SOUTH

Wing Thai Supermarket

⌨ *13 Electric Avenue, SW9*

☎ *020 7738 5898*

🚇 *Brixton LU/Rail*

🕐 *Mon-Sat 10am-7pm*

Tucked away behind the bustling fruit and veg stalls outside, this roomy store has a small fresh produce section and fish-counter at the front but is particularly strong on bottled, tinned and frozen goods.

EATING PLACES

L ondon's Chinese restaurants offer predominantly Cantonese food. As a result several places serve excellent dimsum – an assortment of steamed and fried dumplings traditionally eaten at lunchtime – which are a speciality of Canton.

With Chinatown overrun by tourists, standards have slipped in many of its restaurants, though some continue to offer superb meals. If you enjoy good Chinese food, then you should also head for Bayswater, where a cluster of high quality Chinese restaurants attract enthusiastic and discerning diners.

CENTRAL

China China   *££*

3 Gerrard Street, W1

020 7439 7511

Leicester Square LU

A busy, efficient restaurant offering straightforward down-to-earth Cantonese food.

China City *££*

White Bear Yard, 25a Lisle Street, WC2

020 7734 3388

Leicester Square LU

Tucked away in a courtyard off a Soho side-street, this roomy restaurant offers good dimsum and an extensive Cantonese menu.

Ecapital *£££*

8 Gerrard Street, W1

020 7434 3838

Leicester Square LU

Unusually for London's Chinese restaurant scene, this smart, brightly decorated restaurant specialises in Shanghai rather than Cantonese cuisine. These include classic dishes such as cold starters (including pig's ear and jellyfish), beggar's chicken and complemented by a carefully chosen wine-list. The courteous staff are happy to explain.

Fung Shing *£££*

15 Lisle Street, WC2

020 7437 1539

Leicester Square LU

A peaceful, civilized restaurant noted for its authentic food, offering impeccable versions of dishes such as black bean braised hotpot and duck and plum sauce hotpot.

Golden Dragon *££*

28-29 Gerrard Street, W1

020 7734 2763

Leicester Square LU

Large, gaudily-decorated with splendid writhing dragons and efficiently staffed, this is a quintessential Chinatown restaurant. It's renowned for its dimsum and is correspondingly busy at lunchtime on a Sunday.

Hakkasan *££-£££*

8 Hanway Place, W1

020 7927 7000

Tottenham Court Road LU

Intriguingly situated down a back-street alley, this glamorous restaurant (set up by Wagamama-founder Alan Yau) with its night-club décor and popular cocktail bar, is noted particularly for its dainty lunchtime dim-sum.

Hunan   *££££*

- 🏠 *51 Pimlico Road, SW1*
- ☎ *020 7730 5712*
- 🚇 *Sloane Square LU*

This upmarket veteran Pimlico-based restaurant, run with considerable charm by the velvet-gloved and iron-handed Mr Peng offers a rare chance to sample deliciously fresh and flavourful Sichuanese food.

Jen   *££*

- 🏠 *7 Gerrard Street, W1*
- ☎ *020 287 8193*
- 🚇 *Leicester Square LU*

Distinctly dapper with polite staff, the menu features more unusual dishes, such as yam-stuffed spring rolls.

Memories of China   *£££*

- 🏠 *65-69 Ebury Street, SW1*
- ☎ *020 7730 7734*
- 🚇 *Victoria Station LU/Rail*

Founded by acclaimed Chinese food writer Ken Lo, this sleekly elegant restaurant is an attractive showcase for the considerable cooking talents of Chef Butt. The cooking here is refined but flavourful, with signature dishes including lobster with hand-pulled noodles.

New World   *££*

- 🏠 *1 Gerrard Place, W1*
- ☎ *020 7434 0396*
- 🚇 *Leicester Square LU*

Vast and bright, New World offers straightforward Cantonese food and dimsum, served from trolleys.

Poons   *££*

- 🏠 *4 Leicester Street, WC2*
- ☎ *020 7437 1528*
- 🚇 *Leicester Square LU*

A vintage Chinatown name, tucked away in a side-street, this restaurant continues to offer reasonably-priced, flavourful Cantonese food including speciality wind-dried meats.

EAST

Old Friends   £££
⌨ *659 Commercial Road, E14*
☏ *020 7790 5027*
🚇 *Limehouse DLR*

Claiming to be London's oldest Chinese restaurant, this Cantonese eaterie is a remnant from the days when the city's Chinese community was concentrated around the Limehouse area. Food is standard Cantonese fare.

Shanghai   ££
⌨ *41 Kingsland High Street, E8*
☏ *020 7254 2878*
🚇 *Dalston Kingsland Rail*

What was formerly an eel and pie shop has now been transformed into a busy Chinese restaurant. Good dimsum and a bargain lunchtime buffet pull in the punters.

NORTH

Green Cottage   ££
⌨ *9 New College Parade, Finchley Road, NW3*
☏ *020 7722 5305*
🚇 *Finchley Road LU*

A down-to-earth restaurant serving Chinatown-standard Cantonese food in a North London setting.

Vegetarian Cottage   ££
⌨ *91 Haverstock Hill, NW3*
☏ *020 7586 1257*
🚇 *Belsize Park LU*

An attractive restaurant offering traditional Chinese Buddhist vegetarian dishes, including many that mimic meat in texture. Service is pleasant and the food, including several bean curd dishes, flavourful.

WEST

Hung Toa £££

⌨ *51 Queensway, W2*

☎ *020 7727 5753*

🚇 *Bayswater LU or Queensway LU*

A small, no-nonsense outfit offering excellent one-plate meals, from noodles in soup to congee (savoury rice porridge).

Mandarin Kitchen £££

⌨ *14-16 Queensway, W2*

☎ *020 7727 9468*

🚇 *Bayswater LU or Queensway LU*

Peering in through the large windows to the dimly-lit interior, one is reminded of an aquarium. Appropriately so, as this large, busy restaurant specialises in Cantonese seafood such as succulent steamed scallops in the shell, and fresh crab with ginger.

Royal China £££

⌨ *13 Queensway, W2*

☎ *020 7221 2535*

🚇 *Bayswater LU or Queensway LU*

Such is the fame of the dimsum here that at the weekend queues start forming before the restaurant opens its doors at noon. Inside, the large, roomy restaurant is decorated with 70s opulence: shiny black tiled walls festooned with golden lacquerwork and masses of mirrors. Service is efficient, which is just as well considering how busy it gets. Dimsum dishes are spot on: from delicate mangetout dumplings (filled with pea-shoots) to soft, spongy char siu bau.

Branch at: 40 Baker Street, W1

COOKBOOKS

Sichuan Cookery *by Fuchsia Dunlop*
This elegantly written, attractively packaged cookbook provides a
fascinating and appetising insight into Sichuan cuisine.

Chinese Cookery *by Ken Hom*
An accessible, basic introduction to Chinese cooking.

The Chinese Kitchen *by Deh-Ta Hsiung*
Offering a considerable insight into Chinese cuisine, this attractive,
well-illustrated book features extensive information on Chinese
ingredients plus a most appetising range of recipes.

Classic Chinese Cookbook *by Yan-Kit So*
A truly classic cookbook by a wonderful food writer who knew
how to share her knowledge in the most accessible way, this book is
both lucidly written and well-illustrated with mouthwatering,
workable recipes.

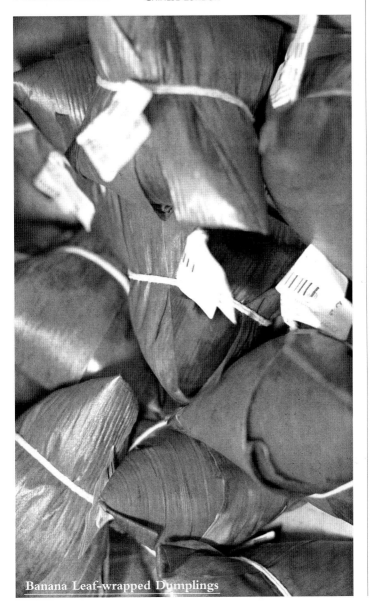

Banana Leaf-wrapped Dumplings

FRENCH LONDON

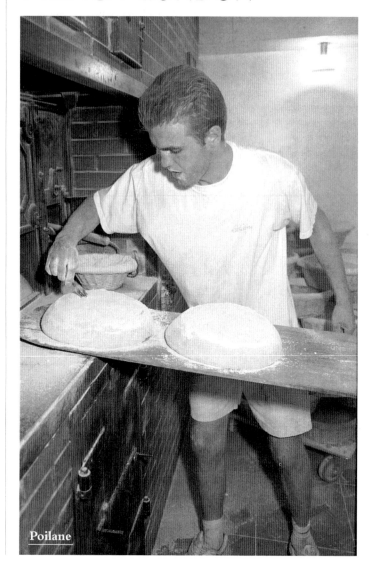

Poilane

London's first serious experience of the French was when it fell under Norman rule following the 1066 Conquest. French became the language both of the Court and local government. London saw an influx of merchant traders from northern France and a number of religious orders, including the influential Knights Templar, established themselves in the city.

The next major increase in London's French community was due to the arrival of French-speaking Protestants, known in France as 'Huguenots', who came to England to escape Catholic persecution. In France, the limited privileges granted to Huguenots by the 1598 Edict of Nantes were gradually eroded, with restrictions placed on Protestant worship. In 1680 many Huguenots fled, and Charles II offered them asylum in 1681. Four years later in France, the Edict of Nantes was revoked and Protestant churches were ordered to be destroyed. Following this, between 40,000 and 50,000 Huguenots moved to England, with half of them thought to have settled in London. By the year 1700, Huguenots formed around five per cent of London's population.

Spitalfields and Soho were the two main areas in London in which the Huguenots settled. Spitalfields (also home to a community of Flemish weavers), attracted the Huguenot weavers, who eventually contributed to a prosperous period in the British silk industry. In Soho, where the Huguenots took over a chapel built for Greek Christians and used it until 1822, the new immigrants were craftspeople, such as watch and clockmakers, bookbinders and gold and silversmiths.

Our popular perception of the French as stylish and fashionable was noticeable even then, with a 1700 report declaring, 'The English have now so great an esteem for the workmanship of the French refugees that hardly any thing vends without a gallic name'. Huguenot merchants, alongside other immigrants, played an important part in London's financial life. When the Bank of England was founded in 1694, a number of the founder directors were Huguenots. In addition to influencing crafts and business, Huguenot academics played a notable role in the worlds of science and technology, with many joining the Royal Society.

London's French community also received subsequent groups of refugees, with an influx of royalists fleeing the 1789 French Revolution, and political refugees escaping the 1870 Commune. Gradually, further institutions catering to French expats were set up, from a chapel in the French Embassy to French schools in Lisle Street in 1865. In 1867, the

French Hospital and Dispensary in Shaftesbury Avenue was established, while 1893 saw the completion of the French Protestant Church in Soho Square. Paul Villars wrote in 1905 in *Living London* of the French community that 'In London, as in France, they use the café as a club' – the Café Royal was a favourite haunt. During the eighteenth and nineteenth centuries, however, the French community slowly became assimilated into English society. Huguenot families such as the Courtaulds and Oliviers became established members of British society. Today, Spitalfields' gracious Georgian houses and Huguenot names like Fournier Street are reminders of the area's former prosperity under the silk merchants.

During the Second World War, Soho, once home to the Huguenots, was a focal point for the French Resistance, with the York Minster pub acting as the headquarters of the Free French Forces. Generally known 'the French pub' it has now been renamed the French House; General de Gaulle used to shop for his coffee at Angelucci's around the corner on Frith Street.

Today, London's French enclave is in elegant, affluent South Kensington, with the French Lycée on Cromwell Road and the French Institute at Queensberry Place providing two focal points. Serving this community are a cluster of upmarket food shops, including butchers selling French cuts of meat and chic pâtisseries offering decent croissants and delectable cakes.

FRENCH CUISINE

French cuisine has been highly influential throughout Europe, with Britain especially living in its shadow. As the current edition of the Larousse Gastronomique baldly states, 'At the beginning of the twentieth century, French cookery gained supremacy throughout the world.' Today the language of the kitchen continues to be French, from 'chef' to culinary terms such as 'sauté'.

Still a predominantly agricultural country, France has retained many of the regional foodstuffs such as cheeses, hams or herbs which give its cuisine character and flavour; markets still abound with locally-grown seasonal produce. Standards of produce have remained high and the simple pleasures of life, such as a decent loaf of bread and some good cheese, are easily found.

An enduring regionalism means that even in the twenty-first century local dishes are cherished, rather than discarded in a mass move towards uniformity. As a result, French cuisine contains wonderfully contrasting strands: from the Mediterranean flavours of Provençal cooking, laden with tomatoes, basil and olive oil; to the dishes of Normandy, flavoured with cider and calvados and rich with the area's famous dairy products.

French cooking can be divided broadly into 'haute cuisine', the cookery of grand restaurants and hotels; 'cuisine du terroir', regional cooking found in provincial restaurants; and 'cuisine grandmère', the everyday food found in people's homes and in cheap, down-to-earth bistros. Haute cuisine has influenced chefs and cookery schools around the world. Naturally, it has followed trends and fashions. In the 1970s and 1980s 'nouvelle cuisine' - a move away from the over-rich dishes of the classic cuisine - was highly influential, although reviled in some quarters for its affectation. In contrast, regional and home cooking continue to stick to a traditional repertoire of classic French dishes, such as cassoulet or tarte tatin.

GLOSSARY

Anchovy (anchois): a small seafish, generally available salted in cans or jars, filleted or whole. Its strong flavour plays a key part in dishes like tapenade and pissaladiere.

Bayonne ham: a famous salt-cured, smoked ham, originally from Bayonne but now manufactured all over France.

Butter: pale, unsalted 'sweet' butter from Normandy is highly prized in French pastry-cooking.

Calvados: a spirit distilled from cider traditionally from Normandy. Pays d'Auge Calvados is a particularly high-quality brand.

Capers: the unopened buds of a Mediterranean shrub, used pickled either in brine or vinegar to provide a distinctive sour flavouring.

Celeriac (céleri-rave): the white, firm-textured, bulbous root of a variety of celery with a distinctive nutty flavour.

Cep (cèpe): a brown-capped, thick-stemmed edible wild boletus mushroom, valued for its rich flavour and meaty texture.

Cheeses: French cheeses are one of the glories of this cuisine. There are hundreds of different French cheeses, with the following only a tiny selection. *Beaufort*, a Gruyère-like hard cow's milk cheese from the mountain pastures of the Savoie; *Brie*: a circular, soft, unpressed cow's milk cheese, with its origins in the 1200s; *Brie de Meaux,* a classic brie farm-made from unpasturised milk; *Camembert*, a round, flat, soft cheese, traditionally from Normandy; *chèvre*, goat's milk cheese (mi-chèvre means cheeses made with a mixture of goat's and cow's milks); *comte*, a Gruyère-type cow's milk cheese from the Jura mountains; *crottin de chavignol*, a soft goat's milk cheese made in Sancerre, shaped like a small flattened ball; *explorateur*, a mild, cylindrical, triple-cream cow's milk cheese; *Fourme d'Ambert*, a semi-soft, cow's milk veined cheese; *fromage frais*, fresh curd cheese made from cow's milk, used in cooking; *livarot*, a soft Normandy cow's milk cheese; *lucullus*, a soft, cylindrical cow's milk cheese; *munster*, a soft cheese from the Alsace with an orange-red rind; *pont l'Eveque*, a square-shaped, soft cow's milk cheese from Normandy; *Roquefort*: a famous veined, semi-soft sheep's milk cheese, ripened for three months in the limestone caves of Les Causses.

Chervil: a subtly-flavoured green herb, with fine fronds, resembling a delicate continental parsley.

Crème fraîche: soured cream containing a minimum of 30 per cent butterfat.

Dandelion (dent-de-lion, pissenlit): a jagged-leafed, wild meadow plant, dismissed as a weed in England but eaten when young as a salad leaf in France.

Lard de poitrine: a fatty version of streaky bacon used for flavouring dishes such as stews; also available smoked.

Marrons glacés: sweet, glazed, syrup-poached chestnuts, eaten as a costly sweetmeat and used in desserts. Available whole, in pieces or in purée form.

Mustard (moutarde): pale yellow *Dijon mustard,* made from black or brown mustard seeds, verjuice and white wine; mild, aromatic dark-brown *Bordeaux mustard*; and grainy-textured *Meaux mustard* made from mixed mustard seeds.

Olive oil: although a small producer, France's olive oil is well-regarded, with the best thought to come from Provence.

Pâtés: *pâté de campagne*, coarse-textured pâté; *pâté de foie*, containing 15 per cent pork liver and 45 per cent fat.

Purslane (pourpier): a green salad vegetable with rounded, clover-shaped leaves.

Puy lentil: a prized small, green-brown lentil which retains its shape and has a good flavour when cooked.

Rocket (roquette): a peppery, jagged green salad leaf; a traditional element of Provençal mesclun (a wild leaf salad).

Salt cod (morue): dried, salted cod which needs pre-soaking before cooking and is used in classic dishes such as brandade.

Saucisson: dried sausages including: *Jésus*, a large pork sausage; *saucisson d'Arles*, made from pork and beef; *saucisson de campagne*, made with pork, fat, garlic and spice; *rosette*, a slowly-matured pure pork sausage.

Sausages: *andouillette*, a thick, bumpy sausage, sometimes smoked; *boudin blanc*, a creamy white sausage containing meat such as veal, chicken or pork; *boudin noir*, a dark-skinned blood sausage made from pig's blood; *cervelas*, a short, stocky pork sausage; *merguez*, a spicy red-coloured Algerian lamb and beef sausage; *Toulouse*, a popular pork cooking sausage, used in cassoulet.

Shallot: a small, russet-skinned, mild member of the onion family.

Snails (escargot): an edible gastropod, enjoyed by the Gauls, available canned or frozen and sometimes found fresh.

Sorrel: a green, leafy herb with a distinctive sour flavour, used to flavour soups, omelettes and salads.

Tarragon: a fine-leafed green herb with a distinctively, aromatic, faintly aniseed flavour.

Truffle (truffe): rare and costly black and white tubers, with a distinctive aroma and flavour. Black Périgord truffles are particularly prized.

Vanilla sugar: vanilla-flavoured caster sugar, available commercially but easily made at home by placing two or three vanilla pods in a jar of caster sugar and leaving it to infuse.

Wine vinegar: red and white wine vinegars are key flavourings in French cookery, essential in salad dressings. Orleans wine vinegars are particularly valued.

FOOD SHOPS

As one would expect from a country famous for its baking, several of London's distinctly French food shops are elegant pâtisseries – offering Londoners an all too rare and welcome chance to enjoy authentic croissants, mouthwatering cakes and proper bread.

CENTRAL

Bagatelle Boutique

⌨ *44 Harrington Road, SW7*
☎ *020 7581 1551*
🚇 *South Kensington LU*
🕐 *Mon-Sat 8am-8pm, Sun 8am-6pm*

Immaculately elegant, with tempting counter displays and helpful, courteous staff, this large shop sells its own high-quality viennoiserie, pâtisserie, breads and cakes (all made with Normandy butter and French flour). In addition, there is a traiteur counter offering dishes such as salmon quenelles and homemade foie gras. A counter of fine French chocolates completes the picture.

Comptoir Gascon

⌨ *61-63 Charterhouse Street, EC1*
☎ *020 7608 0851*
🚇 *Farringdon LU*
🕐 *Mon-Fri 8am-8pm, Sat 9am-6pm*

This discreetly smart shop, with its distressed walls, stone floor and dark wood shelving, arrives with an excellent pedigree, linked as it is to the Michelin starred restaurant Club Gascon. Pride of place here goes to an array of homemade foie gras, with the sweet wines stocked here specifically chosen as good accompaniments to foie gras. Own-made traiteur dishes range from pig's cheek in Armagnac to Gascony pies. On-site bakers produce very competitively priced viennoserie, a range of breads, cakes and pastries, including cannelle, a speciality from South Western France.

Fileric

⌷ *57 Old Brompton Road, SW7*
☏ *020 7584 2967*
🚇 *South Kensington LU*
🕐 *Mon-Sat 8am-7pm, Sun 9am-7pm*

This tiny, dainty pâtisserie and salon de thé, much-frequented by the local French community, sells a small but select range of viennoiserie, pâtisserie and cakes.

La Fromagerie

⌷ *2-4 Moxon Street, W1*
☏ *020 7935 0341*
🚇 *Baker Street LU*
🕐 *Mon 10.30am-7.30pm, Tue-Fri 9.30am-7.30pm, Sat 9.30am-7pm, Sun 10am-5pm*

This new Central London branch of Patricia Michelson's acclaimed North London cheese shop (see p.121) will feature not only a tempting range of cheeses and other edibles but also a café area in which one can sit and sample the fine foods on sale in the shop.

Madeleine

⌷ *5 Vigo Street, W1*
☏ *020 7734 8353*
🚇 *Piccadilly Circus LU*
🕐 *Mon-Sat 8am-10pm, Sun 11am-7pm*

A smart, roomy pâtisserie-cum-café with a tempting window display of French pastries and cakes all freshly made on the premises.

Maison Bertaux

⌷ *28 Greek Street, W1*
☏ *020 7437 6007*
🚇 *Leicester Square LU*
🕐 *Mon-Sat 9am-8pm, Sun 9am-7pm*

Established for well over a hundred years, this small pâtisserie is the last food shop link to Soho's nineteenth-century French community. Tucked away down a side-street, it has a loyal clientele who enjoy the excellent pastries, good coffee and Bohemian atmosphere, lovingly sustained by Michelle, the manager. As one sits sipping coffee, trays of freshly-made croissants or fruit tarts are brought out from the kitchen and regulars pause at the till for a few moment's gossip.

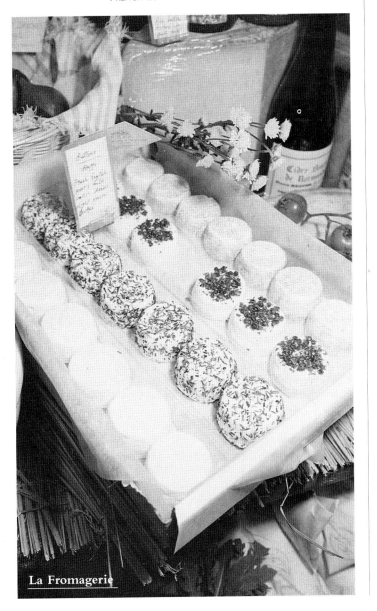

La Fromagerie

Du Pain Duvin

⌨ *31 Paddington Street, W1*
☎ *020 7224 1758*
🚇 *Baker Street LU*
🕐 *Mon-Wed & Sat 10am-6pm, Thurs & Fri 10am-8pm*

This small prettily tiled food shop (formerly Wholefood Butcher's) offers a tempting range of edibles, reflecting owner Eric Duvin's interest in good food. Stock includes pâtés, charcuterie, fresh fruit and vegetables, premium French cheeses (from Brie de Meaux to chèvre), wines and baked quiches and fruit tarts, made on the premises with French flour, butter, sugar and cream.

Paul

⌨ *29 Bedford Street, WC2*
☎ *020 7836 3304*
🚇 *Covent Garden LU*
🕐 *Mon-Fri 7.30am-9pm, Sat & Sun 9am-9pm*

An alluring window display of fruit tarts draws the eye at this, the first London branch of a well-established French chain of bakers. Elegant in a very continental way, Paul's combines a bakery with a spacious salon-de-thé in which to indulge in a coffee éclair or sample a slice of proper Quiche Lorraine. All the goods are baked on the premises, indeed diners can watch the baker busy at work in the backroom bakery. Breads, which range from flute baguettes to rye and wheaten flour 'rustic' bread, are carefully made using traditional techniques.
Other branch: 115 Marylebone High Street, W1, Tel: 020 7836 3304

Poilane

⌨ *46 Elizabeth Street, SW1*
☎ *020 7808 4910*
🚇 *Sloane Square LU, Victoria Station LU/Rail*
🕐 *Mon-Fri 7am-7.30pm, Sat 7.30am-6pm*

This daintily elegant shop is the first London branch of a much-loved Gallic institution. An exact replica of the famous Lionel Poilane's famous bakery on Rue du Cherche-Midi in Paris the shop's basement contains a huge, wood-fired brick oven where the master baker works through the night. Here one can buy the huge, distinctive tangy sour-dough loaves (sold whole, halved, quartered or by the slice) for which

Poilane is famous as well as a select choice of viennoiserie, bags of Guerande sea-salt and simple but utterly more-ish punitions (biscuits).

Villandry

- 170 Great Portland Street, W1
- 020 7631 3131
- Great Portland Street LU
- Mon-Sat 8.30am-10pm, Sun 11am-4pm

This swish deli-cum-eaterie has a strong Gallic element to its upmarket stock. Highlights are the excellent range of French farmhouse cheeses and huge assortment of French dairy products.

NORTH

La Fromagerie

- 30 Highbury Park, N5
- 020 7359 7440
- www.lafromagerie.co.uk
- Highbury & Islington LU/Rail
- Mon 11am-7.30pm, Tue-Sat 9.30am-7.30pm, Sun 10am-4.30pm

Under a dark blue awning, a window filled with appetising tarts and pastries marks the presence of this attractive shop. As the name suggests, cheese is the shop's forte and it stocks between 150-200 seasonal farmhouse cheeses in its cool backroom, of which around 60 per cent are French. A particular speciality is the selection of Alpine cheeses including a "proper Beaufort". Owner Patricia Michelson, whose passionate enthusiasm for cheese is genuine and infectious, makes a point of sourcing cheeses herself, direct from small farms and suppliers. The front room is crammed with delicious Gallic edibles including delicate walnut oil, French raw milk, Poilane bread, superb Normany cider and wines chosen to complement the cheeses on sale. Sweet treats include exquisite French jams and compotes, fine chocolates and fragrant crystallised violets.

SOUTH

Le Tour de France
⌨ *135 Sunnyhill Road, SW16*
☎ *020 8769 3554*
✍ *www.letourdefrance.co.uk*
🚇 *Streatham Rail*
◷ *Mon-Fri 9am-8pm, Sat 10am-8pm, Sun 10am-2.30pm and 7pm-9pm*

Tucked away down a quiet residential Streatham side-street, this small, neat shop, knowledgeably run by its amicable owners Regine and Jean-Pierre Bruyas, is packed with Gallic goodies. Luxury items include fresh Brittany oysters, goose fat, sel gris de Guerande and vintage Armagnacs, but it's also strong on basics such as vinegars, fruit juices and fresh sausages.

Fileric Delicatessen
⌨ *12 Queenstown Road, SW8*
☎ *020 7720 4844*
🚇 *Clapham Common LU*
◷ *Mon-Sat 8am-8pm, Sun 8am-2.30pm*

A pleasantly old-fashioned, shop-cum-café with a delicatessen section offering a range of French cheeses, sausages, salamis and pâtés. The pastry counter offers classic French pastries and cakes, such as tarte citron.

WEST

Maison Blanc
⌨ *102 Holland Park, W11*
☎ *020 7221 2494*
🚇 *Holland Park LU*
◷ *Mon-Wed 8am-7pm, Thurs & Fri 8am-7.30pm, Sat 7.30am-7pm, Sun 8.30am-6pm*

An eye-catching display of the most elegant cakes draws customers into this attractive French pâtisserie-cum-salon de thé, the first London branch of this well-established chain. Goods on offer include rustic-style French breads and exquisitely stylish cakes and pastries including a classic tarte au citron. Buches de Noel (at Christmas) and Tarte Bonne Femme are among the tempting traditional French goodies.

EATING PLACES

CENTRAL LONDON

Elena's L'Etoile   *£££*

30 Charlotte Street, W1

020 7636 7189

Goodge Street LU

In the heart of Fitzrovia this unashamedly cosy, unfashionably comfortable restaurant, with its red plush seating and signed celebrity portraits, is the sort of restaurant which inspires loyalty in its regulars. The rich, classic French food – such as scallops with celeriac purée – and charming service, presided over by famous maître d' Elena Salvoni, match the surroundings to perfection.

La Galette   *£££*

56 Paddington Street, W1

020 7935 1554

Baker Street LU or Bond Street LU

This attractive, smart crêperie offers distinctly superior pancakes; both galettes with savoury fillings and sweet crêpes, such as crêpe Suzette.

Maison Bertaux   *£*

28 Greek Street, W1

020 7437 6007

Leicester Square LU

Vintage Soho café in which to enjoy a café au lait or freshly squeezed orange juice and a freshly baked pastry such as one of their famous almond croissants.

Madeleine   *£*

5 Vigo Street, W1

020 7734 8353

Piccadilly Circus LU

In a side-street away from the bustle of Regent Street, this bright café, with polite French staff, offers 'Les Snacks', including croque monsieur and a tempting range of pâtisserie.

Paul £

⌨ *29 Bedford Street, WC2*
☎ *020 7836 3304*
🚇 *Covent Garden LU*

Paul's backroom salon-de-thé is something of a haven; a civilized place in which to enjoy a slice of proper Quiche Lorraine or a tempting pastry.

NORTH

Almeida £££ £

⌨ *30 Almeida Street, N1*
☎ *020 7354 4777*
🚇 *Highbury & Islington LU/Rail*

Owned by Terence Conran, this Islington restaurant focuses on classic French food, hence hand-carved jambon du Bayonne with celeriac remoulade, superior steak au poivre, buttery potato gratin and a spectacular range of tarts, presented (tongue-in-cheek) on a trolley.

Le Crêperie de Hampstead £

⌨ *Corner of Hampstead High Street*
and Perrins Lane, NW3
🚇 *Hampstead LU*

This corner stall is something of a Hampstead institution, serving excellent take-away sweet and savoury crêpes, such as classic Crêpe Suzette. Customers stand mesmerised watching pats of butter sizzle and melt on the griddles, then a thin pool of batter spread and metamorphosise into a crêpe. Often attracts a queue, particularly when the pubs close.

Paris-London Café ££

⌨ *5 Junction Road, N19*
☎ *020 7561 0330*
🚇 *Archway LU*

Tucked away in an unlikely spot just near Archway Road's busy junction, this small friendly café attracts a steady stream of regulars by offering decent bistro dishes – from Lapin à la Bourguignonne to sautéed celeriac – at bargain prices.

WEST

Maquis *££££*
⌨ *111 Hammersmith Grove, W6*
☎ *020 8846 3850*
🚇 *Goldhawk Road LU or Hammersmith LU*

A sister-restaurant to Clerkenwell's acclaimed Moro restaurant, this spacious eaterie offers an 'au point' menu, featuring simple classics such as gruyère fondue or charcoal-grilled sea bass with tapenade.

COOKBOOKS

Bistro Cooking *by Patricia Wells*
A wonderfully appetising book of bistro cooking

Charcuterie and French Pork Cooking *by Jane Grigson*
A mixture of scholarly knowledge and practical food writing.

Cooking For Friends *by Raymond Blanc*
An illustrated cookbook containing recipes from the chef of Manoir aux Quat' Saisons.

Cuisine Courante *by Bruno Loubet*
An accessible chef's cookbook.

French Country Cookery *by Elizabeth David*
Traditional French cooking.

French Provincial Cookery *by Elizabeth David*
A classic cookbook.

Larousse Gastronomique
A fascinating gastronomic encyclopaedia.

Mastering the Art of French Cookery (Vols 1 & 2),
by Simone Beck, Louisette Bertholle & Julia Child
A well-respected, practical classic.

GREEK LONDON

Michli

The Greek community in London today is about 160,000 strong and largely made up of Greek Cypriots; its growth has been a purely twentieth-century phenomenon. Historically, however, there was a small mainland Greek presence in London which dated back to the eighteenth century. Bishop Timotheus Catsiyannis, of the Cathedral of Aghia Sophia on Moscow Road, has traced back the histories of such prominent Greek families as the Rallis. Pandias Ralli (1793-1865), a prosperous merchant from Chios, came to Britain to expand the family business. He was a leading figure in the early Greek community in Britain, becoming Consul of Greece in 1835.

The Greek community used the Russian Chapel for their religious services and ceremonies until 1837 when a Greek Chapel of Our Saviour was established at 9 Finsbury Circus, where the Ralli brothers had their business. As London's Greek community grew, Pandias felt this chapel to be inadequate and in 1843, proposed building a new church. Seven years later the Greek Church of Our Saviour was opened at London Wall, an historic moment for London's Greek community. This was followed, in 1878, by the completion of the imposing Cathedral of Aghia Sophia in Moscow Road.

The real growth in London's Greek community came much later, as a result of Britain's relations with Cyprus. This strategically important Mediterranean island was leased to the British government in 1878 by the Ottomans, and annexed as a colony by Britain in 1914. During the period of British rule, the lack of opportunities in Cyprus drove many Cypriots to Britain. In the 1930s, the Christian Cypriot Brotherhood was founded in London to offer support to this expat community. The number of Cypriots coming to Britain increased notably after the Second World World and during the 1950s. Many found work as kitchen hands and waiters, and in the garment industry. Soho, with its restaurants and cheap accommodation, was an early focal point. During the late 1940s, however, there was a shift to Camden Town and in 1948 the Greek Cypriots took over the Church of All Saints on Pratt Street. In 1960, Britain withdrew from Cyprus and many of the jobs linked to the naval and military bases disappeared. The economic pull to Britain hit a high point during 1961, when 25,000 Cypriots came to this country. The Turkish invasion of Cyprus in 1974 caused the next major influx, with hundreds of dispossessed refugees fleeing to Britain to seek refuge with family and friends.

During the 1960s the Greek community moved out from Camden, many of them heading north to Turnpike Lane, Wood Green and Palmers Green. Green Lanes, a long road in Haringey, was traditionally a focal point for Greek Cypriots. Today however, though a few veteran Greek Cypriot shops remain, Green Lanes now houses a Turkish and Kurdish community while the Greek community has dispersed through London's north-eastern suburbs.

GREEK CUISINE

The cuisine of ancient Greece, chronicled by the second-century writer Athenaeus, has now been overlayed by other influences. A history of occupation by the Romans, Venetians and Turks has left distinct traces: pasta dishes, kebabs, coffee and honey pastries. There is a clear overlap between Greek and Turkish cooking, especially apparent in Cypriot cooking, and the debate over who originated which dish still continues today. There are also differences: alcohol and pork, prohibited to the Turks under Islam, are used in Greek cooking in dishes like stifatho and afelia. Easter, the most important religious festival in the Greek calendar, is marked by a host of traditional Greek dishes such as mayeritsa: a soup made from lamb head, heart, liver, lungs and intestines; and tsourekia: a braided loaf decorated with a red-dyed, hard-boiled egg, evoking the colour of Christ's blood.

The physical geography of Greece has also shaped its cuisine. The long coastline of the mainland and the islands, shared between three seas, means an abundance of fish and seafood dishes. Mediterranean fish soups, such as bouillabaisse, may be Greek in origin. The lack of grazing ground meant that, traditionally, meat was scarce and had to be ingeniously spun out: minced and layered with aubergine in moussaka or with macaroni in pastitio, or cubed and skewered in kebabs. Goats and sheep, able to thrive on the rocky hills, were more prevalent than cattle, with their need for pasture.

From Arcadia onwards this pastoral tradition has continued, and dairy products such as yogurt and cheese still play an important, nutritious part in Greek cookery. The pungent flavour of sheep's, and goat's, milk provides a characteristic sharp note. In agriculture the olive and vine, able to flourish on the rocky hill tops, continue to dominate as they have done for centuries. Their products are essential to Greek cooking: olives on the table, mellow-flavoured olive oil, wine for drinking and cooking and vine leaves for dolmathes. The host of nut trees that thrive in Greece, such as almond, pistachio, walnut and stone pine, play their part, adding flavour and texture to both sweet and savoury dishes.

The lemon, also grown plentifully, sounds one of the keynotes of Greek cooking. Its fresh, sharp flavour characterises dishes such as avgolemono sauce and soup. The fragrant herbs that grow wild on the hill tops are another source of flavour. Athenaeus wrote of herbs being scattered on fish and grilled meat; rigani, or oregano, 'joy of the mountain' is especially popular. The hills are also the source of horta: wild green leaves such as dandelion, wild mustard and chicory, popularly eaten boiled with a dressing.

One Greek influence that has been embraced in kitchens all over the West stems from the Middle Ages. Cooks who entered the monasteries but continued their culinary vocation adopted tall white hats to distinguish themselves from the black-robed and hatted monks – hence the origin of the chef's white hat. The lavish feasts described by Athenaeus or Hesiod the Epicurean in one of the world's first cookbooks are no longer perceived as characteristic Greek cooking. Instead, Greek food today is valued for its flavourful simplicity.

GLOSSARY

Bastourma: dark, short, spiced sausages.

Bulgar (pourgori): parboiled, cracked wheat grains, available either coarse or finely ground.

Cheeses: *anari*, a soft cheese, similar to Italian ricotta; *feta*, a salty, crumbly white cheese made from cow's, sheep's or goat's milk, often stored in brine to retain its freshness; *halloumi*, a firm white cheese with a rubbery texture, often flavoured with mint.

Colocassi: a large, brown, fibrous tuber with a distinctive white stump, which is a staple of Cypriot cookery.

Filo: paper-thin pastry, sometimes spelled 'phyllo', used in both sweet and savoury dishes. It's usually available frozen, but occasionally fresh filo can be found. When using filo, be careful not to let it dry out and become brittle.

Glyko: preserved fresh fruit, such as quinces and cherries, in a sweet syrup. Traditionally offered to guests with coffee.

Kataifi: a vermicelli-like pastry, formed by pouring batter through a fine sieve onto a hot surface; usually found frozen.

Loukanika: thin sausages popularly flavoured with allspice, savory and orange peel or coriander seeds.

Loundza: smoked pork loin, a traditional Cypriot Christmas food.

Louvana: a type of vetch, recognisable by its curly tendrils, eaten as a salad leaf.

Mahlepi: the fragrant kernel of the blackcherry stone, sold in husked form and added to sweet yeast breads.

Mastic: the fragrant resin of an evergreen tree, sold in powdered form for use in sweet yeast breads.

Olive oil: in Greek mythology the olive tree was a gift from Athena (the goddess of wisdom and warfare). The rich, fruity oil adds a distinctive flavour to Greek cookery.

Olives: *Kalamata*, named after the city, are the famous, large, purple-black olives. *Tiasis*, or cracked olives, are partially-crushed olives which have been marinated, often with olive oil, lemon slices, garlic and cumin seeds.

Ouzo: clear, anise-flavoured liquor, distilled from grapes. When diluted, this potent aperitif becomes white and cloudy and is nicknamed 'lion's milk'.

Parsley: the flat-leafed, flavourful variety known as 'continental parsley' is a basic herb in Greek cookery.

Pasta: dried pasta is a legacy of the Italian influence on Greek cookery. Shapes include macarona, long thick tubes of pasta and manestra, pasta kernels and vermicelli, often cooked with bulgar.

Purslane (glysterida): a green salad vegetable with rounded clover-shaped leaves, sometimes called 'Cypriot watercress'.

Retsina: wine with a distinctive resin flavour, traced back to the days when wine was kept in goat skins sealed with pitch.

Rocket (rocca): a green salad leaf with a distinctive peppery flavour, which is now very fashionable.

Savory: a peppery-flavoured herb, which looks similar to thyme.

Tahini: a smooth paste made from pounded sesame seeds.

Tarama: smoked grey mullet roe or, more commonly, cod roe, used to make taramasalata.

Trahani: brown, stubby, crumbly tubes made from fermented cracked wheat and yogurt. They have a tangy flavour and should be soaked before using.

Vine leaves: large, distinctively-shaped leaves, used principally to make dolmathes. Occasionally found fresh but usually preserved in brine, when they need soaking to rinse off excess salt.

Yogurt: thick, creamy Greek yogurt, made from sheep's or cow's milk.

FOOD SHOPS

NORTH

Clocktower Store

⌨ *52 The Broadway, N8*

☎ *020 8348 7845*

🚇 *Finsbury Park LU, then the W7 bus*

🕐 *Mon-Fri 8.30am-7pm, Sat 8.30am-6pm, Sun 10am-5pm*

This friendly, bustling Cypriot greengrocer's, just by Crouch End's landmark Clock Tower, offers an excellent range of fruit and veg, from bunches of fresh herbs to huge watermelons. Inside are staples such as village bread, feta and olive oil.

Andreas Michli & Sons

⌨ *405-411 St Ann's Road, N15*

☎ *020 8802 0188*

🚇 *Harringay Green Lanes Rail*

🕐 *Mon-Sat 9.30am-7.30pm (Fri until 8.30pm), Sun 11am-3.30pm*

Tucked away just off Green Lanes, this small, characterful row of shops offer everything from foodstuffs to barbecue equipment and Greek statuary. Andreas takes particular pride in the fresh produce, which includes delights such as bergamot lemons, sweet, juicy un-waxed oranges and bunches of the fresh herbs essential to Greek cooking.

Halepi

⌨ *24 Grand Parade, Green Lanes, N4*

☎ *020 8800 9272*

🚇 *Manor House LU*

🕐 *Daily 9.30am-8pm*

This Greek bakery, which is over 25 years old, is something of an institution, and especially famous among the Greek community for its monumental, multi-tiered, lavishly-iced wedding cakes, a display of which is kept upstairs.

Tony's Continental Stores

Milia Wholesale Co Ltd
⌨ *200-202 St Ann's Road, N15*
☎ *020 8802 7654*
🚇 *Seven Sisters LU*
🕐 *Mon-Sat 9am-8pm*

The bright blue walls signal a Greek presence here on this long main road. Milia specialises in everything for Greek barbecues – from sacks of charcoal by the door to savoury bastourma and louganika sausages and halloumi cheese, plus stacks of Greek and Cypriot beers.

Tony's Continental Stores
⌨ *140 High Road, N2*
☎ *020 8444 5545*
🚇 *East Finchley LU*
🕐 *Mon-Fri 8am-7pm, Sat 8am-6.30pm, Sun 10am-1pm*

From watermelons and figs in the summer to quinces and huge field mushrooms in the autumn, there is always a good range of produce at this self-service greengrocer's, run with friendly courtesy by the Athanasiou family.

WEST

Adamou
⌨ *126 Chiswick High Road, W4*
☎ *020 8994 0752*
🚇 *Turnham Green LU*
🕐 *Daily 8.30am-6.45pm*

This Chiswick institution has an attractive display of produce outside: from rocket and avocados to bunches of flowers. Inside, there is a good range of general groceries: olives, pasta, cheeses and cured meats.

Athenian Grocery
⌨ *16a Moscow Road, W2*
☎ *020 7229 6280*
🚇 *Bayswater LU*
🕐 *Mon-Sat 8.30am-7pm, Sun 9.30am-1pm*

Down the road from St Sophia is this charming corner shop, its blue-painted exterior and boxes of vegetables striking an attractive Mediterranean note. Established for over 40 years, its stock includes seasonal items such as green almonds and fresh vine leaves, as well as basic staples. Banter is the name of the game here and insults are genially exchanged with regular customers, but service is friendly and heavy bags are carried out to waiting cars.

SOUTH-EAST

Andreas

⌂ *18 Lordship Lane, SE22*

☏ *020 8299 2214*

🚇 *East Dulwich Rail, then the 40, 176, 185, or 484 bus*

🕐 *Mon-Sat 9am-9pm, Sun 10am-8pm*

Crates of fresh fruit and vegetables such as colocassi and aubergines signal the presence of this roomy Cypriot grocers. The deli-counter is crammed with Greek cakes, cheese and cured meats and there is a good range of basic stock.

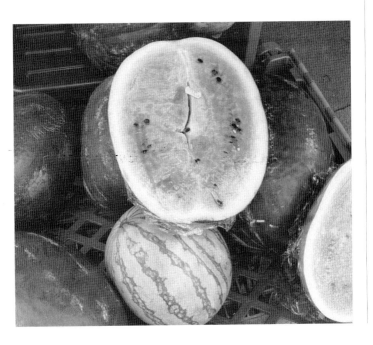

EATING PLACES

EAST LONDON

The Real Greek *££££*
🖂 *15 Hoxton Market, N1*
☎ *020 7739 8212*
🚇 *Old Street LU/Rail*

In the heart of hip Hoxton, chef-patron Theodore Kyriakou offers a fresh, flavourful insight into Greek cookery.

NORTH LONDON

Daphne *££*
🖂 *83 Bayham Street, NW1*
☎ *020 7267 7322*
🚇 *Camden Town LU*

An unreconstructed convivial Greek restaurant serving decent Greek food, popular for both romantic tête-à-têtes and parties of friends.

Lemonia *££*
🖂 *89 Regent's Park Road, NW1*
☎ *020 7586 7454*
🚇 *Chalk Farm LU*

With its lively atmosphere, friendly staff and fresh-tasting food this is everyone's idea of what a Greek restaurant should be and accordingly pulls in the revellers.

Vrisiaki *££*
🖂 *73 Myddleton Road, N22*
☎ *020 8889 8760*
🚇 *Bounds Green LU*

Warmly recommended by Cypriot friends, at first sight this looks solely like a take-away kebab house. Venture in, however, past the busy charcoal grills and it opens into a large, busy restaurant. Those with gargantuan appetites should opt for mezedes, a seemingly never-ending array of dishes, starting with nibbles such as tahini and cracked olives and working up via seafood to a platter of grilled meats.

COOKBOOKS

Flavours of Greece *by Rosmary Barron*
An evocatively written collection of over 250 recipes for Greek dishes, ranging from aromatic giant beans to olive bread.

A Book of Mediterranean Food *by Elizabeth David*
A knowledgeable and evocative book which, although not solely about Greek cookery, captures the flavours of the Mediterranean.

Mediterranean Seafood *by Alan Davidson*
A fascinating and knowledgeable guide to Mediterranean seafood.

The Taste of Cyprus *by Gilli Davies*
A charmingly-written cookbook, combining evocative personal memories with straightforward recipes.

Mediterranean Cookery *by Claudia Roden*
A well-written and attractive book, dealing with Mediterranean cuisine as a whole.

The Greek Cook *by Rena Salaman*
Attractively illustrated with mouth-watering photographs this appetising cookbook offers a seasonal look at Greek cuisine.

ITALIAN LONDON

I. Camisa

Italian links with London date back to the Roman invasion in AD 43 and the creation of a settlement named 'Londinium'. Over subsequent centuries Italians came to live in London, but particularly so in the first half of the nineteenth century when waves of political refugees arrived in the capital. The community continued to grow through the turbulent times of Italian Unification and war with Austria – by 1900 there were around 10,000 Italians in London.

The historical Italian quarter, founded in the mid-nineteenth century, was in Clerkenwell and Holborn, known to outsiders as 'Little Italy' and to its residents as 'The Hill'. The nickname 'The Hill' came from two important streets in the community: Back Hill and Eyre Street Hill. St Peter's Church was the community's focal point, erected in 1864 with money donated by Italian immigrants; its importance in celebrating and commemorating the births, lives and deaths of the Italian community continues to this day. Although the Italian population has now dispersed from Clerkenwell, the legacy of this period is still visible in the area around King's Cross and Holborn where red, white and green signs over barber's, cafés and shops patriotically signal Italy.

Every year in July on the feast day of Our Lady of Mount Carmel, a religious procession in her honour takes place through Clerkenwell from St Peter's, followed by a 'sagra' or fête. One of the few religious processions to take place in London, it has been enacted since the 1880s and older Italians have fond memories of attending it as children. Even today, the procession draws Italians back to Clerkenwell from all over Britain. There is a great sense of community, with the different generations all present and participating. Stalls are set up on the streets selling delicious Italian snacks such as polenta e salsiccie (cornmeal and sausages), freshly-roasted porchetta (pork) and slices of savoury tarts, with glasses of wine adding to the celebratory atmosphere.

The other traditional Italian area in London was Soho, which also saw an influx of Italians in the 1860s. Despite the internment of Italian residents as 'enemy aliens' during the Second World War and the tragic death in 1940 of 470 Italian internees being deported to Canada when the Arandora Star was sunk by the Germans, the Italian community continued to maintain its links with Britain. In the 1950s and 1960s, during the espresso bar boom, a wave of immigrants, mostly from the south of Italy, came to London seeking work and settled in Soho as waiters and restauranteurs.

ITALIAN CUISINE

Italian cuisine is very much a regional cuisine; the different parts of Italy, united only in the nineteenth century, have their own dishes and even their own ingredients. The historical divide between the prosperous, industrial north and the poor, rural south also extended to foodstuffs. Rice, polenta made with cornmeal, and fresh egg pasta were the staples of the north while in the south factory-made, dried durum wheat pasta was eaten. Cooking fats varied: the north used butter, middle-Italy pig fat, and the south, olive oil. With the post-war migration of labour from south to north and the growth of mass-production, regional eating patterns became less rigid. Today the Mediterranean diet, stemming from the south, is valued for its health-giving qualities. Dried pasta and olive oil, low in saturated fats, are now eaten throughout Italy.

Despite this blurring of the north-south divide, regional characteristics are still apparent. Tuscan cuisine comprises of rustic, peasant food such as bean soup (the Tuscans are nick-named 'mangiafagioli', bean-eaters), bruschetta and charcoal-grilled meat such as bistecca fiorentina, a T-bone steak traditionally from the Val di Chiana. Rice dishes are still popular in the north, where rice was traditionally grown, and in Lombardy you find risotto alla Milanese, flavoured with saffron, wine and stock. Roman cuisine is that of the 'quinto quarto', the fifth quarter, with the poor eating what was left after the rich had eaten, hence strongly-flavoured offal dishes. Sicily has a rich, varied culinary inheritance due to a history of invasions by the Greeks, Romans, Arabs and Normans. The Arab legacy is particularly noticeable, with sultanas, aubergines, pistachio nuts and spices being popular ingredients in Sicily.

Italian cooking is noted for its emphasis on clear, simple flavours. Good ingredients are the key to Italian cooking and seasonality is valued. Foods continue to be associated with the regions, towns or villages that have traditionally produced that ingredient: the best radicchio from Treviso, with its annual radicchio festival; balsamic vinegar from Modena; prosciutto from Parma or San Daniele; fontina cheese from Val d'Aosta; and costly white truffles from Alba.

GLOSSARY

Baccala: pungent salted, dried cod which needs soaking before cooking.

Balsamic vinegar: an aromatic brown vinegar made from wine and must historically come from Modena. Traditionally-matured balsamic vinegar is very expensive while cheaper, commercially produced balsamic vinegar compresses the maturing process into a few years.

Ciabatta: a flavourful, distinctively-textured bread, named after a house-shoe because of its flattened, oval shape.

Colomba: a dove-shaped cake similar to panettone, but traditionally eaten at Easter.

Focaccia: a flat, salty bread flavoured with olive oil and sometimes additionally with rosemary, onions or sage; known as schiacciata in Tuscany.

Fontina: a semi-soft cow's milk cheese, traditionally from Val d'Aosta, and famously used to make fonduta, a fondue flavoured with white truffles.

Marscapone: an extremely rich cream cheese, an essential ingredient for the popular dessert tiramisu.

Mortadella: a large pink sausage, traditionally from Bologna, flavoured with peppercorns, garlic and pistachios. It can be eaten like a salami or used in cooking.

Mozzarella: a bland white cheese with a rubbery texture that is famously used on pizzas. Buffalo's milk mozzarella is more expensive than the more easily found cow's milk version. Baby mozzarellas are called 'bocconcini'.

Olive oil: a key ingredient in Italian cooking, olive oil is labelled according to its acidity levels. Extra Virgin must have no more than 1% acidity. As with wine, different regions produce different-flavoured olive oils, with Tuscan olive oil being famously piquant.

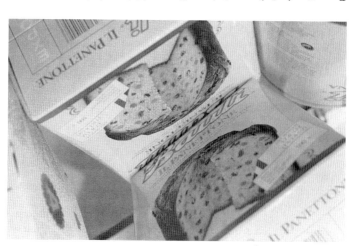

Pancetta: the Italian equivalent of bacon, this is made from the same cut of – pig belly.

Panettone: a light, brioche-style cake, containing sultanas, traditionally given at Christmas time, which is when the Italian delis stock several varieties.

Parmesan: the best-known Italian cheese and also the largest and longest-matured cheese produced in Italy, this hard-grating cheese comes traditionally from around Parma. Grana padano is a similar cheese produced in Lombardy. Buy chunks of Parmesan and keep them refrigerated, wrapped in foil, to be used as required.

Pasta: this famous Italian staple comes both fresh and dried and in a multiplicity of forms. Fresh pasta, made with eggs, can be bought ready-made from delicatessens. Dried pasta should be made from durum wheat and popular Italian brands include Barilla and Da Cecco.

Pecorino: a hard sheep's milk cheese. Pecorino Romano is most commonly found but there is also Pecorino Sardo, from Sardinia, and Toscana, from Tuscany.

Pine nuts: small ivory-coloured kernels from the stone pine tree, with a distinctive flavour.

Polenta: a Northern Italian staple made from maize, polenta flour is available in fine or coarse versions. Pre-cooked polenta flour, scorned by purists, is also available.

Porcini: wild Boletus mushrooms, prized for their flavour and priced accordingly. Dried porcini mushrooms, often in pieces, are easily found, while fresh porcini are much rarer.

Prosciutto Crudo: the most famous of these salt-cured hams is *Parma ham*, cured for 14 months. *San Daniele*, cured for 12 months, is considered another fine prosciutto.

Ricotta: a light, bland sheep's whey cheese, drained in baskets which give it its distinctive woven markings. It is used in both sweet and savoury dishes.

Rocket: known as 'rucola', this peppery, jagged leaf is increasingly available as a chic salad leaf. Italians are fond of pointing out that in Italy it grows wild as a weed.

Salami: ready-to-eat, salt-cured sausages, available in a range of sizes and flavours, such as fine-textured *Milano* or *finocchiona*, flavoured with fennel.

Salsicce: Italian sausages, usually made from pork. *Luganega*, is a mild sausage from Lombardy, sold in long narrow coils, while in the South chilli is often added as a flavouring.

Sun-dried tomatoes: as their name suggests, these are dried tomatoes, available either in their dry state or preserved in olive oil.

Truffles: these rare tubers with their overwhelming and distinctive flavour are astronomically expensive, especially when sold fresh. White truffles from Alba are particularly prized. Tinned and bottled truffles are available as is truffle-flavoured olive oil.

FOOD SHOPS

The older Italian delicatessens in London grew out of the community's needs, starting as everyday corner-shops supplying foods that had to be specially imported. In some cases the shop acted as an informal community centre, lending money, explaining English laws and providing advice. As the Italian community have become assimilated into British life this role has disappeared. With Italian food now enjoying a huge wave of fashionable popularity, newer, more upmarket delicatessens are entering the market now aimed primarily at the English.

CENTRAL

Angelucci

- 23b Frith Street, W1
- *020 7437 5889*
- *Leicester Square LU or Tottenham Court Road LU*
- *Mon–Wed 9am–5pm, Thurs 9am–1pm, Fri–Sat 9am–5pm*

A Soho institution, founded in 1929 by Signore Angelucci and in these premises since 1931 this veteran coffee business is still run by the Angelucci family. This small old-fashioned shop, with its vintage coffee-grinders on the counter, smells enticingly of roasted coffee, of which they sell 36 varieties at remarkably reasonable prices. The most popular is Mokital, for cappuccinos and espressos, which is freshly ground as required. If you want to sample Mokital, drop into Bar Italia two doors away and have one of their much-famed espressos or cappuccinos. Over the decades, customers have included General du Gaulle and numerous Dire Straits fans, drawn by the reference to Angelucci's in the song The Wild West End.

I Camisa & Son

- 61 Old Compton Street, W1
- *020 7437 7610/4686*
- *Leicester Square LU or Tottenham Court Road LU*
- *Mon–Sat 9am–6pm*

On this bustling Soho thoroughfare, Gaby presides genially over this classic Italian deli. Established over thirty years ago, this small shop has a seemingly perpetual queue of loyal regulars, attracted by the quality of

the cheeses (including excellent Parmesan), meats and delicious home-marinated olives. Bags of fresh rocket and stunningly sweet Sicilian cherry tomatoes are another draw. Fresh pasta includes pappardelle, parma ham tortellini and gnocchi and there are homemade sauces such as pesto, lepre (hare) and porcini.

Carluccio's

▢ *28a Neal Street, WC2*
☎ *020 7240 1487*
🚇 *Covent Garden LU*
🕐 *Mon-Thurs 11am-7pm, Fri 10am-7pm, Sat 10am-6pm*

Set up by restauranteur and funghiphile Antonio Carluccio (also of the neighbouring Neal Street Restaurant) and his wife Priscilla, this sleek shop offers an appetising selection of regional Italian foods, including a counter of ready-made dishes and fresh pasta. Everything, from the Calabrian stuffed figs to the rustic loaves of bread, is beautifully packaged and presented. Naturally, there is also a fine seasonal range of fresh wild mushrooms and truffles.

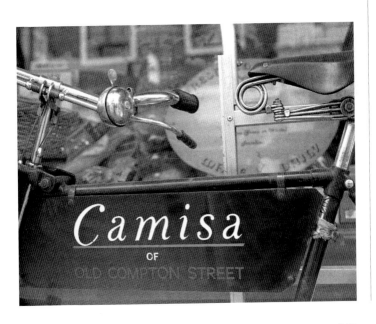

Exeter Street Bakery

🖻 *15 Exeter Street, WC2*
☎ *020 7379 1881*
🚉 *Charing Cross LU/Rail*
🕐 *Mon-Fri 10am-7pm*

Tucked away in a side-street just off the Strand, this smart shop, with its natty chrome shelving, offers an excellent range of authentically flavourful Italian breads, made using traditional recipes and methods including the use of a natural starter. Dark-crusted Pugliese is a bestseller, but one can also buy classic ciabatta, stirato (Italian baguette) and raisin or olive breads. Slices of thin-crusted freshly-cooked pizza, such as pizza bianca (flavoured simply with olive oil, sea salt and rosemary) or sweet crostata (jam tart) can be eaten at the tiny counter or taken away.

Gastronomeria Italia

🖻 *8 Upper Tachbrook Street, SW1*
☎ *020 7834 2767*
🚉 *Pimlico LU & Victoria LU/Rail*
🕐 *Mon-Fri 9am-6pm, Sat 9am-5pm*

This homely delicatessen is well-used by Italians and Spaniards from the local community. As well as a good basic stock of Italian ingredients, they sell tasty Italian snacks to cater to the lunchtime market. The fresh slices of pizza are particularly popular.

Gazzano G. & Son

🖻 *169 Farringdon Road, EC1*
☎ *020 7837 1586*
🚉 *Farringdon LU*
🕐 *Mon & Sat 8am-5pm, Tue-Fri 8am-5.30pm, Sun 10am-2pm*

This venerable shop was set up in 1901 in the heart of the Clerkenwell Italian community. The shop retains its down-to-earth roots with clearly-arranged stock: salamis and sausages in one counter, cheeses in another, and dried pasta along the wall.

Lina Stores

⊡ *18 Brewer Street, W1*

☎ *020 7437 6482*

🚇 *Leicester Square LU, Oxford Circus LU or Piccadilly Circus LU*

🕐 *Mon-Fri 7am-5.45pm, Sat 7am-5pm*

The pistachio-coloured facade and the 1930s lettering tell you this is a long-established shop. Customers return as much for the friendly, leisurely atmosphere as for the delicious food. It is famous for its exquisite fresh pasta, made on the premises every morning. The speciality is pumpkin tortelloni, a dish from Piacenza where the Filippi family come from. Groceries are wide-ranging – you feel you could ask for any Italian ingredient and it would be conjured up.

La Picena

⊡ *5 Walton Street, SW3*

☎ *020 7584 6573*

🚇 *Knightsbridge LU*

🕐 *Mon-Fri 9am-7.30pm, Sat 9am-5.30pm*

Tucked away behind Harrods is this refreshingly down-to-earth delicatessen. It is crammed full of good-quality Italian provisions including fresh pasta and top-notch homemade pasta sauces.

L. Terroni & Sons

⊡ *138-40 Clerkenwell Road, EC1*

☎ *020 7837 1712*

🚇 *Chancery Lane LU or Farringdon LU*

🕐 *Tues-Fri 9am-6pm, Sat 9am-3pm, Sun 10.30am-2pm*

Next to St Peter's Church – a focal point for London's Italian community – Terroni's was established in 1890 in the heart of Little Italy. The large shop retains its grocery store roots, offering a good selection of Italian foodstuffs. Owner John Annessa, who took over from the Terroni brothers over 20 years ago, is particularly proud of his selection of around 300 Italian wines. During the week it attracts a largely English clientele while Sunday mornings see it busy with Italians chatting and catching up on the news after the service at St Peter's.

Angelucci

NORTH

Amici Delicatessen

⌨ *78 High Road, N2*
☎ *020 8444 2932*
🚇 *East Finchley LU*
🕐 *Mon-Sat 8am-7pm, Sun 10am-1pm*

A friendly, basic Italian deli, which draws in a lunchtime crowd for its paninis and freshly-made espressos.

Il Boungustaio

⌨ *90 Stroud Green Road, N4*
☎ *020 7263 5705*
🚇 *Finsbury Park LU*
🕐 *Mon-Sat 8am-10pm*

A small, friendly, down-to-earth shop, combining a sandwich bar, deli section and newsagents. Customers return for the generously filled panini – such as pesto and Parma ham in ciabatta and the Italian gelati.

A. Ferrari

⌨ *48 Cross Street, N1*
☎ *020 7226 1951*
🚇 *Angel LU or Highbury & Islington LU/Rail*
🕐 *Mon-Fri 8am-7pm, Sat 8am-6pm, Sun 9.30am-2pm*

Tucked away in an Islington side-street, this small family-run deli has been here for over 30 years. The stock is basic and unpretentious, with a good range of salamis, De Cecco and Barilla dried pasta and traditional cakes such as panettone at Christmas.

Giacobazzi's Delicatessen

⌨ *150 Fleet Road, NW3*
☎ *020 7267 7222*
🚇 *Hampstead Heath Rail*
🕐 *Mon-Fri 9.30am-7pm, Sat 9am-6pm*

The speciality here is ready-made fresh foods, of which there is an appetising display. The dishes are made on the premises by Raffaele Giacobazzi, who, according to his wife Renata, has a particular penchant for char-grilled vegetables ranging from radicchio to onions in balsamic vinegar. Homemade pasta, freshly made every day, includes upmarket treats such as gorgonzola and walnut and porcini, and white truffle tortellini.

149

King's Cross Continental Stores

⌨ *26 Caledonian Road, N1*

☎ *020 7837 0201*

🚇 *King's Cross LU*

🕐 *Mon-Sat 9am-7pm, Sun 10am-1pm*

Leo Giordani has run this pleasantly old-fashioned shop for over 30 years now. Customers who used to live locally but now live in other parts of London still return to catch up with Leo's news and you're more likely to hear Italian being spoken than English.

Mandara

⌨ *20 High Road, N2*

☎ *020 8883 3777*

🚇 *East Finchley LU*

🕐 *Mon-Fri 8am-7pm, Sat 9am-6.30pm, Sun 10.30am-2.30pm*

Strategically positioned just over the road from East Finchley tube, this smart, bright deli has a basic range of foodstuffs and also offers both cappuccini and panini for hungry commuters.

Monte's

⌨ *23 Canonbury Lane, N1*

☎ *020 7354 4335*

🚇 *Highbury & Islington LU/Rail*

🕐 *Mon-Fri 10am-7pm, Sat 10am-6pm, Sun 10am-4pm*

This is a New Wave Italian deli, with mauve walls, black glossy floor tiles, gleaming metal shelving and jazz playing in the background. Stock is distinctly upmarket, from large bowlfuls of marinated olives and insalata di mare to fresh funghi ravioli. Groceries include several olive oils, balsamic vinegars and polentas.

Mauro's Deli

⌨ *229 Muswell Hill Broadway, N10*

☎ *020 8883 2848*

🚇 *Highgate LU, then 134 bus*

🕐 *Tue-Sat 10am-7pm, Sun 11am-4pm*

An eye-catching window display of colourful homemade pasta demonstrates the shop's speciality. In addition to the extensive range of pastas there are homemade sauces and a selection of basic foodstuffs.

Olga Stores

⌨ *30 Penton Street, N1*
☎ *020 7837 5467*
🚃 *Angel LU*
🕐 *Mon-Fri 9am-8pm, Sat 9am-7pm, Sun 10am-2pm*

Run by the charming and knowledgeable Aida, this bright, attractive deli founded in 1988 caters to its Islington clientele with a wide selection of foodstuffs, from marinated olives to breads. Best-selling items include Aida's homemade lasagne, Portuguese-style salt cod fritters and her huge range of sauces, from tomato-based arrabiata and vongole to pesto.

Saponara

⌨ *23 Prebend Street, N1*
☎ *020 7226 2771*
🚃 *Angel LU*
🕐 *Mon-Fri 8am-6pm, Sat 9am-6pm*

Run with friendly courtesy by brothers Marco and Vincenzo Saponara, this roomy deli-cum-bar offers a classic Italian mixture of delicious foodstuffs, from a distinguished range of cured meats to their home-marinated olives 'arrabiata'. Specialities include homemade pesto ("made the traditional way with pine nuts, not other nuts"), pecorino with truffles, fine Italian wines and superior fresh pasta from Italy including rocket tortelloni and panzerotti. There are several tables at which to enjoy a cappuccino and panino, al' Italiano.

Salvino Ltd

⌨ *47 Brecknock Road, N7*
☎ *020 7267 5305*
🚃 *Bus 29, 253 or 10*
🕐 *Mon-Sat 9am-7pm*

A pleasantly unpretentious shop run by the Salvino brothers. As they import Italian food their stock is above average, with a good selection of cured meats, wines and aperitivos.

SOUTH-EAST

Delicatessen Piacenza

⌗ *2 Brixton Road, SW9*

☎ *020 7735 2121*

🚇 *Oval LU*

🕐 *Mon-Sat 9am-7pm, 'alternate Sundays' 10am-5pm*

There has been an Italian deli on this site (which is a few doors away from the Chiesa della Redentore) for over 20 years. This small, traditional shop stocks a good choice of basics.

La Gastronomeria

⌗ *135 Half Moon Lane, SE24*

☎ *020 7274 1034*

🚇 *Herne Hill or North Dulwich Rail*

🕐 *Mon-Fri 9am-7.30pm, Sat 9am-6.30pm, Sun 10am-2.30pm*

This friendly well-stocked Italian deli offers customers a good range of basic groceries, from Italian dried pastas to packets of biscotti. Popular items on the deli counter include the homemade pastas and antipasti, made by their sister shop in West Dulwich.

Branch at: 86 Park Hall Road, SE21, Tel: 020 8766 0494

SOUTH-WEST LONDON

I Sapori

⌗ *146 Northcote Road, SW11*

☎ *020 7228 2017*

🚇 *Clapham Junction Rail*

🕐 *Mon-Sat 10am-7pm*

Distinctly stylish, this smart delicatessen is run by Michelin-starred Italian chef Stefano Cavallini. Traiteur dishes such as roast pigeon with cherry sauce are a particular highlight. Other homemade goodies include ravioli, pasta sauces and cakes and biscuits such as brutti ma buoni. Grocery items are upmarket: artisanal gelati, beautifully packaged chocolates, bottarga di tonno, flavoured honeys and unusual jams.

Luigi's Delicatessen

🖃 *349 Fulham Road, SW10*

☎ *020 7352 7739*

🚇 *Fulham Broadway LU*

🕐 *Mon-Fri 9am-9.30pm, Sat 9am-7pm*

This roomy, cheerful delicatessen attracts a steady stream of loyal customers. The stock is extensive and high-quality: 40 olive oils and over 300 Italian wines, spirits and aperitivos. There is an appetising display of homemade sauces and dishes.

Salumeria Estense

🖃 *837 Fulham Road, SW6*

☎ *020 7731 7643*

🚇 *Parson's Green LU*

🕐 *Mon-Fri 10am-7pm, Sat 10am-5pm*

Warmly recommended by Italian food historian Anna del Conte, this pretty, friendly delicatessen run by Mr and Mrs Gorini has stylish stock including upmarket olive oils, vinegars and wines. Pasta (including tagliatelle, linguini, paglia e fieno) is freshly made on the premises "using only Italian flour and Italian eggs – no semolina or water" and there is also a range of char-grilled vegetables and excellent homemade sauces.

Salumeria Napoli

🖃 *69 Northcote Road, SW11*

☎ *020 7228 2445*

🚇 *Clapham Junction Rail*

🕐 *Mon-Sat 9am-6pm*

A friendly corner shop with an appetising deli-counter containing olives, homemade red and green pesto sauces and a good selection of salamis and cured meats.

Tony's Continental Delicatessen

🖃 *South Lambeth Road, SW8*

☎ *020 7582 0766*

🚇 *Vauxhall LU*

🕐 *Mon-Fri 7am-6.30pm, Sat 8am-5.30pm*

This down-to-earth corner deli has been serving the local Italian community for over 10 years now. On offer are deli basics, from dried pasta to chunks of Parmesan. There is fresh Italian bread and also panini, made up with salami and cheese from the deli counter.

Valentina

⌨ *210 Upper Richmond Road West, SW14*

☎ *020 8392 9127*

🚆 *Mortlake Rail*

🕐 *Mon-Fri 9am-7pm, Sat 8.30am-6pm, Sun 9.30am-3pm*

The Borfecchia's attractive, friendly delicatessen has a loyal local following. Particularly popular are the home-prepared dishes, from grilled vegetables to baked pasta dishes. There is a good range of grocery items and luxuries such as fresh truffles when they are in season.

WEST LONDON

Exeter Street Bakery

⌨ *1B Argyll Road, W8*

☎ *020 7937 8484*

🚆 *High Street Kensington LU*

🕐 *Mon-Sat 8am-7pm, Sun 9am-6pm*

This smart shop does a roaring trade in authentically tasty slices of pizza, Illy espressos and classic Italian breads such as pane Pugliese and ciabatta.

Speck

⌨ *2 Holland Park Terrace, W11*

☎ *020 7229 7005*

🚆 *Holland Park LU*

🕐 *Mon-Fri 9am-8.30pm, Sat 8.30am-7pm*

This small, sleek shop offers upmarket stock, from an attractive display of homemade dishes such as marinated grilled vegetables to a good assortment of balsamic vinegars, Cipriani dried pasta and fine olive oils.

MAIL ORDER

✍ *www.esperya.com*

Specialising in artisanal Italian produce, Esperya inspires with the immense range of products on offer and the quality of what's available. Efficient delivery completes a truly impressive picture.

EATING PLACES

O ver the last 15 years London's Italian restaurant scene has undergone a transformation. A whole new wave of elegant, smart and expensive restaurants have opened up offering authentic, delicious and regional Italian cooking – rather than the 'Britalian' fare on offer before.

CENTRAL

Bar Italia £

□ *22 Frith Street, W1*

☎ *020 7437 4520*

🚌 *Leicester Square LU or Tottenham Court Road LU*

Despite its cult status as the place for a late night espresso, Bar Italia remains thankfully down-to-earth, complete with fruit machines, a giant video screen for Italian football and Rocky Marciano glowering down from behind the bar.

Carluccio's Caffe *££*

⌨ *8 Market Place, W1*

☎ *020 7636 2228*

🚇 *Oxford Circus LU*

The first in what is now a chain of successful café-cum-delis, this pleasantly stylish, family-friendly eatery offers excellent value Italian food, from spaghetti alla vongole with fresh clams to fresh lemon sorbet.

Locanda Locatelli *££££*

⌨ *8 Seymour Street, W1*

☎ *020 7935 9088*

🚇 *Marble Arch LU*

This sophisticated and elegant restaurant is a showcase for the considerable culinary talents of acclaimed Italian chef Giorgio Locatelli. Deftly executed dishes such as ravioli all'ossobuco or monkfish with walnut and caper sauce exhibit the flavourful simplicity of classic Italian cooking. Equally Italian is the welcome extended to children, with Saturday lunchtime particularly popular with families.

Passione *££££*

⌨ *10 Charlotte Street, W1*

☎ *020 7636 2833*

🚇 *Goodge Street LU or Tottenham Court Road LU*

Chef Gennaro Contaldo's intimate Fitzrovia restaurant, which opens onto Charlotte Street, offers classically flavourful Italian food in attractively atmospheric surroundings.

Pizza Express *££*

⌨ *29 Wardour Street, W1*

☎ *020 7734 7215*

🚇 *Leicester Square LU or Tottenham Court Road LU*

Opened in 1965 by Peter Boizot, this was the first restaurant in successful Pizza Express chain, all of which offer excellent Italian-style pizza with thin, crispy bases and tasty toppings. Consult a phone book for your nearest branch.

Sardo   £££
- 45 Grafton Way, W1
- ☎ 020 7387 2521
- Warren Street LU

Sardinian specialities, including traditional pasta dishes such as spaghetti bottariga or malloreddus, are on offer here in this intimate, friendly restaurant.

Spiga   £££
- 84-86 Wardour Street, W1
- ☎ 020 7734 3444
- Tottenham Court Road LU

A smart, rather hectic restaurant offering the chance to sample delicious pasta dishes (such as linguine with crab and chilli) and authentically thin-crust, wood-fired pizzas with sophisticated toppings.

La Spighetta   £££
- 43 Blandford Street, W1
- ☎ 020 7486 7340
- Baker Street LU

Tucked away on a peaceful side-street this roomy restaurant serves excellent, authentic Italian pasta and pizza.

Strada   £-££
- 15-16 New Burlington Street, W1
- ☎ 020 7287 5967
- Oxford Circus LU or Piccadilly Circus LU

Pleasantly informal restaurant with a menu offering pasta, grilled meat and (their speciality) flavourful Italian-style pizzas, cooked, as is traditional, in a wood oven with carefully chosen toppings ranging from speck to buffalo mozzarella.

Zafferano   ££££
- 15 Lowndes Street, SW1
- ☎ 020 7235 5800
- Knightsbridge LU

A pioneer of fine Italian food in London, this rustically chic restaurant continues to produce excellent Italian cooking

NORTH

Florians   *LL-LLL*
⌸ *4 Topsfield Parade, Middle Lane, N8*
☎ *020 8348 8348*
🚌 *Bus W7*

A pleasant, roomy bar-cum-restaurant offering regional Italian cooking, predominantly from the north, such as Venetian fish pie.

Marine Ices   *LL*
⌸ *8 Haverstock Hill, NW3*
☎ *020 7485 3132*
🚌 *Chalk Farm LU*

A nautically-named gelateria set up by Gaetano Mansi in 1930. He had been a fruiterer and the family myth goes that he began making water-ices from left over fruit. This family business prides itself on its range of flavourful Italian ice creams, using ingredients such as Van Houten cocoa, dark-roasted Mocha and fresh mangoes and oranges. Grander desserts such as tartufo and cassata Siciliana have traditionally been brought for many a family occasion by London's Italian community. There is also a relaxed family-friendly restaurant area serving good tasty pizza and pasta, such as spaghetti alle vongole.

La Porchetta Pizzeria   *LL*
⌸ *147 Stroud Green Road, N4*
☎ *020 7281 2892*
🚌 *Finsbury Park LU*

The gargantuan, tasty, bargain-priced pizzas on offer here ensure a vibrant, bustling atmosphere.

Refreshment House   *L*
⌸ *Golders Hill Park, North End Road, NW3*
☎ *020 8455 8010*
🚌 *Golders Green LU*

Popular with families with young children and old age pensioners alike, this large Italian café serves up cappuccini, panini and a few pasta dishes. The star attraction, however, is their own ice cream – fresh-tasting gelati from refreshing melon to sweet, more-ish marron, studded with pieces of marrons glacés.

SOUTH

Eco Brixton Ltd £
- *4 Market Row, SW9*
- ☎ *020 7738 3021*
- ▦ *Brixton LU & Rail*

Tucked away amongst the hustle and bustle of Brixton Market, this tiny, relaxed pizzeria offers authentic Italian thin-based pizzas, generously topped with gourmet treats like fresh rocket or roasted red peppers. Food is served until 5pm.

Branch at: Eco, 162 Clapham High Street, SW4, Tel: 020 7622 6848

Pizza Metro ££
- *64 Battersea Park Rise, SW11*
- ☎ *020 7228 3812*
- ▦ *Clapham Junction Rail*

Neapolitan food at its best, from aubergine parmigiana to mozzarella in carrozza, and splendid wood oven-baked pizzas.

Pizzeria Castello ££
- *20 Walworth Road, SE1*
- ☎ *020 7703 2556*
- ▦ *Elephant and Castle LU*

An appetising waft of garlic signals this popular pizzeria. Regulars return for the excellent crisp pizzas and lively service.

WEST

Assaggi ££££
- *The Chepstow, 39 Chepstow Place, W2*
- ☎ *020 7792 5501*
- ▦ *Notting Hill Gate LU*

Located above a pub this small restaurant is noted for its flavourful, authentic Italian food.

Riva £££

169 Church Road, SW13

020 8748 0434

Barnes Bridge Rail

A restaurant pioneer of regional Italian cooking, Riva continues to offer imaginative and tasty dishes in an elegant setting, and has a loyal clientele.

The River Café £££££

Thames Wharf, Rainville Road, W6

020 7381 8824

Hammersmith LU

Informally stylish, this acclaimed restaurant, housed in a Richard Rogers'-designed wharf complex by the River Thames, continues to thrive. Owners and chefs Ruth Rogers and Rose Gray make a point of using the finest quality, seasonal produce, from the best Italian cheeses and olive oil to the freshest of salad leaves. A number of best-selling 'River Café' cookbooks and a television series have ensured that its fame has spread far beyond Hammersmith.

COOKBOOKS

Complete Italian Food *by Antonio and Priscilla Carluccio*
An attractively illustrated guide to Italian ingredients complete with
recipes by Italian chef Antonio Carluccio and his wife Priscilla.

The Classic Food of Northern Italy
Gastronomy of Italy
Secrets of an Italian Kitchen
by Anna del Conte
Anna del Conte's books are at once wonderfully appetising and
authoritatively informative. The first title is a lovingly-written look at
the foods of her home region, the second an authoritative encyclopaedia of Italian food and the third, an imaginative cookbook arranged by
ingredients such as 'polenta', 'olives and olive oil' and, quintessentially
Italian, 'edible weeds'.

Italian Food *by Elizabeth David*
Although first published in 1954, her comments on the essence of
Italian cookery remain perceptive and valid. A classic.

The River Café Cook Book *by Rose Gray and Ruth Rogers*
This stylish cookbook by the owners of London's famous River Café
restaurant features classic Italian dishes, with the focus very much on
the quality and seasonality of ingredients.

Italian Regional Cookery *by Valentina Harris*
A lively and informative recipe book.

The Classic Italian Cookbook
The Second Classic Italian Cookbook
Marcella's Kitchen
by Marcella Hazan
Wonderful books by a highly respected author: a great source of knowl-
edgeable writing about Italian cookery and delicious recipes. Essential.

The Food of Italy *by Claudia Roden*
A beautifully-written guide to the regions of Italy and their local
dishes; both evocative and deliciously useable.

JAPANESE LONDON

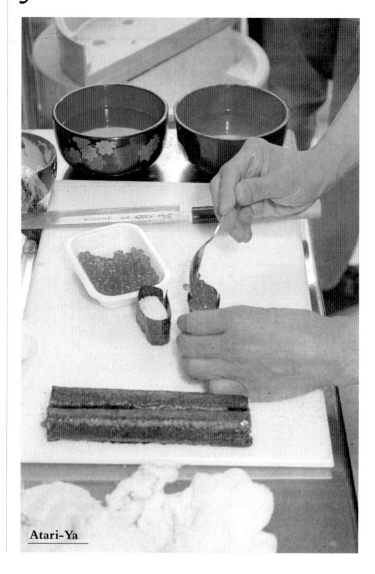

Atari-Ya

The Japanese presence in London is a comparatively recent phenomenon. Japan's deliberate cultural isolation for hundreds of years was broken down in the seventeenth century by Portuguese traders and missionaries, but contact with the West remained limited. It was during Japan's post-Second World War business boom, as the country restored and developed its economy, that a community developed in London. It is primarily a business community, consisting of families on postings for large companies and banks. The temporary nature of most of these postings has kept the community transitory and relatively rootless. Social life, as in Japan, is conducted largely round the golf course and at business lunches.

It used to be said that the Japanese lived on the Northern Line, which provided access to all their needs, from the City for work to the leafy suburbs of Finchley and Golders Green for housing, with much-valued golf courses nearby. The presence of the Oriental City shopping plaza at Colindale was prompted by the growth of this North London community. The shifting of the Japanese School to Acton, however, has opened up a new area of suburban London for the Japanese community and the Northern Line is no longer the sole axis. Acton's Japanese community are now catered for by two kindergartens and primary schools, as well as Japanese shops and restaurants. The past decade has also seen a growing Japanese presence in the West End, with shops opening specifically to cater for the influx of prosperous Japanese tourists.

Japanese Cuisine

This highly refined cuisine, which developed in isolation for hundreds of years, is both aesthetic and ascetic. In Japan's codified society, a meticulously disciplined approach governs food preparation as well as other aspects of life. Presentation is all-important: small portions of foods are carefully arranged, delighting both the eye and the palate. Nouvelle cuisine borrowed greatly from Japanese culinary aesthetics.

'Kisetsukan' is the Japanese term for a sympathy with nature, important in Japanese culture. Dishes are designed to echo nature, perhaps creating a miniature landscape or simply a natural gracefulness. A great value is placed on freshness and seasonality. Fish and vegetables, two key foodstuffs, are at their best fresh. Sashimi, raw fish served with a dipping sauce, epitomises this emphasis. Even though modern preserving techniques have robbed seasonality of its practical imperative, it continues to be valued. There is a whole range of dishes, such as cherry blossom rice or oden, eaten in appropriate months and seasons, with even preserved ingredients such as pickles and miso pastes changing according to the time of year. The flavour of individual ingredients is emphasised in the cooking rather than disguised. Even a Japanese stew retains the separate flavours of ingredients rather than blending them into a whole.

The range of seasonings in Japanese food is limited, falling into three broad categories: salty (provided by shoyu and dashi), sweet (from sugar, mirin and sake) and citrus (from yuzu and dai dai fruits). Shiso leaves and sansho provide an extra aromatic touch. These flavourings are used over and over again in different combinations. Pickles are carefully chosen to go with particular dishes. Fish and seafood, as befits a nation of islands, play a large part in the cuisine, from the basic soup stock to fishcakes and sausages. An extension of this love of seafood has been the use of seaweeds or sea-vegetables, a hallmark of Japanese cooking.

Many of the unique aspects of Japanese cuisine come from the fact that it developed to a great extent in isolation. However, over centuries, a number of foreign influences filtered through. China, between the sixth and eighth centuries, had an effect on many aspects of Japanese life including food – hence chopsticks, tea, the nutritious soya bean, rice and noodles. Zen Buddhism provided both the aesthetic criteria of Japanese cuisine and the emphasis on vegetables. It was only in the nineteenth century that the Japanese began eating red meat more widely. Certain dishes can be traced directly to outside sources, although most have been refined into something quintessentially Japanese. Portugese missionaries in the sixteenth century are said to have requested gambas fritta, fried prawns. From this developed the dish tempura: whole prawns and slices of vegetables cooked briefly in an exquisitely light batter so that the flavour and freshness of the ingredient is highlighted rather than disguised.

GLOSSARY

Agar agar (kanten): a vegetarian setting agent obtained from seaweed, available either in powdered form or in translucent strands.

Azuki Beans: small dark red beans. In a sweetened paste form (an), they form a principal ingredient in Japanese cakes.

Bean curd (tofu): an ivory-coloured soy bean product with a firm custard texture, available either fresh or vacuum-packed.
Kinu or silk tofu has a more delicate texture than momen or cotton tofu.
Koyadofu is freeze-dried tofu, dull brown with a spongy texture.
Aburage are thin deep-fried sheets of bean curd.

Bonito: a member of the tuna fish family, dried bonito flakes, together with kombu seaweed, are used to make dashi soup stock and also as a garnish. *Dashi-no-moto,* is an instant granule form of dashi stock, available in packets.

Burdock (gobo): a long slender root vegetable, available fresh and canned.

Chrysanthemum leaves (shungiku): the leaves of the edible garland chrysanthemum (not to be confused with our inedible ornamental one), used as a garnish and a vegetable.

Daikon: a large, long, mild, white radish, also called *mooli* in greengrocers. Dried daikon strips, called *kiriboshi daikon,* need soaking before use.

Fish and seafood: raw fish, either in *sashimi* or *sushi*, is one of the most famous elements of Japanese cuisine. Popular fish include mackerel (saba), salmon (sake) and tuna (maguro), with the latter graded according to its fattiness. Grilled eel (unagi) is a prized delicacy. Popular seafood includes abalone (awabi), horse clams (mirugai), scallops (hotategai), salmon roe (ikura), octopus (tako) and squid (ika).

Fishcakes and fish sausages: boiled, baked and deep-fried fishcakes and sausages come in various forms, and are often found in the deep freeze section. Popular varieties include: *naruto maki*, a fish sausage with a spiral pink or yellow pattern running through it; *satsuma-age*, oval-shaped fried fishcake; and *chukuwu*, a fish sausage.

Flours: rice flour (joshinko) is used for savoury doughs. Glutinous rice flour (mochiko) and soya bean flour (kinako) are used mainly for desserts.

Gingko nuts (ginnan): maidenhair tree kernels. Fresh gingko nuts (which need shelling) are ivory-coloured, while tinned, shelled gingko nuts are pale green.

Kabocha: Japanese pumpkin, often sold deep-frozen.

Kampyo: dried gourd or winter melon strips, used for tying food.

Kinome: prickly ash tree leaf, used as a garnish.

Konnyaku: a bland, glutinous substance made from the root of the devil's tongue plant, often labelled 'alimentary paste' and found in the chilled section or freezer. Konnyaku noodles, called *shirataki* (meaning white waterfall), are sold packaged in water.

Kuzu: a white starch made from the kuzu vine root, sometimes labelled 'kuzu arrowroot'.

Lotus root (renkon): a crunchy root with a decorative tracery of holes, available fresh, in sausage-like links, or tinned.

Mirin: a sweet Japanese rice wine, used as a glazing ingredient.

Miso: fermented soya bean paste, available in a variety of colours and flavours. It is usually found in the chilled or freezer section and should be stored in the fridge.

Mochi: cooked glutinous rice, pounded to a paste.

Mountain yam (yama no imo): a large, pale-skinned, sweet-flavoured tuber, which comes in different shapes.

Mushrooms: these include large, brown-capped *shitake* (available both fresh and dried), tiny white-capped clusters of *enokidake*, light brown *shimeji* and large, brown *matsutake*.

Natto: fermented soya beans with a pungent smell and sticky texture.

Noodles: *harusame*, fine cellophane noodles made from mung beans whose Japanese name means 'spring rain'; *soba*, brown buckwheat noodles; *somen*, fine wheatflour noodles, sometimes flavoured with green tea; *udon*, thick, white wheatflour noodles.

Pickles: *sudori shoga*, pickled ginger, traditionally eaten with sushi; *takuan*, pickled daikon, often bright yellow in colour.

Ponzu: a citric vinegar.

Potato starch (kataturika): strongly-binding sweet potato starch.

Rice: short grain, slightly glutinous rice is the staple. A very sticky glutinous 'sweet rice' is used to make desserts and cakes.

Rice vinegar (su): delicate rice vinegar, used in making sushi.

Sake: rice wine, both drunk and used as a flavouring in cooking.

Sansho: known as 'Japanese pepper' this is the seed of the prickly ash tree.

Seaweeds: *kombu*, a dark large-leafed seaweed used in making dashi stock; *nori*, thin green sheets of dried seaweed used for sushi, available untoasted or toasted; *wakame*, dried lobeleaf seaweed.

Shichimi togarashi: a piquant seven-spice mix containing chilli.

Shiso: the aromatic red or green leaves of the perilla or beefsteak plant, used to add both flavour and colour.

Soya beans: *edaname*, raw soya beans, available frozen, are a snack food; *daizu*, dried soya beans which need long cooking.

Soy sauce (shoyu): Japanese soy sauce, available both dark and light, has a different flavour from Chinese soy sauce. Kikkoman is a reputable shoyu manufacturer.

Trefoil (mitsuba): a leaf herb, often found freeze-dried.

Umeboshi: small, deep red, pickled plums, with a tart flavour.

Warabi: young edible sprouts of bracken, picked before they have uncurled, available dried or vacuum-packed.

Wasabi: a pungent green root, compared to horseradish, sold in paste or powder form.

Wheat Gluten (fu): wheat gluten forms, often coloured, used rather like croutons in soups and simmered dishes.

Yuzu: an aromatic citrus fruit, used to flavour oil.

FOOD SHOPS

Japanese food shops, aimed at the ex-pat business community, demand high prices at which the Japanese themselves grumble. Many of the foodstuffs are imported from Japan and all of these are beautifully packaged, from rice-paper packets of ribbon-wrapped noodles to gaudy, wacky packets of sweets, shaped like robots or calculators. Fish and meat counters are a beautiful sight, with finely-sliced meat and aesthetic displays of seafood, from a gracefully-coiled octopus tendril to a mosaic of mackerel fillets, arranged skin-side up.

In general Japanese food shops are well ordered, with ingredients grouped together: flavourings, pickles, noodles. Often, the goods have small labels giving the English names.

CENTRAL

Arigato

- 📧 *48-50 Brewer Street, W1*
- ☎ *020 7287 1722*
- 🚇 *Leicester Square LU or Piccadilly Circus LU*
- 🕐 *Mon-Sat 10am-9pm, Sun 11am-8pm*

Neat and airy, this friendly supermarket-cum-take-away caters for Japanese office workers in the area. The stock covers basics from miso paste to soba noodles. The take-away sushi counter is especially popular.

Minamoto Kitchoan

- 📧 *44 Piccadilly, W1*
- ☎ *020 7437 3135*
- 🚇 *Piccadilly Circus LU*
- 🕐 *Daily 10am-7pm (Saturday until 8pm)*

This dainty shop specialises in Japanese confectionery: exquisite-looking concoctions made from red bean paste, rice flour and fruit and bean jelly, tastefully wrapped and packaged. Prices are high, reflecting the fact that these items are traditionally given as gifts. There is a small seating area where you can sit and enjoy green tea and a cake, such as their bestselling Tsuya (a soft round pancake filled with red bean paste).

Natural House

🖳 *Japan Centre, 212 Piccadilly, W1*
☎ *020 7434 4218*
🚇 *Piccadilly Circus LU*
🕓 *Mon-Sat 11am-7.30pm, Sun 10am-6pm*

Tucked away in the Japan Centre's basement is this well-stocked, busy shop. Homesick Japanese stock up with brightly packaged sweets, with names such as 'Kiss Mint' or 'Vessel in the Fog'. More functional food-stuffs are also well-represented, from noodles to pickled plums and miso, a Yoshino fresh fish counter and freezers crammed full with seafood and fish cakes and sukiyaki beef. A deli-counter offers take-away snacks.

NORTH

Atari-Ya Foods

🖳 *15-16 Monkville Parade, Finchley Road, NW11*
☎ *020 8458 7626*
🚇 *Golders Green LU, then bus 82, 102, 260*
🕓 *Mon-Fri 10am-6.30pm, Sat & Sun 10am-7pm*

This neatly arranged shop is particularly strong on store-room staples such as rice, noodles, seaweeds and condiments, though there is a small fresh fish counter. Sunday's sushi counter is popular with the local Japanese community.

Atari-Ya Foods

🖳 *595 High Road, N12*
☎ *020 8446 6669*
🚇 *West Finchley LU, bus 263*
🕓 *Tue-Fri 10am-6.30pm, Sat & Sun 10am-7pm*

A neat shop dominated by a long fish counter, with the staff behind it expertly preparing the fish. In addition, there is a limited selection of groceries and a small chilled cabinet containing essentials such as fresh tofu.

Wing Yip (London) Ltd

⌗ *395 Edgware Road, NW2*
☎ *020 8450 0422*
🚇 *Colindale LU*
🕐 *Mon-Sat 9.30am-7pm, Sun 11.30am-5.30pm*

This massive Oriental supermarket, located just off Staples Corner, contains basic bottled and tinned Japanese ingredients: noodles, sauces, tea and sake.

Supermaz Ltd

⌗ *Oriental City, 399 Edgware Road, NW9*
☎ *020 8200 0009*
🚇 *Colindale LU*
🕐 *Mon-Sat 10am-8pm, Sun 12 noon-6pm*

Located in the shopping centre formerly known as Yaohan Plaza (which comes complete with a SegaDome and a large Japanese bookshop), this is London's largest Japanese supermarket. Brightly spic and span, the store is coherently laid out and goods are clearly labelled in English. There is an excellent array of fresh produce, from burdock and lotus root to clusters of tiny enokidake mushrooms, and a fresh fish counter. Stock is comprehensive: from the aisles of noodles, teas, and condiments to the chilled counters with their neatly-packaged fresh fish and meat.

WEST

Atari-Ya Foods

⌗ *7 Station Parade, W3*
☎ *020 8896 1552*
🚇 *West Acton LU*
🕐 *Tue-Fri 10am-6.30pm, Sat 9am-7pm, Sun 10am-7pm*

West London's Japanese community are served by this friendly food shop, with stock including fresh fish and a good range of basic foodstuffs.

Eating Places

Once Japanese restaurants in London were exclusive, elitist, expensive affairs. Two recent trends – the noodle bar and conveyor-belt sushi restaurant – mean that affordable, accessible Japanese food is now widely available.

Central

Abeno *££*

□ *47 Museum Street, WC1*

☎ *020 7405 3211*

🚇 *Holborn LU or Tottenham Court Road LU*

Located on a peaceful Bloomsbury street, this small, tranquil restaurant offers a chance to sample 'okonomi-yaki': tasty Japanese pancakes made from a thick batter containing shredded cabbage, then topped with ingredients ranging from meat to seafood. Each okonomi-yaki is freshly cooked to order on a table griddle in front of the diner and the staff are charming and helpful.

Ginnan *££*

□ *1-2 Roseberry Court, 36a Roseberry Avenue, EC1*

☎ *020 7278 0008*

🚇 *Farringdon LU/Rail*

Discreet and sedate, this civilized eaterie serves up spanking fresh sushi, tasty noodles and feather-light tempura to a predominantly Japanese clientele.

Ikkyu *££*

□ *67 Tottenham Court Road, W1*

☎ *020 7636 9280*

🚇 *Goodge Street LU*

Tucked away in a basement next to the Scientology Centre this pleasantly informal Japanese restaurant has a loyal following. Sushi is freshly prepared behind a counter while the set lunch menu includes bargains such as miso ramen, a huge bowl of garnished noodles in a flavourful stock.

Kulu Kulu £ £

▢ *76 Brewer Street, W1*

☎ *020 7734 7316*

🚇 *Piccadilly Circus LU*

A classic example of a kaiten (revolving) sushi bar where diners browse on sushi plucked from a slowly-moving conveyor-belt. The strength here is the quality of the fresh, handmade sushi.

Satsuma £ £

▢ *56 Wardour Street, W1*

☎ *020 7437 8338*

🚇 *Leicester Square LU or Piccadilly Circus LU*

From the Wagamama school of refectory-style dining: a sleek, streamlined affair with long wooden tables and benches. Staff are lively and the food, ranging from chicken Teriyaki to sushi, well-presented and tasty.

Ten Ten Tei £ £

▢ *56 Brewer Street, W1*

☎ *020 7287 1738*

🚇 *Piccadilly Circus LU*

Tucked away from the hustle of Piccadilly, this friendly, relaxed restaurant serves up good value Japanese food with all the classics on offer, from sashimi to tempura.

Yo! Sushi! £ £

▢ *52-53 Poland Place, W1*

☎ *020 7287 0443*

🚇 *Oxford Circus LU*

Bright and buzzy high-tech restaurant, offering robotic drinks trolleys and conveyor-belt sushi in a frenetic atmosphere.

NORTH

Jin Kichi   *£££*
⌖ *73 Heath Street, NW3*
☏ *020 7794 6158*
🚇 *Hampstead LU*

A relaxed restaurant, predominantly a yakitori bar, offering a range of tastily salty-sweet skewered foods including chicken and prawns.

Oriental City Food Court   *£*
⌖ *Oriental City Plaza,*
399 Edgware Road, NW9
☏ *020 8200 0009*
🚇 *Colindale LU*

A busy, noisy indoor 'courtyard' dominated by a huge central TV with CNN news and the noise of vendors shouting out their clients' orders, surrounded by food stalls offering a range of Far Eastern cuisines including Japanese. The spanking fresh sushi from the sushi bar next to the supermarket is particularly good.

Sushi-Say   *££££*
⌖ *33B Walm Lane, NW2*
☏ *020 8459 2971*
🚇 *Willesden Green LU*

In deepest Willesden, Sushi-Say, with its pretty, rustic décor is something of an oasis. It has a considerable regular clientele, drawn back by the delicious, freshly prepared Japanese food and the pleasantly relaxed and convivial atmosphere,

Wakaba   *££££*
⌖ *122a Finchley Road, NW3*
☏ *020 7722 3854*
🚇 *Finchley Road LU*

The elegant façade, a curve of smoked glass, and the stark interior comply with one's expectations of Japanese aesthetics. The food is cooked with flair, including impressively fresh seafood.

WEST

Momo *£££*
 14 Queen's Parade, W5
 020 8997 0206
 North Ealing LU

With the Japanese School close by, this pleasant restaurant caters for the local Japanese community and offers deliciously authentic food at reasonable prices.

Sushi-Hiro *££*
 1 Station Parade, Uxbridge Road, W5
 020 8896 3175
 Ealing Common LU

Handily situated just across the road from the tube station is this spic and span sushi restaurant, discreetly hidden behind a frosted glass facade, offering excellent value sushi either to eat in or take-away.

COOKBOOKS

Food of Japan *by Shirley Booth*
An illuminating, lucidly written look at Japanese cuisine with recipes and much detailed ingredient information.

Way of the Noodle *by Russell Cronin*
A cultish, entertaining insight into the Wagamama noodle bar ethos.

Easy Sushi *by Emi Kazuko*
Attractively illustrated, accessible guide to the joys of homemade sushi.

The Heart of Zen Cookery *by Soei Yoneda*
An exploration of the centuries-old vegetarian cuisine of the Zen temples.

Japanese Cookery *by Elizabeth Lambert Ortiz*
A clearly-written cookbook; a useful introduction to the cuisine.

Step-by-Step Japanese Cooking *by Leslie Downer and Minoru Yoneda*
An easy to follow primer.

Jewish London

Platters

The Jewish presence in England dates back to the eleventh century when French Jews followed William the Conqueror and settled here. They were legally restricted to certain trades and professions but moneylending, forbidden to Christians, was allowed, indeed encouraged, and became the basis for a prosperous and established community. Persecution of the Jews grew, however, and in 1290 all Jews were expelled from England by Edward I.

Following the expulsion of Jews from Spain in 1492, some Sephardi Jews (Mediterranean Jews) accepted the Christian faith but continued to practice Judaism in secret. They became known as Marranos and a small community of them settled in London. In 1655 Rabbi Menassah ben Israel, resident in Holland, appealed to Oliver Cromwell to permit Jewish resettlement. In June of the following year Cromwell declared that Judaism would again be allowed in England and a small community of Sephardi merchants, bankers, bullion dealers and gem importers settled in London. The Sephardi community's first synagogue was in a house at Creechurch Lane in the East End. In 1701, when this had become too small, the Bevis Marks synagogue was built – and continues in use to this day.

The Jewish community was also expanded by the immigration of Ashkenazi Jews from Eastern Europe, who followed a different liturgy. In general they were artisans, peasants, tailors and shoemakers. By 1690, they had established their own synagogue in Dukes Place. George I encouraged German Jews to come to England and by the middle of the eighteenth century the Ashkenazi community outnumbered the Sephardi.

Aldgate and Houndsditch were popular Jewish areas, although in the first half of the nineteenth century a move took place among the established and prosperous Jewish families, such as the Rothschilds and Montefiores, who left St Swithins Lane for the fashionable West End. In 1858, a special parliamentary resolution enabled Lionel de Rothschild to take his seat in the House of Commons, which marked a watershed in Jewish emancipation in Britain. During the late nineteenth century middle-class Jews moved into the new suburbs and by 1882, the St John's Wood synagogue was in operation.

For the poorer Jewish immigrants, however, the East End remained the focus. As Stephen Brook puts it in his fascinating book, The Club, 'Jews tend to live in enclaves not out of natural gregariousness but because they want to be close to institutions vital to the life of the community. Religious Jews will not ride or drive on the Sabbath so they wish to live within easy walking distance of a synagogue. They also needed convenient access to Jewish schools (there were seven in existence in 1851) and kosher butchers. Naturally new arrivals tended to join fellow Jews in the areas favoured by those who had arrived before them.'

Following the assassination of the liberal Russian Tsar Alexander II in 1881, a series of pogroms was unleashed in Russia and Poland, which continued into the early twentieth century. Thousands of Jews fled westwards, many aiming for and reaching America, but some coming to Britain instead of continuing their journey. Between 1881 and 1914 the Jewish population of the East End swelled by well over 100,000 people. These were Orthodox, Yiddish-speaking, semi-skilled or unskilled Jews; and the already established Anglo-Jews felt ambivalent about the influx, fearing an anti-Semitic backlash.

The Ashkenazi immigrants moved into the East End, especially around Whitechapel. Food shops sold the herrings and pickles of their homelands and the number of chevras (small synagogues) grew. The United Synagogues established dispersal committees to encourage Jewish immigrants to move out of the East End into the expanding suburbs of Dalston, Stoke Newington and Hackney. In the 1920s there was a move northwards from the East End into Stamford Hill and then into the newly established suburbs of Golders Green, Edgware and Ilford. The rise of anti-Semitism in the 1930s brought in around 70,000 Jews from Central Europe, with the influx increasing sharply after Germany's 1938 Anschluss (unification) with Austria and the Kristallnacht pogrom. These were prosperous middle-class refugees who settled in north-west London in areas such as Hampstead, St John's Wood and Swiss Cottage. The decline of the Jewish East End community was hastened by the war. Bombing destroyed both families and property. Instead of returning after service or evacuation, many East End Jews opted for the suburbs with their by now well-established Jewish communities. By the 1970s the population of the East End Jewish community had shrunk to less than 5,000; today, around a third of Britain's Jewish population lives in north-west London.

JEWISH CUISINE

J ewish cuisine reflects the widely-dispersed Jewish community by containing a range of dishes and styles of cooking from around the world. Two broad and diverse strands stem from the culinary traditions of the Ashkenazi and the Sephardi. The former, influenced by long, cold winters, features preserved and pickled dishes such as rollmop herrings and smoked salmon; while the latter delights in aromatic spices and Mediterranean produce such as aubergines, peppers and olive oil. Common to all Jewish food, however, are the Kashrut, the strict dietary laws governing the preparation and consumption of food, which stem from biblical injunctions. They have been adhered to over the centuries.

Leviticus permits certain fish and meat: 'Any animal that has true hoofs, with clefts through the hoofs, and that chews the cud such you may eat' and 'Anything in water, whether in the seas or in the streams, that has fins and scales these you may eat'. Cattle, sheep and most fish, therefore, are permitted, but pigs, rabbits and shellfish are not, neither certain birds nor anything that crawls or swarms. Permitted animals and birds must be ritually slaughtered in a way that allows as much blood as possible to drain from the carcass. As the consumption of blood is forbidden, raw meat must be 'koshered' by being soaked in water, treated with salt, drained and then rinsed.

The injunction 'Thou shalt not boil a kid in its mother's milk' has been interpreted to mean that meat and dairy products may not be consumed together. Food containing dairy products may not be eaten after meat until at least three hours have passed. This extends to separating kitchen equipment used for meat products from that for dairy products. 'Pareve' means neutral and refers to foods that may be eaten with either meat or dairy products.

The commandment that 'On the seventh day thou shalt do no work, neither thy maidservant nor thy manservant' has produced a range of characteristically Jewish dishes that are prepared the day before they are eaten. Cholent is one of the most famous of these dishes: a Sabbath stew traditionally cooked slowly overnight. Harry Blacker, in his book of East End reminiscences Just Like It Was, writes of the cholent being 'carried to the nearest bakehouse, where for a small consideration (about 2 pence), the baker would put the pan in the oven to cook until the following midday'.

Religious festivals also influence Jewish cuisine. At Pesach (Passover), when wheat flour is banned, dishes are made with ground nuts, matzo meal or potato flour. Certain symbolic foods and dishes are eaten both during the weekly Shabbat (Sabbath) and the festivals. During Pesach, which celebrates the Jewish delivery from slavery to the Egyptians, a 'Seder' plate is assembled made up of symbolic ingredients such as haroset, a sweet fruit paste representing the mortar used by Jewish slaves when they worked on the Pharoah's cities, and a bitter herb, such as endive, representing the bitterness endured during slavery. Matzos, the unleavened bread used during Pesach, represents the bread which didn't have time to rise as the Jews fled.

Another element common to Jewish cookery across the continents is its ingenuity, born out of the poverty and lack of ingredients which Jewish communities often suffered. Meat, in particular, was eked out in resouceful dishes such as helzel, stuffed chicken neck skin, and koureven, stewed chicken gizzards.

GLOSSARY

Bagels: circular bread rolls with a distinctive, chewy texture which comes from being first boiled then baked. Increasingly available both plain and flavoured.

Bulka: the 'everyday' cholla loaf, made from the same dough as bagels but shaped differently.

Cholla: a symbolic plaited loaf made from an egg-rich dough, and with a brown glaze. It plays a prominent part in most Jewish festivals and is especially associated with Shabbat, the weekly Sabbath.

Chopped liver: a tasty mixture of finely-chopped liver, onion and hard-boiled egg.

Falafel: small, savoury chick-pea croquettes, now regarded as an Israeli national dish.

Gefilte fish: minced fish balls, either poached or fried.

Herrings: a staple fish, preserved by salting or pickling. *Chopped herring*, a sweet-sour mixture of herrings, onions, apple, sugar and vinegar; *roll-mops* or *Bismarcks*, pickled herrings rolled round onion rings; *schmaltz herrings* or *matjes*, smoked young herrings, often ready-filleted.

Kreplach: triangular dumplings with a meat or cheese filling. The three corners symbolise the three patriarchs: Abraham, Isaac and Jacob. These can be found ready-made in freezer sections.

Latkes: shredded potato fritters associated with Chanucah.

Lokshen: egg noodles, used in soups and also to make lokshen kugel, a rich baked pudding, traditionally baked overnight for Shabbat.

Mandlen: from Yiddish for 'almonds', these are fried or baked dough 'soup nuts', used like croutons as a garnish.

Matzos: a flat unleavened bread, similar in texture and taste to a water biscuit. It is the main element in Passover cookery, which forbids the use of leavened grain. The entire process of matzo-making must take no longer than 18 minutes, otherwise fermentation may start.

Matzo balls (knaidlach): walnut-sized, matzo-meal dumplings.

Matzo meal: a binding element made from finely ground matzos.

Rye bread: bread made from rye, with a distinctively rich flavour.

Salt beef: boiled and pickled beef, usually brisket. Available freshly-made or in packets.

Smoked salmon (lox): traditionally served in a fresh bagel with cream cheese. Available pre-sliced or freshly sliced.

FOOD SHOPS

The food shop has always been important in Jewish life, both to satisfy religious dietary needs and as a focus of identification. The food that we find in Jewish shops in Britain is predominantly Ashkenazi rather than Sephardi. In East End Story, A. B. Levy remembers the aromas that 'wafted through the open fronts of delicatessen shops, from smoked salmon and roe, barrelled cucumbers and sauerkraut, and herrings in various guises, kippered, schmaltz, chopped and pickled.' These items continue to be familiar Jewish deli fare but nearly all the East End shops have gone and the delicatessens are now found in the North-London suburbs.

Perhaps what is most baffling for a non-Jew are the varying degrees of kosherness. The Kashrut are strict dietary laws which govern the preparation and consumption of foods. Certain food shops display certificates to show that they are supervised or licensed by authorities such as the Kedassia, the Joint Kashrus Committee of the Union of Orthodox Hebrew Congregations, the Adam Yisroel Synagogue and the Golders Green Beth Hamedrash Congregation. These are the shops and eating places that I have called 'kosher' in my guide, but readers should satisfy themselves as to the standards of Kashrut observed. Some shops have a large range of kosher foodstuffs without being supervised while others carry a range of non-kosher Jewish foods. Interest in kosher food is reviving among younger Jews and the shops are responding to this. Kosher food, nowadays, is an increasingly sophisticated business and the range of kosher items available has grown enormously, from tandoori chicken to champagne.

EAST

Brick Lane Beigel Bake

⌨ *159 Brick Lane, E1*
☏ *020 7729 0616*
🚇 *Liverpool Street LU*
🕐 *Daily 24 hours*

This small, reasonably-priced bakery is a culinary reminder of the East End's Jewish history. Piled high with bagels and chollas it remains enormously popular. A trip to Brick Lane market on a Sunday simply wouldn't be complete without one of their bagels – a fact confirmed by the perpetual, straggling queue.

183

Ilford Kosher Meats

▣ *7 Beehive Lane, Ilford, IG4*

☎ *020 8554 3238*

▦ *Gants Hill LU*

🕑 *Mon & Fri 6.30am-1pm, Tue-Thurs 6.30am-6pm, Sun 7am-1pm*

This large butcher's shop, run with genuine enthusiasm by Brian Brown, has an excellent selection of kosher meat products. Everything is made on the premises, from the lamb and mint sausages to the de-boned stuffed chicken. Traditional dishes include helzel (chicken neck stuffing) and, a family speciality, Russian Verrainitz: pastry-wrapped mashed potato, liver and onion from an old recipe handed down by Mr Brown's grandmother.

NORTH

Amazing Grapes

▣ *94 Brent Street, NW4*

☎ *020 8202 2631*

▦ *Hendon Central LU*

🕑 *Mon-Wed 9am-6pm, Thurs 9am-7pm, Fri 9am-6pm in summertime (11/2 hours before Shabbat in winter), Sun 10am-2pm*

This well-stocked kosher off-licence sells kosher wines from all over the world, reflecting the increasing range available. They stock Kiddush, the strong, sweet red wine used for sacramental purposes, and Israeli wines.

La Boucherie (Kosher) Ltd

▣ *4 Cat Hill, East Barnet, EN4*

☎ *020 8449 9215*

▦ *Cockfosters LU*

🕑 *Mon 8.30am-2.30pm, Tue-Thurs 8.30am-5pm, Fri 8am-1pm, Sun 8.30am-1.30pm & 3.30pm-7.30pm*

This vast, sleek, scrupulously-clean shop is one of London's leading kosher butchers and consequently bustles with customers. There are 40 staff altogether, including six chefs working behind the scenes on ready-made dishes such as Boeuf Wellington and the kofte kebabs for which La Boucherie is famous.

Carmelli Bakeries

⌖ *128 Golders Green Road, NW11*

☎ *020 8455 3063*

🚇 *Golders Green LU*

🕑 *Mon-Wed 6.30am-1am, Thurs 6.30am-Friday 4pm,*
Sat 11pm-Mon 1am

Smart and glitzy, this famous kosher bakery continues to attract crowds
of customers. Noted for its bagels, it also offers a host of breads, cakes,
pastries, quiches and biscuits. It is divided into a Parev or 'non-milky'
counter and a 'milky' counter, while behind-scenes bustles with bakers
producing the goods.

J. A. Corney Ltd

⌖ *9 Hallswelle Parade, Finchley Road, NW11*

☎ *020 8455 9588*

🚇 *Golders Green LU*

🕑 *Tue-Thurs 7.30am-5pm, Fri 7.30am-4pm, Sat & Sun 7.30am-1pm*

This well-established fishmongers has been in the Corney family for over
40 years. It stocks a large range of fish, such as St Peter's fish and carp, plus
minced fish (a mix of haddock, whiting and bream) – with more expensive fish minced on demand. Staff are friendly and knowledgeable.

Daniel's Bagel Bakery

⌖ *13 Halleswelle Parade, Finchley Road, NW11*

☎ *020 8455 5826*

🚇 *Golders Green LU*

🕑 *Sun-Wed 7am-9pm, Thurs 7am-10pm, Fri 7am-11/2 hours before Shabbat*

A busy kosher bakery noted for its top-notch bagels as well as a good
range of cholla, rye bread and pastries.

Hendon Bagel Bakery

⌖ *35-7 Church Road, NW4*

☎ *020 8203 6919*

🚇 *Hendon Central LU*

🕑 *Mon-Thurs 7am-11pm, Fri 8am-3pm, Sat open 7pm-Sun 11pm*

A well-established and popular kosher bakery, selling bulka, dark and
light rye breads and a wide range of bagels. On Thursdays and Fridays,
piles of freshly baked chollas lie temptingly on the racks.

Louis Mann and Son Ltd

⌨ *23 Edgwarebury Lane, HA8*

☎ *020 8958 4910*

🚇 *Edgware LU*

🕐 *Mon 7am-1pm, Tue-Thurs 7am-5pm, Fri 7am-1pm, Sun 7am-1pm*

A smart, well-established kosher butcher, run with friendly efficiency by the Mann family. Salt beef, sold hot on Sundays, and hot roast chickens, sold daily, are especially popular.

Panzer's

⌨ *13-19 Circus Road, NW8*

☎ *020 7722 8162/8596*

🚇 *St John's Wood LU*

🕐 *Mon-Fri 8am-7pm, Sat 8am-6pm, Sun 8am-2pm*

Warmly recommended by Evelyn Rose, the doyenne of Jewish cookery, this large bustling delicatessen has been established since 1955, with Peter Vogel carrying on the family tradition. In its range and depth of stock, Panzer's is more like a supermarket than a deli, stocking everything from Hershey chocolate bars (for the area's ex-pat American community) to Israeli wine. Although not supervised, there is a large selection of kosher lines plus traditional Jewish foodstuffs. The large deli-counter offers six types of herring and four grades of smoked salmon among its delicacies, and its smoked salmon bagels are a must for aficionados.

Platters

⌨ *10 Halleswelle Parade, Finchley Road, NW11*

☎ *020 8455 7345*

🚇 *Golders Green LU, then bus 82, 102. 260*

🕐 *Mon-Sat 8.30am-4.30pm, Sun 8.30am-2pm*

This friendly, well-established business, run by the eponymous Platters family, offers a range of fresh, own-made, classic, Jewish deli fare, from more-ish fried gefilte fish to chopped liver. A particular highlight is the hand-carved smoked salmon, skillfully sliced by Len (now in his eighties), which attracts regular customers from as far away as Birmingham. Other branch: 83-85 Allitsen Road, NW8, Tel: 020 7722 5352

Ivor Silverman

⌨ *4 Canons Corner, London Road, Stanmore, HA8*

☎ *020 8958 8682/2692*

🚇 *Stanmore LU*

🕐 *Mon, Fri & Sun 8am-1pm, Tue-Thurs 8.30am-5.30pm*

An elegant and upmarket kosher butcher's which, in addition to freshly-cut meat and poultry, offers a large range of prepared meat dishes.

Steve's Kosher Kitchen

⌨ *5 Canons Corner, London Road, Stanmore, HA8*

☎ *020 8958 9446*

🚇 *Stanmore LU*

🕐 *Mon, Tue-Thurs 8.30am-5.30pm, Fri 8am-3pm (summer) 8am-1pm (winter), Sun 8am-1.30pm*

A kosher delicatessen with an excellent selection of homemade foods. Specialities include chopped liver, salt beef and shallow-fried fish 'like granny used to do'.

Sam Stoller and Son

⌨ *28 Temple Fortune Parade, NW11*

☎ *020 8458 1429*

🚇 *Golders Green LU, then bus 82, 102, 260*

🕐 *Mon 8am-1pm, Tue-Thurs 7am-5pm, Fri 7am-1 hour before Shabbat, Sun 8am-1pm*

Mr Sam Stoller opened his first fishmongers in 1932. He took over this attractive tiled shop in 1947 and is known as one of the leading kosher fishmongers. The smoked salmon is particularly good, plus the 'prime kosher fish' such as St Peter's fish and Israeli carp.

EATING PLACES

CENTRAL

The Knosherie   £-££
🖾 12-13 Greville Street, EC1
☎ 020 7242 5190
🚇 Chancery Lane LU

Bustling and lively, this down-to-earth 'deli diner' specialises in generous portions of homely Jewish food, with salt beef sandwiches a particular forte.

NORTH

Aviv   ££
🖾 87 High Street, HA8
☎ 020 8952 2484
🚇 Edgware LU

A well-established kosher restaurant that specialises in Israeli food, hence there is a definite Middle-Eastern flavour to the menu which offers mezze (including excellent houmous) and grilled meats.

Blooms   ££
🖾 130 Golders Green Road, NW11
☎ 020 8455 1338
🚇 Golders Green LU

Opened in 1965, this Golders Green institution has survived its better-known Whitechapel counterpart and continues to offer traditional kosher Jewish food. The salt beef is famous and portions are generous – homely food in a vintage atmosphere.

Chit Chat   ££
🖾 85 Golders Green Road, NW11
☎ 020 8731 6255
🚇 Golders Green LU

A contemporary restaurant serving excellent Mediterranean Jewish foods: lots of the salads so beloved by Israelis and large portions of tasty grilled meats.

Harry Morgan's *£-££*

⌨ *31 St John's Wood High Street, NW8*

☎ *020 7722 1869*

🚇 *St John's Wood LU*

Dapper, well-established restaurant offering all the classics: chicken noodle soup with dumplings, salt beef and latkes.

Taboon *£*

⌨ *17 Russell Parade, Golders Green Road, NW11*

☎ *020 8455 7451*

🚇 *Golders Green LU*

Thoroughly unpretentious, Taboon does a roaring trade in take-away falafel: deliciously juicy, freshly-fried chickpea rissoles garnished with good salad and tahini – a world away from the small, hard, dry rissoles normally on offer.

COOKBOOKS

The Book of Jewish Food *by Claudia Roden*
A fascinating and absorbing look at Jewish food around the world, taking in both Sephardi and Ashkenazi traditions.

Jewish Cooking from Around the World *by Josephine Bacon*
A lively and accessible cookbook exploring both Sephardi and Ashkenazi cooking.

The Jewish Holiday Cookbook *by Gloria Kaufner Greene*
An informative look at festival and holiday dishes.

The Complete International Jewish Cookbook *by Evelyn Rose*
An excellent basic and reliable cookbook by the doyenne of Jewish cookery.

New Jewish Cuisine *by Evelyn Rose*
A straightforward look at Jewish recipes.

The Jewish Heritage Cookbook *by Marlena Spieler*
A well-illustrated cookbook filled with appetising recipes, including classics like gefilte fish, hamantashen and chopped eggs and onion.

MIDDLE-EASTERN LONDON

Le Marrakech

The Middle-Eastern community in London comprises several different nationalities. Egyptians came to Britain in the 1940s and 1950s both for education and work. The Turkish community is predominantly Turkish-Cypriot – many came to Britain because they were displaced following the Turkish invasion of Cyprus in 1974. They are mainly based in Islington, Hackney and Haringey, with the Stoke Newington end of Green Lanes being a particular focal point. Many of the cafés and kebab houses remain male preserves, with the sound of backgammon being played behind the scenes.

The oil boom in the 1970s and the discovery by Arab countries of new sources of wealth and power meant an increasingly wealthy Arab presence in London, mainly focused around Mayfair and Kensington. A series of political disturbances has also contributed considerably to the Middle-Eastern presence here. The overthrow of the Shah and the Iranian revolution brought in an influx of wealthy Iranian families who were able to use their money and connections to escape, many to America but some to London. They were followed by political opponents of the Ayatollah, seeking refuge. The civil war in Lebanon resulted in a substantial Lebanese presence in London. Edgware Road, Bayswater, Mayfair, Knightsbridge and Kensington together form the heartland of the Middle-Eastern community, served by a splendid assortment of restaurants, fruit juice bars, cafés, banks, shops and clubs.

MIDDLE-EASTERN CUISINE

This is an ancient cuisine, in which recipes can be traced back hundreds of years. An Egyptian recipe for melokhia soup, for example, dates from the time of the Pharoahs. The former spice routes which passed through the Middle East have left a fragrant legacy in the region's cooking.

Claudia Roden, an authoritative and knowledgeable writer on Middle-Eastern cookery, identifies four main strands: Iranian or Persian, Arab, Ottoman Turkish and North African. Iranian cuisine is subtle and refined, a product of ancient Persia. Rice forms the heart of the cuisine and is carefully cooked and exquisitely garnished. The combination of meat with fruit or nuts is a hallmark of the Persian kitchen, shown in dishes such as koresh-e-fesenjan, chicken in walnut and pomegranate sauce. Arab cuisine is very flavourful, using strong-tasting herbs such as mint and coriander and fragrant spices such as cardamom, cinnamon and allspice. Grilled meats are popular, served with rice, burghul or flat breads.

During the Ottoman Empire, Turkish cuisine reached luxurious heights. Cooking at the Topkapi Palace in Istanbul followed a strict pattern of rules, still adhered to by chefs today. Ottoman food was spread through the Empire by the army and its followers, with shish kebab said to date back to these warlike days, when Turkish soldiers cooked over their camp fires. This culinary legacy includes numerous stuffed vegetables, such as imam bayaldi (an aubergine dish named after a priest who swooned with delight upon trying it); and layered nutty pastries in sweet syrups, beloved throughout the Middle East. North-African cooking, in contrast to the other cuisines, has a fiery element, produced by hot sauces such as harissa. It is also a cuisine of subtle and delicate spicing.

The influence of Islam means that certain dietary laws are observed throughout the Middle East. Pork is forbidden and meat must be ritually slaughtered and drained of blood. Lamb is the most highly-prized meat throughout the region. Yogurt is widely used: as a refreshing drink, in hot and cold soups, and in salads and marinades.

Saffron

GLOSSARY

Allspice: round berry, similar to peppercorns, with a flavour of nutmeg, cinnamon and cloves.

Apricot paste sheets (amretin): translucent orange sheets made from apricots which, when diluted with water, make a refreshing drink. Especially popular during the fasting month of Ramadan.

Arab bread (khoubz): flat round bread

Barberries (zerezhk): tart, red berries, used dried in Iranian cooking to add colour and flavour.

Burghul (bulgar): parboiled, cracked grains of wheat, available both coarse or finely ground.

Coriander: a flat-leafed green herb, similar to continental parsley but with a distinctive sharp taste.

Couscous: fine yellow cereal made from semolina.

Dibbis: thick, dark brown syrup made from dates.

Dill: a caraway-scented herb with fine, feathery green fronds.

Dried limes (limoo): hard, brown, dried limes, used to add a distinctive flavour to Iranian and Iraqi soups and stews.

Filo: paper-thin fine pastry usually found frozen but occasionally available fresh.

Freekeh: roasted green wheat

Harissa: a fiery, red pimento paste.

Kashk: stony lumps of pungent-smelling dried buttermilk, used in soups and stews. Also available in powdered form.

Konafa (kadaif): a vermicelli-like dough, white in its raw state but resembling shredded wheat once cooked.

Labne (lebne): thick, strained concentrated yogurt (usually sold bottled) which has been shaped into balls, and floats in oil.

Mahlab: small pale brown seeds which are the kernels of blackcherry stones, with a spicy fragrance.

Melokhia: a green, leafy vegetable, similar in appearance to mallow, used in making a famous eponymous Egyptian soup. Fresh melokhia is sometimes found, while dried is readily available.

Merguez: a spicy sausage from North Africa.

Okra: tapering, ridged green pods, available fresh, dried, tinned or frozen.

Onion seeds (sharmar): small, black teardrop-shaped seeds, not related to onions!

Orange-flower water: a fragrant flavouring made from orange flower essence, used in sweets, drinks and desserts.

Orange peel: fine strips of dried orange peel, traditionally from sour (Seville) oranges.

Pine nuts: small, ivory-coloured kernels, with the fine, long Lebanese pine nuts being particularly prized.

Pistachio: a small, green-coloured nut, indigenous to Iran.

Pomegranate syrup: made from the concentrated juice of sour pomegranates and used in Iranian cooking.

Pulses: *black-eyed beans*, with characteristic black markings; *chickpeas*, rounded yellow peas; *Egyptian brown beans (ful)*, small brown broad beans.

Quince: a hard yellow-skinned fruit, resembling a large, craggy pear. Usually cooked, whereupon its flesh turns pink.

Rice: long-grain rice is a Middle-Eastern staple. Fine-quality Iranian rice is hard to get over here, with Basmati rice being the closest substitute.

Rose water: an essential scented flavouring made from rose essence and used in sweets and desserts.

Saffron: a costly spice made from the stigmas of a particular crocus variety, sold in thread or powdered form.

Salep: a thickening agent made from dried, crushed orchid roots, used in Iran to thicken ice cream.

Sumac: a dark red powdery spice, made from crushed berries, with a tangy flavour. Sometimes diluted and used as a lemon equivalent.

Tahini: sesame-seed paste.

Tamarind: a brown pod with sour, dark brown, pulpy flesh and seeds. Available in de-seeded pulp form or as a paste. Also used to make a syrup, which is then diluted into a refreshing drink.

Turmeric: an orange-fleshed root, usually sold in its ground form as a yellow-orange powder. It has a harsh, flat taste and is used to add flavour and a distinctive yellow colour to dishes.

Vine leaves: large, distinctively-shaped leaves of the vine. Occasionally found fresh, but more usually sold in packets, preserved in brine, when they require soaking in water.

Yogurt: tangy sheep's and goat's yogurt as well as cow's yogurt is widely used in Middle-Eastern cooking.

Zahtar: a spice mix made from thyme, salt, sumac and sometimes roasted sesame seeds, often baked on the top of breads.

FOOD SHOPS

Attractive greengrocers-cum-delis selling everything from bunches of fresh herbs to pretty pastries, as well as bakers and halal butchers all serve the Middle-Eastern community in London.

CENTRAL

Bustling Edgware Road is lined with Middle-Eastern grocers, cafés and restaurants, and is well worth exploring if you're at all interested in Middle-Eastern food. Drive up it late at night and you'll see a lively, metropolitan scene – with drivers pulling in to get a take-away kebab and people sitting on pavement tables watching the world go by.

Green Valley

- *36 Upper Berkeley Street, W1*
- ☎ *020 7402 7385*
- *Marble Arch LU*
- *Daily 8am-10pm*

Warmly recommended by cookery writer Claudia Roden, this spacious Lebanese shop just off the Edgware Road has an eye-catching array of pastries, arranged temptingly in the window. Stock is impressively comprehensive: fresh produce, groceries, a halal meat counter and an in-house bakery. Customers with a sweet tooth are well-catered for with an ice-cream counter, pastry counter and a plethora of prettily packaged nougats, candied nuts and Turkish delight. There's even a small coffee counter at which to enjoy an aromatic cardamom-flavoured Lebanese coffee.

EAST

Turkish Food Centre

- *89 Ridley Road, E8*
- ☎ *020 7254 6754*
- *Dalston Junction Rail*
- *Mon-Sat 9am-7.30pm, Sun 8.30am-7pm*

A large, down-to-earth, competitively-priced Turkish supermarket, complete with a halal meat counter selling lamb, mutton and quails; a cheese counter and piles of fresh fruits and vegetables – including bunches of leafy greens, vine tomatoes and watermelons. The large bakery section does a roaring trade in kibbeh and loaves of flat 'pide' bread.

NORTH

Antepliler

⌨ 47 Grand Parade, Green Lanes, N4

☎ 020 8809 1004

🚇 Manor House LU

🕒 Daily 8am-10pm

Bright and cheery, this bakery-cum-café is famous for its high quality Turkish pastries, truly luxurious nut-filled syrup-laden concoctions such as pistachio baklava baked on the premises.

Other branch: 33A Newington Green, N16, Tel: 020 7226 9409

Hormuz

⌨ 5 Ashbourne Parade, Temple Fortune, Finchley Road, NW11

☎ 020 8731 8230

🚇 Golders Green LU, then 82, 102, 260 bus

🕒 Daily 9am-9pm

Next-door to an Iranian bookshop of the same name, this neatly arranged Iranian grocery is recommended by Claudia Roden as "having a lot of good things". Inside there is a good cross-section of Iranian foodstuffs: jams (including barberry), teas, pulses, flower waters and syrups, pastries, pickles and dairy products.

Sahand

⌨ 74 Ballards Lane, N3

☎ 020 8343 3279

🚇 Finchley Central LU

🕒 Mon-Sat 8am-9pm, Sun 9am-9pm

This small, neatly arranged Iranian food shop offers a good range of Iranian ingredients: packets of tea, bottles of scented waters and syrups, pulses and an attractive display of pastries. The courteous manager is happy to offer advice.

Yasar Halim

⌨ *493-495 Green Lanes, N4*
☎ *020 8340 8090*
🚇 *Manor House LU*
🕐 *Mon 8am-9.30pm, Tue-Sun 8am-10pm*

'Haringey's best supermarket!' declares a sign inside this bustling, well-established Turkish food store, which usefully combines a bakery, greengrocer's, deli and halal meat counter. Here one can find everything from fresh green almonds and spanking fresh flat-leafed parsley to tubs of sheep's yogurt and jars of quince jam. The bakery here remains a vibrant focal point, with customers queueing up for the freshly baked, huge, round loaves of village bread and sweet and savoury pastries such as guzleme, brought into the shop still warm from the oven. Fresh filo and kadaif is also on sale. Staff are numerous and friendly.

SOUTH

Mediterranean Food Centre

⌨ *45 A & B Streatham Hill, SW2*
☎ *020 8678 1385*
🚇 *Streatham Hill Rail*
🕐 *Daily 6am-1am*

This large corner store serves the local community by offering, as its sign declares, 'English, Turkish, Greek, West Indian Food'. Fresh fruit and vegetables include quinces and pumpkin alongside chow-chow and yams. The comprehensive stock features pulses, dairy products, dried fruit, nuts and spices. Next door is the bakery, selling freshly baked pide, and a halal butcher's counter.

WEST

Lebanese Food Centre

⌨ *153 The Vale, W3*
☎ *020 8740 7365*
🚇 *Acton Central Rail*
🕐 *Daily 8am-10pm*

A large down-to-earth shop resembling a small supermarket, complete with a halal meat counter and an adjoining kebab restaurant. The stock is strong on basics such as pulses, spices and dried herbs with a modest selection of fresh fruit and vegetables outside on the pavement.

Le Marrakech

🏠 *64 Golborne Road, W10*

☎ *020 8964 8307*

🚇 *Ladbroke Grove LU*

🕐 *Mon-Sat 8.30am-7.30pm, Sun 10am-4pm*

An attractive front-of-shop display of earthenware tagines indicates this foodshop's Moroccan roots. Inside, this friendly establishment offers delights such as olives with kumquats, pomegranate molasses and pickled lemons, with cookware including couscoussiers and gilded tea-glasses. Lanterns, chandeliers and wall-hangings create something of a bazaar atmosphere – compounded on my visit by one of the staff pulling out a box of Moroccan leather slippers and offering them to an interested punter.

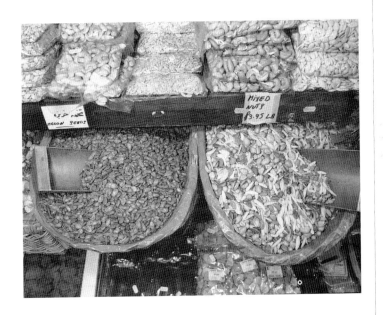

Reza Patisserie

⌨ *345 Kensington High Street, W14*
☎ *020 7602 3674*
🚇 *Kensington High Street LU*
🕐 *Daily 8.30am-9pm*

A delectable assortment of pastries are on offer here, including both Arabic pastries, characterised by nuts and honey, and Iranian, which are simpler and more subtle. The freezer contains Iranian ice creams, flavoured with rose water and saffron, while the shelves hold a variety of nuts, sweetmeats and dried fruit, such as Iranian sour cherries.

Super Bahar

⌨ *349a Kensington High Street, W14*
☎ *020 7603 5083*
🚇 *Kensington High Street LU*
🕐 *Daily 9am-9pm*

This well-stocked Iranian greengrocer's-cum-grocer's is warmly recommended by food writer Margaret Shaida, author of the Glenfiddich Award-winning The Legendary Cuisine of Persia. Here she says 'you can find everything you need for Persian cooking'. Outside are tempting piles of fruit, herbs and vegetables such as tiny green grapes and baby okra, while inside the stock is extensive, with pride of place going to a back-counter display of Iranian Caviar in splendid blue tins. The owner, Margaret adds, is 'extremely helpful'.

Zaman

⌨ *347 High Street Kensington, W8*
☎ *020 7603 8909*
🚇 *Kensington High Street LU*
🕐 *Daily 9am-10pm*

This attractive shop's Iranian roots are clearly signalled with a bright fluorescent sign saying 'Persian Caviar' in the window, a colourful fresh fruit and vegetable display in front of the shop and the sound of Persian music floating through the door. Long and narrow, it extends to a downstairs halal meat counter. Along the way stock includes a self-service counter resplendent with nuts, seeds and dried fruit such as mulberies and figs, a chilled cabinet with labne and yogurt drinks and an assortment of pickles with their characteristic sour scent. Non-edible items also on sale include inlaid backgammon boards, splendid Iranian teapots and tea-glasses and a basement room of CDs and tapes.

EATING PLACES

Londoon's thriving Middle-Eastern restaurants cater very much for the ex-pat community and as a result, standards are generally high. The range is such that you can enjoy simple but good street food such as a succulent lamb kebab washed down with fresh fruit juice, or a leisurely meal of sophisticated Lebanese mezze in elegant surroundings.

CENTRAL

Al-Hamra *££££*
🏠 *31-33 Shepherd Market, W1*
☎ *020 7493 1954*
🚇 *Green Park LU*

Elegant surroundings, efficient service and fine Lebanese food combine in one of London's best-known Lebanese restaurants, with prices reflecting the affluent location. The mezze are superb (including delicacies such as walnut-stuffed baby aubergines) but the atmosphere and service can be on the chilly side.

Al Sultan *££££*
🏠 *51-52 Hertford Street. W1*
☎ *020 7408 1155*
🚇 *Green Park LU*

This intimate, upmarket Lebanese restaurant is a perfect place in which to sample exemplary mezze, from smooth-as-silk houmous Shawarma, topped with pine nuts and tender pieces of lamb to gutsily garlicky foul (beans). The dainty dessert pastries are similarly not to be missed.

Ali Baba *££*
🏠 *32 Ivor Place, NW1*
☎ *020 7723 5805*
🚇 *Baker Street LU*

This small, modest café, with its bargain-priced food, is recommended by Claudia Roden for its 'real Egyptian' food, in particular the 'melokhia' and the 'falafel'.

Efes Kebab House   *LL*

⌨ *80 Great Titchfield Street, W1*

☎ *020 7636 1953*

🚇 *Great Portland Street LU or Oxford Circus LU*

This enormous Turkish restaurant – very much an institution – continues to run with smooth efficiency. The menu caters for carnivores, with charcoal-grilled kebabs much in evidence.

Iran the Restaurant   *LLLL*

⌨ *59 Edgware Road, W2*

☎ *020 7723 1344*

🚇 *Edgware Road LU*

A chance to enjoy top-notch Persian cooking – such as rich Chicken Fesanjoon (in a walnut sauce) and deliciously moreish flat Persian bread freshly-baked in the huge clay oven – in wonderfully glitzy surroundings.

Maroush   *LLLL*

⌨ *21 Edgware Road, W2*

☎ *020 7723 0773 or 020 7262 1090*

🚇 *Marble Arch LU*

Very much an Edgware Road fixture, this smart Lebanese restaurant serves up high-quality food, complete with live entertainment at weekends.

Meshwar   *LLL*

⌨ *128 Edgware Road, W2*

☎ *020 7262 8304*

🚇 *Marble Arch LU*

At the front, the take-away section (frequented predominantly by besuited Lebanese men) serves excellent lamb and chicken kebabs. The back room offers the chance to try some tasty Lebanese food, courteously served in pleasant surroundings.

Ranoush Juice Bar   *L*

⌨ *43 Edgware Road, W2*

☎ *020 7723 5929*

🚇 *Marble Arch LU*

Gleamingly glitzy with its black marble interior, this take-away bar serves up fresh fruit juices and tasty Lebanese snacks with panache. Pay first, then order your food.

Sofra £ £
- *36 Tavistock Street, WC2*
- ☎ *020 7240 3773*
- *Covent Garden LU*

This spacious Turkish restaurant operates on a successful formula: good, simple Turkish food, polite staff at very reasonable prices, especially given the West End location.

EAST

Anatolya £
- *263a Mare Street, E8*
- ☎ *020 8986 2223*
- *Hackney Central Rail*

A friendly down-to-earth Turkish caff, serving generous portions of gutsy food.

Mangal £
- *10 Arcola Street, E8*
- ☎ *020 7275 8981*
- *Dalston Kingsland Rail*

A famous Stoke Newington eaterie offering tasty charcoal–grilled kebabs. Also at: 4 Stoke Newington Road, N16

NORTH

The Royal Cous Cous House £ £
- *316 Holloway Road, N7*
- ☎ *020 7700 2188*
- *Holloway Road LU*

In an unprepossessing stretch of Holloway Road, this small, friendly restaurant serves up lovingly cooked couscous and tagines.

Yayla £
- *429 Green Lanes, N4*
- ☎ *020 8348 9515*
- *Manor House LU*

Small, cheery corner café serving tasty Turkish food, from kebabs to pide, at remarkably reasonable prices. Bread is freshly made on the premises before your eyes.

NORTH-WEST

Hafez $\mathcal{LL}$
- 559 Finchley Road, NW3
- ☎ 020 7431 4546
- Finchley Road LU

Recommended by Iranian friends for its authentic food, this is the more glitzy sister restaurant of the Hereford Road branch in West London.

SOUTH

Tas $\mathcal{LL}$
- 33 The Cut, SE1
- ☎ 020 7928 2111
- Waterloo LU

This large, New Wave Turkish restaurant offers reasonably priced, tasty Turkish food.

WEST

Adams Cafe $\mathcal{LL}$
- 77 Askew Road, W12
- ☎ 020 8743 0572
- Buses 12, 207 or 266

Operating as a café by day and a restaurant by night, this relaxed restaurant draws a loyal crowd of regulars by offering good-value, tasty Tunisian food at reasonable prices. Freshly fried brik make an excellent starter and there is an impressive array of couscous to choose from.

Alounak $\mathcal{LL}$
- 10 Russell Gardens, W14
- ☎ 020 7603 7645
- Olympia LU

Originally housed in a portacabin in an Olympia car park, Alounak has expanded into more conventional premises. Still on offer, however, is gutsy Persian food – excellent lamb kebabs and flavourful stews.
Other branch: 44 Westbourne Grove, W2, Tel: 020 7229 0416

Hafez £primary£

⌖ *5 Hereford Road, W2*

☏ *020 7221 3167 or 020 7229 9398*

🚇 *Bayswater LU, Notting Hill Gate LU or Queensway LU*

A pleasantly laidback Iranian restaurant offering classic dishes such as 'Persian bread', freshly baked on order in an impressive tiled oven in the corner, grilled meats and Persian stews.

Mohsen £primary£

⌖ *152 Warwick Road, W14*

☏ *020 7602 9888*

🚇 *Earl's Court LU*

Despite an unprepossessing location, opposite a huge Homebase, this small Iranian restaurant is warmly recommended by food writer Margaret Shaida. Diners here can enjoy Persian dishes, including kebabs and stews, at their flavourful best.

Phoenicia £££

⌖ *11-13 Abingdon Road, W8*

☏ *020 7937 0120*

🚇 *High Street Kensington LU*

An attractive Lebanese restaurant, with courteous service. Diners can opt for an array of mezze, such as tangy labneh or tasty aubergine dip, or classic grilled meats.

COOKBOOKS

Lebanese Cuisine *by Anissa Helou*
An appetising cookbook offering an insight into the glories of Lebanese cuisine.

The New Book of Middle Eastern Food *by Claudia Roden*
An invaluable book on Middle-Eastern cookery, evocatively and authoritatively written, with tempting recipes. A classic.

The Legendary Cuisine of Persia *by Margaret Shaida*
This elegant book knowledgeably charts the history of Persian cuisine and is filled with excellent recipes.

POLISH LONDON

Korona Delicatessen

From the eighteenth century onwards, Poland's history of partition, invasion and resistance, created a Polish presence in London – a self-contained, close-knit community, preoccupied with the military. Following the collapse of communism in Poland, however, business opportunities for British-born Poles have increased, and the former sense of exile which characterised the ex-pat Polish community has diminished. London's Polish community, however, retains and cherishes a very strong sense of its Polish roots.

In 1765, Poland was divided up between Austria, Prussia and Russia. Many Polish émigrés fled to France and a few to England, starting a pattern of political exile. A succession of failed insurrections in 1830-1, 1848 and 1863-4 brought more exiles to Britain. In Highgate Cemetery, White Eagle Hill is the resting place of the leaders of the failed 1863-4 uprising. The author Joseph Conrad emigrated first to France and then to Britain after his father's arrest in the period prior to that rebellion. Some Poles came to Britain for purely economic reasons, taking on jobs as artisans or labourers. By the late nineteenth century, a Polish Christian community in London was centred around the Polish Catholic church on Devonia Road in Islington, Our Lady of Czestochowa. Large numbers of Polish Jews entered Britain during this period but they became assimilated into the Jewish community.

The real increase in Britain's Polish community – swelling its numbers from 5,000 to tens of thousands – came with the Second World War. Following the German invasion in September 1939, over 30,000 Poles from the government and the military came to Britain, and a Polish Government-in-Exile under Prime Minister Sikorski was declared. Operational headquarters were set up around South Kensington and the Polish Air Force fought alongside the RAF. Their contribution was extensive: during the Battle of Britain one in seven of the German planes shot down was despatched by Polish airmen. A memorial to the 1,241 Polish airmen who died stands on the edge of Northolt Airport.

The Soviet occupation of Poland and the Treaty of Yalta dispossessed thousands of Poles by handing over Eastern Poland to the Soviet Union, so many Poles who had come to Britain to fight in the war stayed on. The British government offered free domicile to the 250,000

Poles (and their families) who had fought under British command, and over 150,000 accepted. Offers of British nationality were usually refused by Poles on patriotic grounds, in an effort to keep the political situation in Poland a 'live' issue.

Post World-War II, high property prices created a move west from Kensington to Earl's Court, with Cromwell Road becoming known as the 'Polish Corridor'. Polish clubs founded during the war, such as the former magnificent White Eagle Club in Knightsbridge and the aristocratic Ognisko on Exhibition Road, had provided community focal points, but again rising costs edged the Polish community out into Balham, Chiswick and Ealing. Many of the upper and middle-class Poles (who constituted the majority of the community) had to adapt to difficult circumstances following the war.

The completion in 1982 of POSK, the Polish Social and Cultural Centre, at considerable expense, was a source of pride to London's expat Polish community and remains an important focal point for it. The Catholic Church, too, strengthened existing bonds, with around 12 Polish Catholic centres and churches in London.

POLISH CUISINE

The popular perception of Polish cuisine as hearty winter food is a realistic one. The bitter Polish winters mean that many of the essential ingredients are those that can be stored or preserved: grains, root vegetables, sauerkraut, dried mushrooms, and salted and pickled herrings. Flavourful, warming stews and soups are popular, with soups such as krupnik (barley soup), yellow-pea soup and barley soup dating back to the Middle Ages.

Polish food is often described as Russian-influenced. This is a generalisation resented by the Poles, although the cuisines do share many dishes, ingredients and characteristic flavours. Other influences on Polish food, however, include Italian (traced back to the 1518 marriage of King Sigismund to Bona Sforza) and French, with one of the earliest cookbooks published in Poland, The Perfect Cook, being translated from the French.

Meat has always been highly valued in Polish cookery, a sad irony during the post-war years when meat was rationed and scarce. Every bit is used, producing the famous sausages, hams, black puddings, tongues and brawn. The Poles also enjoy game, traditionally hunted in their homeland's numerous forests. Bigos, or huntsman's stew, is a famous dish, made from game, sauerkraut and sausages. When Bona Sforza and her Italian retinue came to live in Poland, they were reputedly horrified at the amount of meat consumed by the Poles. The Italians introduced salads and certain vegetables, and even today 'wloscyzna', the word for basic green vegetables, means 'things Italian'.

Grains and cereals have always been important crops for the Poles, and rye bread is a staple. In her fascinating book Old Polish Traditions in the Kitchen and at the Table, Maria Lemnis writes, 'The popularity of bread in Poland is manifested in the numerous old sayings, e.g. 'bread unites the strongest'; 'bread cries when eaten for free'; 'bread obtained for labour is tasty and filling'; or, sharper in tone, 'whomever bread harms, a stick can cure'. Cereals such as millet, barley and buckwheat are used widely in dishes from soups to kasha, a purée of cooked grains.

The Catholic Church has had a marked influence on Polish cooking. Catholic festivals such as Christmas and Easter are celebrated with a host of special dishes and cakes. The austerity of the various fasts laid down by the church is also an influence, with fish and mushroom dishes eaten instead of meat at certain times of the year. Christmas Eve, for example, is traditionally celebrated with a feast including carp or pike.

Because of the grim economic situation and political isolation following the Second World War, Polish cookery remained frozen in time, restricted by severe food shortages and closed to foreign influences. The recent political changes and the opening up of trade means that Polish cuisine is developing in Poland, with 'modern Polish' cooking offering sophisticated versions of traditional classic dishes.

GLOSSARY

Buckwheat: a triangular brown-green grain. Buckwheat flour is used in blinis.

Cakes: Cakes and pastries are an important feature of Polish life, and a huge variety is made, with some traditionally eaten at Christmas and Easter. *Babka*, a famous Easter yeast cake with a distinctive fluted shape; *cheesecake*, traditionally baked and not oversweet; *makowiec*, poppy-seed roll; *mazurek*, flat, traditionally rectangular cakes eaten at Easter; and *paczki*, Polish doughnuts, often filled with plum jam.

Caraway seeds: tiny, ridged brown seeds, with an aniseed flavour.

Curd cheese: a slightly tangy soft cheese made from curds, used in pierogi and cheesecake.

Dill: a caraway-flavoured herb with delicate, feathery fronds.

Dried mushrooms: hunting for wild mushrooms is a national pastime in Poland. Fresh wild mushrooms are rarely found in the shops, but both dried and pickled mushrooms are widely available.

Juniper berries: aromatic, blue-black berries, used with game.

Kohlrabi: a plump, rounded vegetable, either pale green or deep purple, called a 'cabbage-turnip' by Jane Grigson.

Pierogi: filled pasta pouches, often called Polish ravioli.

Pinhead barley: fine-grained barley.

Polish pure spirit: a powerful spirit – 168 proof – used to make vodka.

Poppy seeds: tiny white or purple-blue seeds, used in vast quantities in Polish baking.

Rye bread: a Polish fundamental. Rich-flavoured, dark brown Ukranian rye is distinctive.

Sauerkraut: pickled, shredded cabbage with a sharp flavour, available fresh or bottled.

Sausages: *boiling ring*, loops of spicy sausages; *kabanos*, long, thin pork sausages; *kielbasa*, pork and beef sausage flavoured with garlic; *krakowska*, garlic sausage, eaten as a salami.

Vodka: flavoured vodkas in Poland include: honey, lemon, *sliwowica* (prune), *winiak* (matured in wine barrels), *wisniak* (cherry), and *zubrowska* (bison-grass, easily identifiable because of the blades of long grass in the bottle).

FOOD SHOPS

Polish food shops have been an important part of the self-contained Polish community in London. As one Polish lady said, 'We Poles like our food', and the shops provide essentials such as rye bread, sausages and cakes as well as acting as a local meeting place. Rumour has it that one Polish shop had a sign declaring 'English Spoken Here'. As the Polish community is declining in size, Polish food shops are becoming scarcer. Some have started to offer 'continental' foodstuffs in addition to Polish ingredients. Many of those listed below have been trading for years and have a pleasantly old-fashioned air about them.

NORTH

Austrian Sausage Centre
📠 *10A Belmont Street, NW1*
☎ *020 7267 3601*
🚇 *Chalk Farm LU*
🕐 *Mon-Fri 7am-5pm, Sat 7am-1pm*

Hidden away on an industrial estate, this functional retail outlet attracts East European ex-pat and English old age pensioners, drawn by the huge array of sausages and cooked and cured meats from brawn to kielbasa.

SOUTH

Korona Delicatessen
📠 *30 Streatham High Road, SW16*
☎ *020 8769 6647*
🚇 *Streatham Hill Rail, bus 159, 109 or 133*
🕐 *Mon-Fri 9am-7pm, Sat 9am-6pm, Sun 9.30am-2.30pm*

Well-established for over 50 years now, this is a pleasantly old-fashioned shop with a fine range of Polish foodstuffs. It is especially noted for its cakes, which include baked cheesecake, chocolate-coated honey cake, poppyseed cakes and Easter specialities such as babka. Specialities include homemade pierogi, filled with curd cheese; meat, sauerkraut and wild mushrooms; stuffed cabbage and flavoured vodkas and gold wasser liqueur complete with flecks of real gold! Owners Mr and Mrs Wicinska are both knowledgeable and helpful.

Panadam Delicatessen

⌂ *2 Marius Road, SW17*

☏ *020 8673 4062*

🚇 *Balham LU*

🕐 *Tue/Thurs/Fri 9.30am-5.45pm, Wed 9.30am-1pm, Sat 9.30am-4pm, Sun 10am-1.30pm*

A charming 20 year-old delicatessen serving Balham's large Polish community. The deli-counter offers a good selection of Polish sausages, meats and herrings, and there is a range of rye breads and cakes. The Sunday opening is explained by the presence round the corner of the Polish church of Christ the King.

WEST

Polanka

⌂ *258 King Street, W6*

☏ *020 8741 8268*

🚇 *Ravenscourt Park LU*

🕐 *Mon-Sat 10am-10pm, Sun 11am-8pm*

A shop-cum-restaurant with a delicatessen counter selling Polish sausages, sweets, cakes, Krakus jams and pickles.

Enca Foods

⌂ *2 Salisbury Pavement, Dawes Road, SW6*

☏ *020 7385 5762*

🚇 *Fulham Broadway LU*

🕐 *Mon-Fri 7am-6pm, Sat 8am-5pm*

Discreetly hidden behind what looks like garage doors is a well-established, family-run Polish food supplier. It is famous for the 30 types of sausages and cooked and cured meats made on the premises – an appetising, savoury smell permeates the shop. Raw carcasses are delivered to the back door to be transformed into specialities such as pork brawn or roasted pork poledwica. There is also a basic grocery stock of Central European foodstuffs: rye breads, cakes, pickles and jams.

Parade Delicatessen

▣ *8 Central Buildings, The Broadway, W5*

☎ *020 8567 9066*

🚇 *Ealing Broadway LU*

🕐 *Mon-Fri 9.15am-6pm, Sat 9.15am-5pm*

There's been a Polish food shop on these premises for over 50 years now. This appetising delicatessen offers an excellent range of Polish foods, including sausages and cured meats, plus a variety of herrings, curd cheese and pierogi. Also on offer is a good choice of groceries, from biscuits and sweets to packet soups and Polish jams.

Prima Delicatessen

▣ *192 North End Road, W14*

☎ *020 7385 2070*

🚇 *West Kensington LU*

🕐 *Mon-Thurs & Sat 9.30am-6pm, Fri 9.30am-7pm*

Founded in 1948, this old-fashioned corner shop is heartily recommended by Polish friends. It has an impressive stock of Polish ingredients: a large counter is filled with sausages and smoked meats, rye breads, cakes and pastries. The chilled section offers pickled wild mushrooms and there is a rack of pulses and seeds including buckwheat and poppy seeds.

EATING PLACES

Many of London's best-known Polish eating places continue to be housed in veteran clubs or institutions, characteristic of the close-knit Polish community.

CENTRAL

Daquise *LL*

⌨ *20 Thurloe Street, SW7*

☎ *020 7589 6117*

🚇 *South Kensington LU*

This sedate café has been a popular Polish meeting place since it was founded in the 1940s and is now an institution. The furniture and fittings, the Polish clientele and the elderly staff, complete the impression that nothing much has changed since the 1950s. The menu offers down-to-earth Polish food such as pierogi and apple strudel.

Ognisko Polskie (Polish Hearth Club) *LLL*

⌨ *55 Princes Gate, Exhibition Road, SW7*

☎ *020 7589 4635*

🚇 *South Kensington LU*

Housed in an elegant high-ceilinged room, the restaurant at this famous Polish club is a bastion of excellent Polish food. The menu offers dishes including barszc, bigos or pierogi, which can be washed down with flavoured vodkas.

NORTH

Primrose Brasserie *LL*

⌨ *101 Regent's Park Road, NW1*

☎ *020 7483 3765*

🚇 *Chalk Farm LU*

A large, relaxed, friendly restaurant which offers huge portions of tasty Polish food at very reasonable prices.

Zamoyski £

86 Fleet Road, NW3
☎ *020 7794 4792*
🚇 *Belsize Park LU*

A pleasant and intimate wine bar and restaurant offering traditional Polish food and vodkas.

SOUTH

Baltic *££££-£££££*

74 Blackfriars Road, SE1
☎ *020 7928 1111*
🚇 *Southwark LU*

Smart contemporary restaurant and vodka bar offering a chic, haute-cuisine version of traditional Polish food.

WEST

Adam & Agusia *£*

258 King Street, W6
☎ *020 8741 8268*
🚇 *Ravenscourt Park LU*

A small, unpretentious café, just a few doors down from the Polish Cultural Centre, offering good down-to-earth fare.

Café Grove *£*

65 The Grove, W5
☎ *020 8810 0364*
🚇 *Ealing Broadway LU*

A pretty café serving Ealing's Polish community and dishing up a tempting range of savoury dishes and classic Polish cakes.

Home *£*

17 High Street, W3
☎ *020 89992 9139*
🚇 *Acton Central Rail*

This jaunty café, with its orange and green walls and round tables, serves both traditional British café nosh and classic Polish dishes: the menu, therefore, features grills, roasts and omelettes alongside bigos, a range of pierogi and assorted vodkas. Prices are reasonable, portions are generous and service is friendly.

Lowiczanka Polish Cultural Centre (POSK) *LL*

⊞ *238-46 King Street, W6*
☎ *020 8741 3225*
🚇 *Ravenscourt Park Rail*

Inside the Polish Social and Cultural Centre is this large restaurant, with a typically Polish menu. Service can be slow so be prepared for a leisurely meal. Prices are reasonable, especially the set lunch.

Patio *LL-LLL*

⊞ *5 Goldhawk Road, W12*
☎ *020 8743 5194*
🚇 *Goldhawk Road LU or Shepherd's Bush LU*

This intimate unpretentious restaurant attracts a loyal following for its generous helpings of tasty Polish food and convivial atmosphere.

Wodka *LLL*

⊞ *12 St Albans Grove, W8*
☎ *020 7937 6513*
🚇 *Kensington High Street LU*

A sleek New-Wave Polish restaurant serving distinctly upmarket food at corresponding prices. As the name implies, a huge range of flavoured vodkas is also on offer.

COOKBOOKS

The Food and Cooking of Eastern Europe *by Lesley Chamberlain*
A clearly-written, overview of East-European cookery.

The Polish Kitchen *by Mary Pininska*
A well-written, knowledgeable book on Polish cookery, with appetising recipes.

SOUTH-EAST ASIAN LONDON

The South-East Asian community in London is widespread and diverse, reflecting the variety of its national origins. The term 'South-East Asia' encompasses Indonesia, Malaysia, the Philippines, Singapore, Thailand and Vietnam. There is no obvious centre, an equivalent to the Chinese community's Gerrard Street, but both Peckham and Dalston are a focal points for the Vietnamese, while Earl's Court is a centre for the Filipino community.

Lack of economic opportunities in their own countries is the main reason for many South-East Asians seeking work in Britain, demon-strated most tragically by the Vietnamese boat people. Much of their work is found in the catering or hotel industries, but the last two Immigration Acts have made it much harder for people from these countries to enter Britain.

SOUTH-EAST ASIAN CUISINE

The term, 'South-East Asian cuisine' is the blanket term used to describe the cuisines of Indonesia, Malaysia, the Philippines, Singapore, Thailand and Vietnam – a simple way to describe a complex set of overlapping national cuisines. Seemingly no dish has a single recipe in South-East Asia: variations abound from country to country, region to region and family to family. Satay in Thailand may be served with toast and a chilli-based dipping sauce, whereas the Indonesian version comes with a spicy peanut sauce, cucumber and cubes of compressed rice. Differences stem from race and religion with, for example pork avoided by the Muslim Malays but enjoyed by the Chinese. These variations help create a rich and diverse set of cuisines, but there are certain shared characteristics.

Both Chinese and Indian cuisines have influenced South-East Asian food in cooking techniques and ingredients. From China comes the balancing of five flavours: sweet, sour, hot, salty and bitter; and, from India, the use of spices and curry pastes. Like both Chinese and Indian cuisines, South-East Asian cuisine is mainly rice-based.

Certain ingredients provide unique flavours that distinguish South-East Asian cooking. Coconut milk, extracted from the flesh of the versatile coconut, is a key ingredient. It is widely used in both savoury and sweet dishes as a marinade, a stock, a curry-base and a dairy equivalent. Fragrant aromatics have a citrus quality: lemon grass, lime juice, kaffir lime leaves and rind. To the Asian trinity of onion, garlic and ginger are added the more subtle rhizomes, galingal and krachai. Chillies, introduced by the Portuguese and Spanish in the sixteenth century, provide a characteristic South-East Asian 'hot' kick.

Seafood is important in South-East Asian cooking and found in abundance. In its dried and fermented forms seafood is used to add saltiness to food. Fish sauce often replaces soy sauce in Thailand, the Philippines and Vietnam, while pungent shrimp paste is used throughout South-East Asia.

Indonesian and Malay cooking are often grouped together, as the majority religion in both countries is Islam. Singapore is distinguished culinarily by Nonya or Straits Chinese cuisine, a unique blend of heavily-spiced dishes combining Chinese and Malay ingredients and techniques. Thai cooking, with its emphasis on aesthetic presentation, is

219

marked by its use of aromatic herbs such as coriander roots, Thai mint and several varieties of basil. Filipino cuisine stands out from the rest of South-East Asia, as it was influenced by the Spanish colonisation of the country from 1521 to 1898, and subsequent American occupation until 1946. The Spanish influence is apparent in Filipino dishes such as adobo and paella while American influences crop up in a predeliction for condensed milk and apple pie. Brightly-coloured rice cakes and desserts are also popular, made with ingredients such as makapuno, soft-fleshed coconut. Vietnamese cuisine is seen to stem largely from the Chinese, with basic ingredients for Vietnamese cooking available in Chinese supermarkets. Vietnamese fish sauce (nuoc mam) is a key ingredient and the generous use of fresh herbs, such as dill and mint, is another distinguishing feature.

Banana Leaves

GLOSSARY

Agar agar: a vegetarian setting agent obtained from seaweed which does not require refrigeration to set, available in either powdered form or translucent strands. Filipino agar agar (gulaman) comes in bright pink and yellow to add colour to desserts.

Annatto (achuete): small red seeds which impart an orange colour.

Banana leaves: used to wrap foods in the way that kitchen foil is used, with the added virtue of also adding flavour to whatever is cooked within.

Basil: a herb used in Indonesian, Thai and Vietnamese cuisines. In Thailand one finds *bai horapa* (similar to European sweet basil), *bai mangluk*, and *bai garapo* or *holy basil*.

Bean curd (tahu, tokua): a nutritious soya-bean product. Fresh, ivory-coloured bean curd has a firm, custard texture and bland flavour and is sold packed in water. Deep-fried bean curd has a golden colour and spongy texture. Both are found in the chilled section.

Candlenuts (kemiri, buah keras): large, white, waxy nuts, used to thicken curry pastes, sold unshelled. Raw macadamia nuts are the closest substitute.

Chilli paste (nam prik pow): a thick sauce made from chillies, onions and sugar.

Chillies (prik, cabe, sili labuyo): introduced from South America by the Portuguese and Spanish in the sixteenth century, chillies are an essential ingredient in South-East Asian cookery. Generally the smallest are the hottest, for instance, the tiny Thai bird's eye chillies.

Coconut milk (santen): this thick white 'milk' is made from the grated flesh of the coconut and not from the cloudy water found inside the coconut. In South-East Asia freshly-made coconut milk is sold in markets; here, tinned coconut milk is the best option widely available.

Creamed coconut and coconut milk powder, both of which need mixing with hot water, are the other options.

Coriander (cilantro, Chinese parsley, daun ketumbar, pak chee): this green flat-leafed herb, similar in appearance to continental parsley, has a distinctive sharp flavour. Both the seeds and the leaves are used throughout South-East Asia.

Custard apple (sweet-sop): an apple-shaped, green-skinned fruit with creamy flesh and plentiful small seeds.

Durian: a notorious large, spiky, green-skinned fruit, prized as a delicacy throughout South-East Asia. It is notable for its pungent smell, described as a cross between Camembert and turpentine and, as a result, is banned on airlines.

Fish sauce (nam pla, nuoc mam, patis): a thin, brown salty liquid, produced from compressed shrimps or small fish, and used similarly to soy sauce as a salty flavouring.

Galingal (Siamese ginger, kenguas, languas, ka): a fleshy rhizome, resembling a creamy-coloured root ginger with pink nodules, and a sharp, medicinal aroma. Available fresh or dried, either in pieces or in powder form (Laos powder).

Ginger: a brown-skinned rhizome, noted for its aromatic flavour and digestive qualities. Lesser ginger (krachai in Thai) is a milder relation and, while similarly-coloured, comes in clusters of small 'fingers'.

Jackfruit: bulky, football-sized fruit with a thick green skin covered in prickles, similar in appearance to durian. Yellow jackfruit flesh is available tinned.

Kaffir limes (jeruk purut, makrut): large limes with a bumpy, dark-green skin. The glossy lime leaves, sold in bunches or packets of loose leaves, are used in South-East Asian cooking and add a distinctive citrus flavour.

Kalamansi: small, round, green citrus fruits used in the Philippines to make a refreshing drink.

Kangkong: water-convolvulus leaves, eaten as a green vegetable.

Lemon grass (serai, sereh, takrai): a fibrous grey-green grass with a white bulbous base and subtle citrus flavour.

Macapuno: a type of coconut with soft, slightly sticky flesh, used in Filipino desserts.

Mango: an orange-fleshed, fragrant fruit, eaten fresh and used in desserts. Pale orange Thai mangoes are particularly prized for their delicate flavour and scoopable flesh.

Mangosteen: an apple-sized fruit with thick purple skin which, despite its name, is no relation to the mango. Inside, it contains white pulpy segments with a delicate, perfumed flavour.

Milkfish (bangus): a bony, white-fleshed fish, cultivated and eaten extensively in the Philippines.

Mooli (daikon): a large, long white radish with crisp flesh.

Noodles: *cellophane noodles* (also known as beanthread, glass or transparent noodles) are fine threadlike noodles made from mung beans, which need soaking before they can be easily cut; yellow *egg noodles* (available fresh and dried); dried white *rice noodles* and *vermicelli; river rice* or *sarhor noodles*, made from ground rice and water. Fresh river rice noodles are sold in clear packets, usually stored near the chilled section.

Palm sugar (gula melaka): a caramel-flavoured, dark brown sugar made from the coconut palm flower, sold in small, hard cylinderical blocks.

Pandan leaves: long, thin, dark-green screwpine leaves, sold fresh in bunches. They add a unique, slightly nutty flavour and green colouring to desserts.

Pawpaw (papaya): a gourd-like fruit, which comes in varying sizes and colours from deep green to orange. Green pawpaw is used in salads by the Thais.

Pea aubergine: tiny pea-sized aubergines with a sharp, bitter taste, used especially in Thai cooking.

Pomelo (shaddock): the largest of the citrus fruits, resembling a huge grapefruit with a flattened end; used in Thai salads.

Prawn crackers (krupuk): flat wafers which puff up when fried. Emping are a slightly bitter Indonesian version, made with melinjo nuts, and used to garnish gado gado salad.

Rambutan: a fruit resembling a hairy, red egg – the name comes from 'rambut', Malay for 'hair'. Inside is a translucent, juicy egg-shaped fruit, prized for its refreshing qualities.

Rice: long-grain rice is commonly used, with the best coming from Thailand. The phrase 'perfumed rice' is an indicator of quality. Short-grained white and black glutinous rice is also used in both savoury and sweet dishes.

Shrimps (dried): small, shelled, dried pink shrimps, with a strong salty flavour.

Shrimp paste (blachan, terasi, bagoong, kapee, mam tan): a paste made from fermented shrimps, available in many forms, from solid, brown blocks to bottled pink-grey liquid. It has an extremely pungent smell and should be stored in an airtight container.

Soy sauce: a dark brown, salty liquid made from fermented soya beans, available as thin, salty *Light Soy Sauce* or as thicker, sweeter *Dark Soy Sauce*. *Kecap manis* is a thick, sweet Indonesian soy sauce.

Starfruit (carambola): a ridged, fleshy fruit which when sliced produces star-shaped slices.

Straw mushrooms: cone-shaped mushrooms, usually available canned.

Tamarind (asam, mak kum): a bean-like fruit from the tamarind tree, available in lumps of de-seeded pulp, and used to add tartness to dishes. Tamarind sauce, although slightly salty, is a convenient version. 'Tamarind slices', from a different fruit with similar qualities, is also available.

Tempe: a pressed fermented soya bean product, with a nutty taste.

Turmeric: a slender, brown-skinned rhizome, with a deep orange flesh. Widely available in dried powdered form, or occasionally found fresh.

Ube: a bright purple, sweet yam used in Filipino cookery.

Yard-long beans: as the name implies, these are long green beans, commonly cut into short lengths before cooking.

Thai Lemon Grass

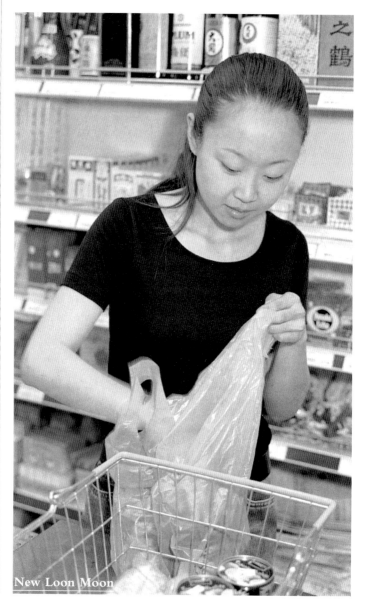

New Loon Moon

FOOD SHOPS

Traditionally the more established Chinese supermarkets have acted as umbrella suppliers, carrying basic South-East Asian ingredients. With the recent boom in Thai cookery, major supermarket chains are also starting to stock ingredients such as tinned coconut milk and fresh lemon grass. For the more unusual items, especially vegetables and herbs, it is necessary to track down a specialist South-East Asian shop.

CENTRAL

New Loon Moon Supermarket

🏠 *9a Gerrard Street, W1*
☎ *020 7734 9940*
🚇 *Leicester Square LU*
🕐 *Daily 10.30am-8pm*

As you enter this pleasantly old-fashioned shop you're greeted by an attractive display of good quality fresh Thai produce, including fresh Thai basils, pea-aubergines, green mangoes and papayas and petai beans. The grocery section includes a decent range of S.E. Asian ingredients, including coconut milk, chilli sauces and, in the back-room, an impressive range of curry pastes.

See Woo

🏠 *19 Lisle Street, WC2*
☎ *020 7439 8325*
🚇 *Leicester Square LU*
🕐 *Daily 10am-8pm*

Although a veteran Chinese supermarket See Woo is a reliable stockist of South-East Asian ingredients including fresh flavourings such as kaffir lime leaves and galingal.

EAST

Alan's Chinese & Vietnamese Grocery

🏠 *199 East India Dock Road, E14*
☎ *020 7515 8909*
🚇 *All Saints DLR*
🕐 *Daily 10am-10pm*

A small Vietnamese grocery, warmly recommended by American food-writer and pho-fan Marlena Spieler, with an excellent range of Vietnamese foodstuffs, including bunches of fresh dill, mint and coriander to a wide selection of dried noodles and rice pancakes.

Hoang-Nam

⌨ *185 Mare Street, E8*
☎ *020 8985 9050*
🚉 *London Fields Rail*
🕐 *Daily 9am-9pm*

Well-stocked Vietnamese supermarket, with store-cupboard staples (rice, noodles, condiments), frozen seafood and a superior array of fresh vegetables and herbs.

NORTH-WEST

Hopewell Emporium

⌨ *2F Dyne Road, NW6*
☎ *020 7624 5473*
🚉 *Kilburn LU*
🕐 *Mon & Wed-Sun 7am-10.30pm*

This large South-East Asian foodstore, run with relaxed friendliness by Tony, specialises in Indonesian ingredients such as tempeh and emping, and caters to the North London Indonesian community whose embassy staff live mainly in Hendon. Fresh produce includes snake beans, banana leaves and pea aubergines, while there is also an excellent range of bottled, tinned and packeted ingredients.

Maysun Market

⌨ *869 Finchley Road, NW11*
☎ *020 8455 4773*
🚉 *Golders Green LU*
🕐 *Mon-Sat 9am-7.30pm*

This small shop stocks a selection of South-East Asian ingredients (predominantly tinned, bottled, frozen or dried) which range from frozen seafood and packets of pig's blood to tins of Alphonso mango pulp.

Wing Yip (London) Ltd

⌨ *395 Edgware Road, NW2*
☏ *020 8450 0422*
🚇 *Colindale LU*
🕐 *Mon-Sat 9.30am-7pm, Sun 11.30am-5.30pm*

This enormous supermarket at Staples Corner contains an impressive range of South-East Asian ingredients, and is particularly strong on bottled, tinned, dried and frozen foods. The greengrocer's section, although small, stocks more unusual items including pandan leaves, Thai basil and fresh tamarind.

SOUTH-EAST

Wing Thai Supermarket

⌨ *13 Electric Avenue, SW9*
☏ *020 7738 5898*
🚇 *Brixton LU/Rail*
🕐 *Mon-Sat 10am-7pm*

Tucked away behind the bustling fruit and veg market stalls outside, this roomy store has a small fresh produce section, but is very strong on bottled, tinned and frozen goods with a range of Vietnamese products such as dried rice wrappers.

SOUTH-WEST

Amaranth

⌨ *346-348 Garrett Lane, SW18*
☏ *020 8871 3466 or 020 8874 9036*
🚇 *Earlsfield Rail*
🕐 *Mon 4pm-10pm, Tue-Sat 11.30am-10pm*

An extension of the popular Thai restaurant next door, this small food-shop stocks basic Thai ingredients, including homemade curry pastes. Tuesday is the best day for fresh Thai produce, such as holy basil or lime leaves, as deliveries from Thailand arrive on Monday evening. The shop's particular forte, and one which pulls in the local commuters, is the homemade, frozen ready-to-cook savouries, such as dainty spring rolls or red duck curry. Staff are friendly and helpful and happy to offer cooking advice.

Talad Thai

- 320 Upper Richmond Road, SW15
- 020 8789 8084
- Putney Rail
- Mon-Sat 9am-10.30pm, Sun 10am-8pm

Upstairs functions as a Thai take-away while downstairs is a basement supermarket with a small back room of fresh vegetables, herbs and fruits – such as Thai basils and pea aubergines. The large freezer section contains meat and seafood while the shelves are lined with noodles, condiments, tinned vegetables and coconut milk. The manageress is friendly and helpful and there are Thai cookery demonstrations every Sunday morning.

Paya Thai

- 101-103 Kew Road, TW9
- 020 8332 2959
- Richmond LU/Rail
- Daily 10am-7pm

This large store has every thing you could want for Thai cooking, from fresh pea aubergines and fragrant Thai basil to bottles of fish sauce and tins of coconut milk.

WEST

Manila Supermarket

- 11-12 Hogarth Place, SW5
- 020 7373 8305
- Earl's Court LU
- Daily 9am-9pm

As the name and the stacks of The Filipino newspaper near the door suggest, this spacious store specialises in Filipino foodstuffs such as purple yam jam, coconut spread and pork sausages, but also stocks an extensive range of general South-East Asian ingredients. One room contains freezers of grated cassava, fresh coconut milk, sweet potato leaves and a variety of fish and seafood. Greengrocer's items include chillies, galingal and banana leaves. Staff are friendly.

Muay

⌨ *8A Hogarth Place, SW5*
☎ *020 7341 3599*
🚇 *Earl's Court LU*
🕐 *Mon-Sat 9am-8pm, Sun 10am-8pm*

This small, cluttered Thai food shop (above a basement hairdressers) has a superb selection of fresh Thai vegetables and herbs, attractively arranged in baskets. Pretty Thai cakes, fresh mangosteens and packets of fresh, moist yellow durian segments when in season are among the treats on offer.

Sri Thai

⌨ *56 Shepherd's Bush Road, W6*
☎ *020 7602 0621*
🚇 *Shepherd's Bush LU*
🕐 *Daily 9am-7pm*

This clearly-arranged shop, run with friendly courtesy by Mr and Mrs Threpprasits, has an impressive stock of Thai ingredients, with a particularly strong selection of fresh Thai produce. Tuesday is the best day to visit for fresh vegetables and herbs jetted in from Thailand, such as bitter melon, fresh Thai basils and galingal.

Tawana

⌨ *16-20 Chepstow Road, W2*
☎ *020 7221 6316*
🚇 *Bayswater LU*
🕐 *Daily 9.30am-8pm*

"There were only two Thai restaurants in London when we started", muses owner Mr Farooqi. Today, Thai cuisine is popular and his roomy, well-stocked shop does a roaring trade in Thai staples such as kaffir lime leaves, coconut milk and lemon grass. Wednesdays and Saturdays are the best days for fresh produce flown in from Thailand, including pea aubergines, banana leaves and holy basil.

Also at: 243-245 Plaistow Road, E15

EATING PLACES

While Thai food seems to have secured a pub restaurant niche, authentic South-East Asian food in London is pretty scarce. With delicious ingredients such as lemongrass, lime leaves and coconut milk to use, it's not so much that the majority of food on offer is unpleasant – rather that it lacks the depth of flavour and gutsiness of the genuine article.

CENTRAL

Mawar *£-££*
✉ *175A Edgware Road, W2*
☎ *020 2762 1663*
🚇 *Edgware Road LU*

Discreetly hidden in basement premises this unpretentious, friendly eating place serves up tasty Malay food at remarkably reasonable prices. A buffet-style lunch and snacks such as colourful kueh and tasty curry puffs attracts Malay students while in the evening one can order à la carte.

Satay House *££*
✉ *13 Sale Place, W2*
☎ *020 7723 6763*
🚇 *Edgware Road LU or Paddington LU*

Tucked away in a quiet side-street, this is a peaceful place in which to enjoy Malaysian dishes such as murtabak (mince-stuffed flat bread) and tasty char kway teow. Sweet tooths can be satisfied with authentic versions of pulot hitam or ice kacang.

Selasih *££*
✉ *114 Seymour Place, W1*
☎ *020 7224 8816*
🚇 *Edgware Road LU*

A bargain lunchtime buffet means that this small, friendly, pretty restaurant fills up fast with local office workers. It's well worth ordering à la carte, however, to sample quality versions of classic dishes such as nasi lemak or spicy baked mackerel.

Silks and Spice *££*

🖾 *23 Foley Street, W1*

☎ *020 7636 2718*

🚇 *Goodge Street LU, Great Portland Street LU or Oxford Street LU*

An attractively-styled restaurant with an extensive menu of South-East Asian dishes, ranging from Malay to Thai. Set-price lunches are good value and the food is flavourful and prettily presented.

Also at:

28 Chalk Farm Road, NW1, Tel: 020 7267 5751

95 Chiswick High Road, W4, Tel: 020 8995 7991

EAST

Thai Garden *££-£££*

🖾 *249 Globe Road, E2*

☎ *020 8981 5748*

🚇 *Bethnal Green LU*

A friendly, unpretentious restaurant offering meat-free Thai dishes, from noodles to curries.

NORTH

O's Thai Cafe *££*

🖾 *10 Topsfield Parade, N8*

☎ *020 8348 6898*

🚇 *Finsbury Park LU, then the W7 bus*

Bright, light and funky, O's attracts a stream of Crouch End diners drawn by the chance to try tasty Thai dishes (such as green chicken curry) at very reasonable prices.

NORTH-WEST

Singapore Garden *£££*
☐ *83-83a Fairfax Road, NW6*
☏ *020 7328 5314*
🚇 *Swiss Cottage LU*

A loyal multi-cultural clientele testifies to this smart restaurant's commitment to admirably authentic Singaporean food. The menu offers predominantly Chinese food, but includes a range of South-East Asian delicacies such as mouth-watering and gloriously messy chilli crab, excellent satay and oyster omelette, and the best cendol (a coconut milk drink) in town.

Southeast W9 *£££-££££*
☐ *239 Elgin Avenue, W9*
☏ *020 7328 8883*
🚇 *Maida Vale LU*

Thai chef Vatcharin Bhumichtr's elegantly airy restaurant, with its pan-South-East Asian menu, offers a chance to sample less familiar dishes such as Laotian laap (minced chicken salad) or Vietnamese Bo Xao Mang (beef with bamboo shoots).

SOUTH

Champor-Champor *££££*
☐ *62 Weston Street, SE1*
☏ *020 7403 4600*
🚇 *London Bridge LU/Rail*

Hidden away down a quiet side-street, this vibrantly decorated, intimate restaurant offers an imaginative take on South East Asian cuisine. Malay chef Amran Hassan serves beautifully presented, creative and flavourful dishes drawing on ingredients and cooking techniques from across the region.

WEST

Bedlington Cafe *LL*
⌨ *24 Fauconberg Road, W4*
☎ *020 8994 1965*
🚇 *Chiswick Park LU or Turnham Green LU, then the E3 or E4 bus*
Originally a standard caff in the day, only offering Thai food at night, its
fame spread to such an extent that now tasty Thai food is available at
both lunch and dinnertime.

COOKBOOKS

Thai Cooking *by Jennifer Brennan*
A classic book on Thai cuisine, lovingly and knowledgeably written.

Far Eastern Cookery *by Madhur Jaffrey*
A well-written exploration of Far Eastern cookery with clear, useable
recipes.

Indonesian Food and Cookery *by Sri Owen*
An authoritative and in-depth book by Indonesian food writer Sri
Owen, attractively illustrated with evocative line drawings.

New Wave Asian *by Sri Owen*
Highly illustrated, this handsome book by Indonesian food writer Sri
Owen offers an insight into the latest cutting edge cuisine from South
East Asia.

The Complete Asian Cookbook *by Charmaine Solomon*
An impressively comprehensive cookbook by an experienced food
writer with recipes from across Asia.

SPANISH & PORTUGUESE LONDON

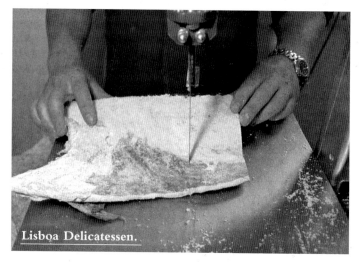

Lisboa Delicatessen.

Although a Spanish presence in London can be traced back to the Middle Ages, the real growth in the capital's Spanish and Portuguese communities came in the twentieth century. Following the Spanish Civil War (1936-9), many Spanish refugees and political exiles came to Britain. Republican exiles set up El Hogar Espanol (The Spanish House) in Bayswater: a cultural, social and political focal point. In addition to political reasons for coming to Britain, economic ones also played their part. During the 1950s and 1960s, millions of working-class Spaniards were forced to leave Spain and look for work abroad because of the lack of opportunities at home. The area around Ladbroke Grove was a focal point for the Spanish community. Many of the Spanish in Britain are from Galicia, the north-west coastal region of Spain which has a seafaring and travelling tradition and which suffered in the post-war depression.

Despite the fact that Portugal is Britain's oldest ally (a tie dating back to the Treaty of Windsor in 1386) the Portuguese community in London is small. It was the decades after the Second World War which saw an influx of Portuguese arriving in London, largely as a result of a lack of economic opportunities in Portugal.

236

One focal point for the city's Iberian community is the area around Golborne Road and Portobello. On these roads, the community is served by a Spanish school, Spanish and Portuguese delicatessens, and cafés and bars in which to meet other members of the community. Stockwell, too, is home to a number of Portuguese food shops, cafés and restaurants.

SPANISH & PORTUGUESE CUISINE

Both Spanish and Portuguese cookery share many characteristic ingredients: salted cod, paprika sausages, rice, beans, garlic and olive oil. The Moorish occupation of the Iberian Peninsula from AD 711 has left its mark on the sweets of both countries, with ground almonds and egg yolks used in desserts and cakes such as the Portuguese touchino de ceu or Spanish tarta de naranja.

Seafood is important in both cuisines, with an extensive range fished on the countries' long coastlines. Many of the famous regional dishes are seafood-based, such as zarzuela (Catalan seafood stew), marmitako (Basque bonito soup) and Northern-Portuguese caldeirada. There is no squeamishness when it comes to seafood. Lampreys are eaten in Northern Portugal in a famous dish, lapreia a moda do Minho; while Spanish calamares en su tinta, calls for squid to be cooked in its own black ink. Absolute freshness is demanded and one traditional Spanish fish dish is nicknamed mato mulo (mule killer) because the fish used in it had to be rushed by mule from the coast to Madrid.

There are some obvious differences between the cuisines and national dishes. From Portugal's former colonies come spices and flavourings such as spicy piri piri sauce – used in both Brazil and East Africa. Tapas, however, are quintessentially Spanish. The term means 'little lid' and is thought to come from the bar tradition of covering glasses with a saucer of olives or nuts. Bars vie with each other to offer good tapas and the discerning Spanish, who both enjoy their food and take it seriously, hunt out their favourites with a passion.

Both Spain and Portugal retain a strong sense of regionalism, with traditional dishes still cherished. Many recipes feature a place name, such as de salmao a Lisboeta, or fabada Asturiana. As in Italian cuisine, certain areas or towns are known for the quality of particular foods or dishes, with the best Spanish seafood from Cadiz or Galicia and the best Portuguese caldo verde from the Minho.

GLOSSARY

Aguardiente (orujo): a potent Spanish spirit, distilled from the left-over grapes and pips after wine has been made.

Anchovies (boquerones, biqueiros): tiny cured fish, usually filleted, with a strong, salty flavour.

Capers (alcaparras): the unopened buds of a Mediterranean shrub, sold and used in their pickled form. Spain is the world's largest producer of capers.

Cava: sparkling Spanish wine made using the champagne method, with Cordoniu and Frexenet among the best producers.

Charcuterie:
Butifarra, a white Spanish sausage, spiced with cinnamon, cloves and nutmeg. *Chorizo or chourico*, a range of paprika sausages, used in cooked dishes, to which they add a distinctive colour and flavour, or eaten as a salami.
Jamon de Serrano, a highly prized, salt-cured Spanish ham, the best of which is made from the acorn-fed pigs of the Estremadura region.
Lomo, cured pork loin from Spain. *Presunto*, a fine salt-cured ham from Portugal, traditionally made from acorn-fed pigs from Tras-os-Montes.

Cheese:
Azeitaio, small Portuguese sheep's milk cream cheeses. *Cabrales*, a famous Spanish blue-veined cheese, made from cow's milk and sometimes with sheep's or goat's milk added. *Evora*, a creamy, strong, salty sheep's milk cheese from Portugal. *Idiazabal*, a much-prized, semi-soft cheese with a dark rind made from sheep's milk in the Basque region of Spain. *Ilha*, a Portuguese Cheddar-like cheese made from cow's milk. *Mahon*, a flavourful Spanish semi-soft cow's milk cheese. *Manchego*, one of Spain's best-known cheeses, made with sheep's milk and sold in three grades depending on age. *Roncal*, a hard, Spanish, sheep's milk cheese. *Serra*, a soft, Portuguese, sheep's milk cheese.

Chickpeas (garbanzos, grado): hazelnut-shaped, yellow peas.

Coriander (coentros): a sharp-flavoured green herb, similar in appearance to continental parsley, widely used in Portuguese cookery.

Madeira: a famous Portuguese fortified wine, from the island of Madeira.

Madelenas: small, sweet, golden-brown cakes, eaten for breakfast in Spain.

Olive oil: olive oil is produced in both Spain and Portugal and is the main cooking oil in both countries. Carbonell, with its elegant Art Nouveau labels, is one of Spain's famous brands.

Olives: green olives stuffed with anchovies are particularly popular in Spain.

Paprika: a bright red powder, made from ground sweet or spicy peppers and used as a spice.

Pine kernels (pinon, pinhao): small, ivory-coloured stone pine kernels, used in both sweet and savoury dishes.

Piri piri: a hot Portuguese sauce made from chillies, a culinary legacy from Portugal's colonial past.

Port: a fortified wine from the Douro valley in North-West Portugal. Its creation can be traced back to the early seventeenth century when, due to Anglo-French hostilities, Portuguese wine rather than French claret was exported to England.

Quince paste (membrillo, marmelo): a thick, golden, jelly-like paste made from quinces, eaten as a sweetmeat or as a classic accompaniment to cheese.

Rice: introduced by the Moors to Spain and Portugal in AD 711. Short-grain rice is used for Spanish paella.

Saffron: a costly spice made from the stigmas of a type of crocus, sold in either thread or powdered form.

Salt cod (bacalao, bacalhau): dried, salted cod traditionally eaten on Fridays for religious reasons. In Portugal it is regarded as a national delicacy and there is said to be a different bacalhau recipe for every day of the year. It should be soaked for 24–36 hours before cooking to remove excess salt.

Sherry: a classic Spanish wine named after the town of Jerez and imported by the British since the fifteenth century.

Tiger nut (chufa): a small, wrinkled rhizome from which *horchata*, a refreshing almond-flavoured drink thought to have been introduced by the Moors, is made.

Turron: Spanish nougat, available in two forms: *alicante*, crisp and textured with chopped nuts, or *jijona*, soft and crumbly, made from ground nuts. Traditionally this is a Christmas treat but it is now available all the year round.

Vinho verde: delicate effervescent wines, both white and red, which form around a quarter of Portugal's wine production.

Pasteis De Nata from Lisboa

FOOD SHOPS

As with the Italian food stores, many of these shops began as corner shops rather than delicatessens, selling everyday ingredients to their community.

CENTRAL

Brindisa
- *32 Exmouth Market, EC1*
- ☎ *020 7713 1666*
- *Farringdon & King's Cross LU/Rail*
- ☺ *Tue-Fri 10am-6pm, Sat 9am-5pm*

This small, stylish shop is a showcase for some of Spain's finest food-stuffs. Here one can find hand-carved Iberico and Serrano hams, fine chorizo, salchicon and cheeses. The emphasis is firmly on flavourful, top quality Spanish foodstuffs, from superb extra virgin olive oils and wine vinegars to dangerously moreish almonds.

Delices de Portugal
- *43 Warwick Way, SW1*
- ☎ *020 7630 5597*
- *Pimlico LU or Victoria LU/Rail*
- ☺ *Mon-Sat 8am-8pm, Sun 9am-2pm*

This pretty delicatessen caters to hungry office workers, offering pasteis de bacalhau and a selection of Portuguese cakes and pastries as well as sand-wiches. There is a large range of deli goods, including huge slabs of bacalhau (cut on demand), packets of 'flan' and a choice of goat's cheeses.

Lisboa
- *6 World's End Place, SW10*
- ☎ *020 7376 3639*
- *Fulham Broadway LU*
- ☺ *Mon-Sat 8am-6pm*

A branch of the well-known Golborne Road establishment.

NORTH

Ferreira

⌨ *40 Delancey Street, NW1*
☏ *020 7485 2351*
🚇 *Camden Town LU*
🕐 *Mon-Sat 8am-9pm, Sun 8am-8pm*

A friendly Portuguese corner store which has something for everybody.
On the counter is a selection of cakes such as pasteis de nata, inside are
Portuguese cheeses and sausages, while behind are shelves of Portuguese
breakfast cereals. In addition, there is a selection of tinned and bottled
groceries, wines and slabs of bacalhau.

Lisboa

⌨ *4 Plender Street, NW1*
☏ *020 7387 1782*
🚇 *Camden Town LU*
🕐 *Tue-Fri 9.30am-6.30pm, Sat 9am-7pm, Sun 10am-2pm*

A branch of the established Portuguese delicatessen (see under West
London for further details).

Villa Franca

⌨ *3 Plender Street, NW1*
☏ *020 7387 8236*
🚇 *Camden Town LU*
🕐 *Mon-Sat 7am-8pm, Sun 9am-7pm*

A small down-to-earth shop-cum-café selling a mixture of Portuguese
and English pâtisserie plus a range of foodstuffs: bacalhau (stored beneath
the counter), cured meats, soft drinks and cheeses such as queijo Evora.
Downstairs is a smoking room from which blares the sound of
Portuguese satellite TV.

Rias Altas

⌨ *97 Frampton Street, NW8*
☏ *020 7262 4340*
🚇 *Edgware Road LU*
🕐 *Mon-Sat 9am-7.30pm*

A long, narrow Spanish delicatessen, well-stocked with foodstuffs such as
Spanish cheeses, cured meats, bacalao and Spanish wines.

SOUTH

Delicias de Portugal

- 280 Wandsworth Road, SW8
- 020 7622 9811
- Wandsworth Road Rail
- Mon-Fri 9am-8pm, Sat 9am-7pm, Sun 10am-7pm

An unpretentious, friendly food shop, filled with a good selection of Portuguese staples.

Sintra Delicatessen

- 146-48 Stockwell Road, SW9
- 020 7733 9402
- Stockwell LU
- Daily 9am-8pm

The scent of bacalhau and the hum of conversation evoke Portugal as you enter this homely shop, which is attached to a down-to-earth café and restaurant. There is a good selection of foodstuffs: chourico, presunto and morcela and Portuguese cakes and bread. The shelves are lined with Portuguese groceries: cereals, olive oil, Portuguese wines and boxes of Ancora crochet yarn.

WEST

Delicias de Portugal

- 1008 Harrow Road, NW10
- 020 8960 7933
- Kensal Green LU
- Mon-Sat 8.30am-7.30pm, Sun 9am-2pm

A pleasant, well-stocked Portuguese food shop.

Garcia R. & Sons

- 48 Portobello Road, W11
- 020 7221 6119
- Ladbroke Road LU or Notting Hill LU
- Tue-Sat 8.30am-6pm

The Garcia family have had a Spanish food shop on Portobello Road for over 40 years. Their present shop is London's largest Spanish delicatessen and retains a pleasantly old-fashioned feel. The deli counter does a roaring trade in Jamon Serrano and costly Jamon Iberico (from acorn-fed black-footed pigs), which are deftly sliced to order. In addition, there are groceries such as chorizo sausages, different pimenton, paella rice, tinned seafood, bacalao and olive oil. Turrons are kept throughout the year, with the range expanding at Christmas time.

Lisboa Delicatessen

🏠 54 Golborne Road, W10
☎ 020 8969 1052
🚇 Westbourne Park LU
🕐 Mon-Sat 9.30am-7.30pm, Sun 10am-1pm

When Carlos Gomes opened this shop over 20 years ago, it was the first Portuguese delicatessen in London and he and his partners 'imported' their own stock in suitcases from Portugal. All the essential ingredients for Portuguese cooking can be found in this characterful shop: pungent bacalhau, pulses including Brazilian black beans, sausages and trayfuls of pickled and salted pig's trotters, snouts, tails and ears. A back-room contains a selection of Portuguese wines and spirits, including port.

Lisboa Pâtisserie

🏠 57 Golborne Road, W10
☎ 020 8968 5242
🚇 Westbourne Park LU
🕐 Daily 8am-8pm

Across the road from the delicatessen, this small, popular pâtisserie supplies a constant stream of customers with delicious Portuguese pastries freshly baked on the premises such as pasteis de nata (custard tarts) and bolo arroz (rice cakes).

P. de la Fuente

🏠 288 Portobello Road, W10
☎ 020 8960 5687
🚇 Ladbroke Road LU or Notting Hill LU
🕐 Mon-Sat 9am-6pm

Just down the road from the large Spanish College, is this small, down-to-earth Spanish food shop with a useful stock of essentials.

Brindisa

EATING PLACES

CENTRAL

Moro *££££*
- 34-36 Exmouth Market, EC1
- 020 7833 8336
- *Farringdon LU/Rail*

Much critical acclaim has greeted this stylish restaurant, which draws on both Spanish and North African cuisines in its inventive menu. Delights include melt-in-the-mouth crab brik and delicious sherry ice-cream.

NORTH

La Bota *££*
- 31 Broadway Parade, Tottenham Lane, N8
- 020 8340 3082
- *Finsbury Park LU, then the W7 bus*

A straightforward tapas bar which attracts a lively crowd.

El Parador *££*
- 245 Eversholt Street, NW1
- 020 7387 3789
- *Camden Town LU*

This tapas bar comes into its own in the summer, when you can sit in the garden at the back and sample a range of tapas washed down with Spanish wines and beers.

SOUTH

The Gallery *££*
- 256A Brixton Hill, SW2
- 020 8671 8311
- *Brixton LU/Rail*

Stockwell's Portuguese community are well served by this friendly, down-to-earth restaurant offering large portions of tasty, authentic food.

Meson Don Felipe *££*
- 🖼 *53 The Cut, SE1*
- ☎ *020 7928 3237*
- 🚇 *Waterloo LU/Rail*

A large, attractive tapas bar, with a central counter piled high with appetising morsels.

Rebatos *££*
- 🖼 *169 South Lambeth Road, SW8*
- ☎ *020 7735 6388*
- 🚇 *Stockwell LU*

An atmospheric and popular well-established tapas bar, with above-average tapas served at the front bar and a large restaurant area at the back.

WEST

Galicia *££*
- 🖼 *323 Portobello Road, SW10*
- ☎ *020 8969 3539*
- 🚇 *Notting Hill LU or Ladbroke Grove LU*

This atmospheric tapas bar-cum-restaurant, popular with the local Spanish community, specialises in food from Galicia, hence the large number of fish and seafood dishes.

Lisboa Pâtisserie *£*
- 🖼 *57 Golborne Road, W10*
- ☎ *020 8968 5242*
- 🚇 *Ladbroke Grove LU or Notting Hill LU*

This delightful Portuguese pâtisserie, with its excellent cakes (including delectable pasteis de nata custard tarts), is usually full of regulars sampling coffee and pastries.

Cookbooks

Portuguese Cookery *by Ursula Bourne*
A basic introduction to Portuguese cuisine.

The Spanish Kitchen *by Nicholas Butcher*
A knowledgeable book conveying the regional diversity of
Spanish cooking.

The Foods and Wines of Spain *by Penelope Casas*
An excellent, comprehensive and appetising survey of Spanish cuisine.

The Gastronomy of Spain and Portugal *by Maite Manjon*
A useful encyclopaedia of Iberian food

The Food of Spain and Portugal *by Elizabeth Lambert Ortiz*
A authorative look at Iberian cooking, with accessible recipes.

The Taste of Portugal *by Edite Vieira*
A wonderfully evocative and appetising cookbook, offering a considerable insight into Portuguese cuisine.

MISCELLANEOUS

AFGHAN

Afghan Kitchen
35 Islington Green, N1
020 7359 8019
Angel LU

This tiny, minimalist, friendly restaurant offers tasty home-style Afghani food at very reasonable prices.

AMERICAN

Panzer's
13-19 Circus Road, NW8
020 7722 8596
St John's Wood LU
Mon-Fri 8am-7pm, Sat 8am-6pm, Sun 8am-2pm

St John's Wood affluent American ex-pat community is shewdly catered to by this large Jewish delicatessen which makes a point of stocking foodstuffs such as grape jelly, Karo syrup, Mr and Mrs T. Bloody Mary mix, flour tortillas and mini-marshmallows.

BELGIAN

Belgo Noord
72 Chalk Farm Road, NW1
020 7267 0718
Chalk Farm LU

Mussels and frites washed down with flavourful Belgian beers are the house speciality at this popular restaurant, with its minimalist décor and bustling atmosphere.

BRAZILIAN

Armadillo

⌂ *41 Broadway Market, E8*

☎ *020 7249 3633*

🚅 *London Fields Rail*

Pleasantly funky restaurant where chef Rogerio David cooks up creative Brazilian fare.

Terra Brasil

⌂ *36-38 Chalton Street, NW1*

☎ *020 7388 6554*

🚅 *Euston LU/Rail*

This jauntily decorated café draws a lunchtime crowd with its bargain buffet dishes, generously and lovingly doled out by its matriarchal owner. Dishes range from stews and fried chicken to flavourful fish soup (on Fridays only).

BURMESE

Mandalay

⌂ *444 Edgware Road, W2*

☎ *020 7258 3696*

🚅 *Edgware Road LU*

This relaxed, friendly restaurant offers a rare chance to sample Burmese cuisine, a fascinating blend of Asian, Chinese and Thai ingredients and cooking techniques. Dwight Ally, who runs the restaurant with his brother, is happy to give menu guidance.

COLOMBIAN

La Tienda

⌂ *81 Praed Street, W2*

☎ *020 7706 4695*

🚅 *Edgware Road LU or Paddington LU/Rail*

🕐 *Mon-Sat 10am-6pm*

This small, laid-back corner store comes complete with a sign which reads 'Parking for Colombians only. All others will be towed'. Beers, spirits and flour are on display, with chorizos and other meats stored in the fridge.

DANISH

Lundum's
⌧ *119 Old Brompton Road, SW7*
☎ *020 7373 7774*
▥ *South Kensington LU*

Warmly recommended by Danish friends this smart restaurant offers excellent Danish food with the Sunday buffet being particularly popular with families.

GERMAN

German Wurst Delicatessen
⌧ *127 Central Street, EC1*
☎ *020 7250 1322*
✎ *germanwurstdelicatessen@btinternet.com*
▥ *Old Street LU*

As the name of this small, neat shop makes clear this is indeed a German sausage specialist, with around 30 different types of sausages made on the premises by Steffen Stirtzel who with his partner Michael Ristau run the business. These are seriously meaty sausages ("no fillers" explains Michael), ranging from 'proper' frankfurters and bratwurst to slicing sausages and brawn, which is proving very popular with English OAPs. Though sausages are the shop's forte, they also stock rye bread, pretzels and a wide range of German mustards.

HUNGARIAN

The Gay Hussar
⌧ *2 Greek Street, W1*
☎ *020 7437 0973*
▥ *Leicester Square LU or Tottenham Court Road LU*

A venerable Soho restaurant, noted for its literary and political clientele as well as its generous portions of authentic Hungarian food, such as chilled cherry soup and Transylvanian stuffed cabbage.

Louis Pâtisserie   £
🖃 *32 Heath Street, NW3*
☎ *020 7435 9908*
🚇 *Hampstead LU*
🕐 *Daily 9.30am-6pm*

Set up by Mr Louis over 30 years ago, this charmingly old-fashioned pâtisserie sells Hungarian cakes and pastries such as dobos (caramel cake) and makos (poppyseed slice), all of which can be enjoyed with a cup of coffee in the tearoom.

The Old Europeans   £££
🖃 *106 High Road, N2*
☎ *020 8883 3964*
🚇 *East Finchley LU*

Wooden panelling, folklorie bric-à-brac and violin music add to the atmosphere of this cosy little restaurant, which serves up generous portions of tasty Hungarian dishes, such as paprika pork with tiny dumplings. Chestnut purée, whipped cream and cherries feature strongly on the dessert list.

KOREAN

Song's Supermarket
🖃 *76-78 Burlington Road, New Malden, Surrey, KT3 4NU*
☎ *020 8942 8471*
🚇 *New Malden Rail*
🕐 *Daily 9am-8.30pm*

New Malden's substantial Korean community are served by a number of restaurants and shops. Song's is next to Jie's Café, an informal Korean café from which the most appetising, savoury aromas waft out. Neatly arranged, Song's has an impressive range of stock: fresh meat and fish counters, fresh fruit, vegetables and herbs and a huge array of groceries. Particularly tempting is the extensive range of chilled, ready-made dishes such as spinach with garlic and chilli.

MAURITIAN

Chez Liline

▫ *101 Stroud Green Road, N4*

☎ *020 7263 6550*

🚇 *Finsbury Park LU*

Laid-back and unpretentious, this is a place to enjoy large portions of delicious Mauritian seafood, combining both tropical and French flavours.

MEXICAN

Cool Chile Company

▫ *P.O. Box 5702, London, W11 2GS*

☎ *0870 902 1145*

🖉 *www.coolchile.co.uk*

(Also at Portobello Market, on a stall on Portobello Road, near the junction with Blenheim Crescent on Saturdays 10.30am-5.30pm and at Borough Market on Saturdays 10am-5pm)

An impressive range of Mexican chillies plus certain key ingredients are on offer from the Cool Chile Company. Dodie is a genuine enthusiast and happy to offer advice and recipes. For a taste of real Mexican street food (rather than the Tex-Mex stuff normally on offer) visit Dodie's stall at Portobello or Borough.

SOUTH AFRICAN

St Marcus

▫ *1 Rockingham Close, Priory Lane, Roehampton, SW15*

☎ *020 8878 1898*

🚇 *Barnes Rail*

🕐 *Daily 9am-6pm*

Lovers of biltong, boerewors and braai can satisfy their cravings at this 'mini-market', run with zest by South African master butcher Emory St Marcus.

South Africa Shop

▭ *15 Henrietta Street, WC2*
☏ *020 7836 2292*
▦ *Covent Garden LU*
🕐 *Mon-Fri 10.30am-6.30pm, Sat 11am-6.30pm, Sun 11am-5.30pm*

This cheery shop, which also stocks Australian and New Zealand goods, offers a small selection of South African edibles, including the inevitable biltong, plus droewors and confectionery.

SWEDISH

Ikea

▭ *2 Drury Way, North Circular Road, NW10*
☏ *020 8451 5611*
🕐 *Mon-Fri 10am-8pm, Sat 9am-6pm, Sun 11am-5pm*

Situated on the North Circular, this popular Swedish furniture store has a small food outlet selling essentials such as huge circular crispbreads, gravadlax, lingonberries and frozen Swedish meatballs.

A Swedish Affair

▭ *32 Crawford Street, W1*
☏ *020 7224 9300*
▦ *Baker Street LU*
🕐 *Mon-Fri 10am-6pm, Sat 10am-5pm*

Patriotically painted in yellow and blue (the colours of the Swedish flag) this pretty shop has a whole range of Swedish edibles, from all-important crispbreads and pickled herrings to treats including liquorice sweets, lingonberry conserve and Swedish ice cream. The hard stuff – such as akvavit (an aromatic spirit) and snuff – is kept behind the counter.

KITCHENWARE

CENTRAL

The Conran Shop

⌨ *Michelin House, 81 Fulham Road, SW3*
☎ *020 7589 7401*
🚇 *South Kensington LU*
🕐 *Mon & Wed-Sat 9.30am-6pm, Tue 10am-6pm, Sun 12noon-5pm*

This stylish store has a seductive kitchen and tableware section. Stock ranges from wacky glass tumblers to exclusive Quaglino china, and wooden-handled tin openers to elegant espresso-makers.

Divertimenti

⌨ *33-34 Marylebone High Street, W1*
☎ *020 7935 0689*
🚇 *Baker Street LU*
🕐 *Mon-Fri 9.30am-6pm (Thurs until 7pm), Sat 10am-6pm, Sun 10am-5.30pm*

This attractive, airy kitchenware store (complete with a café area) offers a delectable, discerningly selected mixture of ceramic tableware, ranging from classic white French porcelain to colourful rustic ware, alongside pots, pans and Magimix and Kitchen Aid gadgets. The downstairs Cookery Theatre hosts a range of cookery classes by well-known food writers and chefs.

Branch at: 139-141 Fulham Road, SW3, Tel: 020 7581 8065

Habitat

⌨ *196 Tottenham Court Road, W1*
☎ *020 7631 3880*
🚇 *Goode Street LU*
🕐 *Mon-Wed 10am-6pm, Thurs 10am-8pm, Fri & Sat 10am-6.30pm, Sun 12 noon-6pm*

Stacks of saucepans, plates and mugs lend a bazaar-like quality to the kitchen section here. Useful for colourful, reasonably-priced tableware, Habitat also stocks basic pots and pans. There is an Eastern element too with a selection of bamboo steamers, woks and Japanese bowls.

Heal's

⌂ *196 Tottenham Court Road, W1*

☎ *020 7636 1666*

🚇 *Goodge Street LU*

🕐 *Mon-Wed 10am-6pm, Thurs 10am-8pm, Fri 10am-6.30pm,*
Sat 9.30am-6.30pm

The elegant kitchen section is strong on stylish gastro-items such as stainless steel Dualit toasters and Waring blenders. It also stocks a select range of cookware and a good choice of attractive tableware.

Jerry's Home Store

⌂ *163-167 Fulham Road, SW3*

☎ *020 7581 0909*

🚇 *South Kensington LU*

🕐 *Mon-Sat 10am-6pm, Sun 12 noon-6pm*

Bright and airy, this all-American store has an interesting selection of upmarket cookware, cheerful tableware, American cookbooks and kitchen utensils and gadgets including Waring blenders, pasta racks and popcorn makers.

John Lewis

⌂ *Oxford Street, W1*

☎ *020 7629 7711*

🚇 *Oxford Circus LU*

🕐 *Mon-Fri 9.30am-6pm (Thurs until 8pm), Sat 9am-6pm*

This large, neatly-arranged kitchenware department has an enviable range of cookware, including Circulon, Prestige and Le Creuset. It also stocks microwave ware, assorted storage jars, knives and baking paraphernalia, as well as gadgets including strawberry hullers, lemon wedge covers and garni bags. Prices are competitive and staff are helpful.

Leon Jaeggi

⌂ *77 Shaftesbury Avenue, W1*

☎ *020 7580 1974 or 020 7434 4545*

🚇 *Leicester Square LU or Piccadilly Circus LU*

🕐 *Mon-Sat 9am-5.30pm*

A large, well-established shop specialising in professional catering utensils and equipment, including tin-lined copperware and an impressive range of knives. Stock is extensive and the staff are helpful and knowledgeable. Note that prices do not include VAT.

David Mellor

🖃 *4 Sloane Square, SW1*
☎ *020 7730 4259*
🚇 *Sloane Square LU*
🕒 *Mon-Sat 9.30am-6pm*

An elegant shop with classically tasteful stock, including a good selection of wooden salad bowls and Mellor's well-designed cutlery.

Pages

🖃 *121 Shaftesbury Avenue, W1*
☎ *020 7379 6334*
🚇 *Leicester Square LU or Tottenham Court Road LU*
🕒 *Mon-Fri 9am-6pm, Sat 9am-5pm*

Eye-catching displays of huge ice-sculpture moulds in the window mark this large, well-stocked shop, aimed primarily at the catering trade but also stocking useful items for home cooks.

NORTH

Japanese Knife Company

🖃 *131-179 Belsize Road, NW6*
☎ *020 7624 0436*
🚇 *Kilburn Park LU*
🕒 *Tue-Sat 10.30am-5pm (other times by appointment)*

A showcase for this cutting-edge (no pun intended) Japanese knife business who offer over 600 knives and sharpeners, including zirconium, ceramic and artisan steel knives. They provide a repair service and custom make knives and handles. Shortly opening in Harrods.

Richard Dare

🖃 *93 Regent's Park Road, NW1*
☎ *020 7722 9428*
🚇 *Chalk Farm LU*
🕒 *Mon-Fri 9.30am-6pm, Sat 10am-4pm*

An attractive kitchenware shop with an appealing range of stock. French ceramic tableware is a particular forte and staff are very helpful.

The Scullery

🖾 *123 Muswell Hill Broadway, N10*
☎ *020 8444 5236*
🚌 *Bus 134*
🕐 *Mon-Sat 9.30am-6pm*

A neat, cheery shop with a wide selection of tableware including Portmerion china and hand-painted dishes, plus kitchen utensils and cookware.

Gill Wing Cookshop

🖾 *190 Upper Street, N1*
☎ *020 7226 5392*
🚌 *Highbury & Islington LU/Rail*
🕐 *Mon-Sat 9.30am-6pm, Sun 10am-6pm*

A friendly kitchen shop with stock ranging from stainless steel saucepans to decorative tableware.
Branch at: 45 Park Road, Crouch End, N8, Tel: 020 8348 3451

SOUTH

La Cuisiniere

🖾 *81-83 Northcote Road, SW11*
☎ *020 7223 4487*
🚌 *Clapham Junction Rail*
🕐 *Mon-Sat 9.30am-6pm*

The thinking behind this Aladdin's cave of a shop is that 'life goes on in the kitchen'. As a result, stock ranges across from kitchen and tableware to specialist gadgets, with friendly staff on hand to proffer advice.

Kooks Unlimited

🖾 *16 Eton Street, TW10*
☎ *020 8940 8448*
🚌 *Richmond LU/Rail*
🕐 *Mon-Sat 9.30am-5.30pm*

This small, cheerful shop is crammed with stock from Le Creuset casserole dishes to kitchen gadgets.

WEST

Kitchen Ideas

- 70 Westbourne Grove, W2
- 020 7229 3388
- Bayswater LU
- Mon-Sat 9.30am-6pm

A down-to-earth shop with stock aimed at the catering trade.
Branch at: 23 New Broadway, W5, Tel: 020 8566 5620

The Kitchenware Company

- 36 Hill Street, TW9
- 020 8948 7785
- Richmond LU/Rail
- Mon-Sat 10am-6pm, Sat 10am-5pm

This well-stocked shop offers a mail order service. Stock ranges from everyday basics and gadgets to specialist equipment.

MAIL ORDER

Lakeland Ltd

- Alexandra Buildings, Windermere, Cumbria, LA 23 1BQ
- 05394 88100
- www.lakelandlimited.co.uk

This well-established, efficient Cumbria-based mail order kitchenware company enjoys a loyal following across the UK. The range of stock is impressive, from essentials to novelties such as expanding toast racks and tea bag squeezers.

MAIL-ORDER & WEBSITES

Mail-ordering food is one way to access specialist ingredients and a considerable number of small producers and specialist importers offer mail-order facilities. The growth of the Web has also seen the rise of gastronomic e-commerce, with a number of specialist food producers and suppliers having web-sites and a delivery service.

CHILLIES

Cool Chile Company

⌨ *P.O. Box 5702, London W11 2GS*

☎ *0870 902 1145*

✎ *www.coolchile.co.uk*

A must for chilli connoisseurs, Dodie Miller's mail-order company offers an extensive range of dried Central American chillies from mild guajillo to intensely hot habaneros, plus Mexican ingredients such as blue Masa Harina.

Peppers by Post

⌨ *Sea Spring Farm, West Bexington, Dorchester, Dorset DT2 9DD*

☎ *01308 897892*

Chilli-enthusiasts Michael and Joy Michaud run a mail-order service selling fresh chillies and tomatillos grown on their own Dorset farm, freshly picked then delivered the following day. On offer are a selection of chillies, including Jalapeno, Hungarian Hot Wax and Serrano.

ITALIAN INGREDIENTS

Esperya

✎ *www.esperya.com*

Widely acclaimed for the quality and range of artisanal Italian ingredients it supplies, this well-designed web-site features regional Italian foodstuffs such as prime mozzarella, vintage balsamic vinegar, superb olive oils. Well worth investigating.

Vyta

✍ *www.vyta.com*

Antonio Tambolin, the visionary founder of Esperya, is currently setting up a new e-commerce project, very much in its initial stages as I write. On offer will be the highest quality, traditional Italian food and drink, with the aim of extending this to include other fine quality produce from other European countries such as France and England.

MEAT, FISH AND GAME

Donald Russell Direct

✉ *Harlaw Road, Inverurie,*
Aberdeenshire, Scotland, AB51 4FR
☎ *01467 629 666*
✍ *www.donaldrusselldirect.com*

Noted particularly for the quality of its traditionally raised, grass-fed prime Scotch beef this reputable Scottish company also supplies game, lamb, pork and seafood.

Fletchers of Auchtermuchty

✉ *Reediehill Farm, Auchtermuchty,*
Fife, Scotland, KY14 7HS
☎ *01337 828369*
✍ *www.fletcherscotland.co.uk*

Nicola and John Fletcher sell prime Scottish venison from deer raised on their own farm in Fife. Their mail-order business stocks venison in numerous forms, from medallions and carpaccio to osso buco or boned and rolled haunch of venison. If you're uncertain how to cook venison, Nicola is only too happy to share her considerable expertise in game cookery.

SMOKED SALMON

H. Forman & Son
📠 6 Queen's Yard, Whitepost Lane, E9
☎ 020 8985 0378
🖋 www.formans.co.uk

Established in 1905 this veteran London-based smokery is renowned for the quality of its smoked salmon (using a mild 'London cure'), in particular its smoked wild salmon, which has a notable depth of flavour and distinctive drier texture.

SPICES

Seasoned Pioneers
📠 101, Summers Road,
Brunswick Business Park, Liverpool, L3 4BJ
☎ Freephone 0800 0682348
🖋 www.seasonedpioneers.co.uk

An intelligently chosen selection of over a hundred spices, spice blends and herbs are on offer from this mail-order company. Spices are dry-roasted in small batches in-house and carefully blended to provide authentic flavours. In addition to more familiar spices, Seasoned Pioneers carry items such as Ras-al-Hanout, sumac, chipotle chillies and curry leaves, with the spices ingeniously packaged in funky re-sealable foil packets.

BOOKSHOPS

The Africa Centre
📠 38 King Street, WC2
☎ 020 7240 6649
🚇 Covent Garden LU
🕐 Mon-Fri 11am-5.30pm, Sat 11am-5pm

This small bookshop stocks some unusual and hard-to-find African cookbooks.

Books For Cooks

⌨ *4 Blenheim Crescent, W11*

☏ *020 7221 1992*

🚇 *Ladbroke Grove LU or Notting Hill Gate LU*

🕐 *Tue-Sat 9.30am-6pm*

This small Notting Hill bookshop, crammed with cookbooks from floor to ceiling, is a mecca for anyone interested in food and cookery. The stock is extensive, ranging across cuisines from Asian to Spanish, and usefully includes American publications. Staff are knowledgeable and helpful and appetising cooking smells waft out from the small back kitchen, where recipes from books stocked in the shop are tested out and sampled in the back room café area.

Cooking The Books

⌨ *The Glen,*
St Brides Netherwent, Caldicot, NP26 3AT

☏ *01633 400150*

✉ *cooking_the_books@msn.com*

Run with genial enthusiasm and depth of knowledge by Brian and Gill Cashman, Cooking the Books is a mail-order business specialising in second-hand and out-of-print cookery books. Their humourously written monthly catalogues offer a huge range of books, from classics to obscure gems, and if you're trying to track down a particular out-of-print title it's well worth approaching them.

The Japan Centre

⌨ *212 Piccadilly, W1*

☏ *020 7434 4218*

🚇 *Piccadilly LU*

🕐 *Mon-Sat 10am-7.30pm, Sun 10am-6pm*

A good selection of Japanese cookbooks.

BIBLIOGRAPHY

The books used for my research include all the cookbooks I've recommended in each section of the book; those listed below are additional sources.

Across Seven Seas *Caroline Adams* (Tharp Books, 1987)

The Best of Thai Cooking *Chalie Amatyakul* (Travel Publishing Asia, 1988)

The British Museum Cookbook *Michelle Berriedale-Johnson* (British Museum Publications, 1987)

Just Like It Was *Harry Blacker* (Vallentine, Mitchell & Co., 1974)

Fruits and Vegetables of the Caribbean *M.J. Bourne, G.W. Lennox, S.A. Seddon* (Macmillan, 1988)

South-East Asian Food *Rosemary Brissenden* (Penguin, 1970)

The Club *Stephen Brook* (Constable, 1989)

Polish Cookbook *Zofia Czerny* (Panstowowe Wydawnictwo Ekonomiczne, 1975)

Galing Galing *Nora and Mariles Daza* (Daza, 1974)

The Fine Art of Japanese Cooking *Hideo Dekura* (Bay Books, n.d.)

Inside Soho *Mark Edmonds* (Robert Nicholson, 1988)

The Streets of East London *William Fishman* (Duckworth, 1979)

Staying Power *Peter Fryer* (Pluto Press, 1984)

Jewish Cookbook *Florence Greenberg* (Hamlyn, 1980).

Jane Grigson's Vegetable Book *Jane Grigson* (Penguin, 1980)

Exotic Fruits & Vegetables *Jane Grigson & Charlotte Knox* (Jonathan Cape, 1986)

Singapore Food *Wendy Hutton* (Times Books International, 1989)

Filipino Cooking Here and Abroad *Eleanor Laquian and Irene Sobrevinas* (National Book Store Inc., 1977)

Old Polish Traditions in the Kitchen and at the Table *Maria Lemnis and Henryk Vitry* (Interpress Publishers, n.d.)

East End Story *A.B. Levy* (Vallentine, Mitchell & Co., 1950)

Guide to Ethnic London *Ian McAuley* (Michael Haag, 1987)

The Peopling of London *Nick Merriman* (The Museum of London, 1993)

Flavours of Korea, *Marc and Kim Millon* (Andre Deutsch, 1991)

A Popular Guide to Chinese Vegetables, *Karen Philipps and Martha Dahlen* (Frederick Muller, 1983)

Fruits of South-East Asia *Jacqueline M. Piper* (Oxford University Press, 1989)

Living London *George Sims* (Cassell, 1904–1906)

The Best of Singapore Cooking *Mrs Leong Yee Soo* (Times Books International, 1988)

Penang Nonya Cooking *Cecilia Tan* (Times Books International 1983)

Sushi Made Easy *Nobuko Tsuda* (John Weatherhill Inc, 1982)

The London Encyclopaedia *Ben Weinreb & Christopher Hibbert* (Papermac, 1987)

Cooking the Polish-Jewish Way *Eugeniusz Wirkowski* (Interpress Publishers, 1988)

Jewish London *Linda Zoff* (Piatkus, 1986)

GASTRO-SOHO TOURS

Aimed at anyone interested in food, Jenny Linford's **Gastro-SohoTours** are guided tours around Soho's diverse and fascinating food shops. The tours start in Chinatown, exploring the rich treasures of exotic fruits and vegetables and unusual ingredients to be found in chinese supermarkets, pauses for coffee then goes on to explore Soho's European food shops, from venerable Italian delicatessens to aromatic coffee shops. Throughout the tour foodwriter Jenny Linford offers ingredient information and recommendations, plus recipe suggestions.

For details of **Gastro-Soho Tours** ring 020 8440 0794

INDEX

Order Form

The following titles are also available from Metro Publications:

Book Lovers' London	£8.99	☐
Gay & Lesbian London	£7.99	☐
A Taste of London	£6.99	☐
The London Market Guide	£5.99	☐
The Guide to Cookery Courses	£7.99	☐
Museums & Galleries of London	£8.99	☐
Bargain Hunters' London	£6.99	☐
The London Theatre Guide	£7.99	☐

Please tick the boxes representing the books you would like to order and fill in your details below:

Name:

Address:

Send your order along with a cheque made payable to Metro Publications to the address below:

Metro Publications,
PO Box 6336, London N1 6PY
E-mail: metro@dircon.co.uk
www.metropublications.com

You can also get our guides via a customer order line on 020 8533 0922 (Visa/Mastercard/Switch)
Open: 9am-6pm; Mon-Fri

Postage is free, please allow 14 days for delivery.

Book Lovers' London
2nd edition
Author: Lesley Reader
£8.99, 320 pp, 30 photos
ISBN: 1 902910 13 3

Metro Publications' latest title is a complete guide to London's bookshops (both new, second-hand and antiquarian), as well as details of all the best book related markets, charity shops, auctions and a listing of bookfairs.

Taste of London
Author: Jenny Linford
£6.99, 144pp, 42 b/w photos
ISBN 0-9522914-7-9

A Taste of London contains over 80 cosmopolitan recipes, many of them recommended by Londoners of diverse ethnic origin and using all the ingredients to be found in the Capital, from dried porcini mushrooms to root ginger and lemon grass. The book also contains a glossary of cooking ingredients.

The London Market Guide
2nd edition
Authors: Andrew Kershman & Ally Ireson
£5.99, 192pp, 40 b/w photos,
80 Maps
ISBN 1-902910-04-4

The London Market Guide contains all the essential information needed to explore London's 70 street markets including maps, photos, travel information, consumer tips, over 90 cafés and full contact details for those wanting to get a stall.

The London Theatre Guide
Author: Richard Andrews
£7.99, 288pp, 50 b/w photos,
1 Area Maps, 50 seating plans
ISBN 1 902910 08 7

This is a complete reference work about the theatres of London. It will not only answer questions a first time visitor would ask, but will also surprise the regular theatregoer with useful and interesting information. Also features seating plans for all West End Theatres.

Museums & Galleries of London
2nd edition
Author: Abigail Willis
£8.99, 288pp, 60 b/w photos,
3 Area Maps & 8 Floor plans
ISBN 1-9029-10-079

This is the first guide to combine detailed reviews of all the museums and galleries of London with listings of the city's commercial galleries, archives and details of London's many art degree shows

Bargain Hunters' London
2nd edition
Author: Andrew Kershman
£6.99, 288pp, 60 b/w photos,
11 Area Maps
ISBN 1-9029-10-06-0

A comprehensive guide to finding bargains in London, including the best charity shops, auctions, designer sales, dress agencies, second-hand bookshops, factory outlets, independent designers and manufacturers and much more.